MAHAYANA BUDDHISM

MAHAYANA BUDDHISM

K S Dwivedi

MD PUBLICATIONS PVT LTD
NEW DELHI
www.mdppl.com

Published by :

MD Publications Pvt Ltd
"MD House", 11, Darya Ganj,
New Delhi - 110 002
Phone : +91-11-45355555
E-mail : contact@mdppl.com
Website: www.mdppl.com

ISBN: 978-81-7533-302-4

Published and Printed by Mr. Pranav Gupta on behalf of MD Publications Pvt Ltd at Mohit Enterprises, Delhi.

PREFACE

Mahayana, literally 'Great Vehicle' is one of the two main existing branches of Buddhism and a term for classification of Buddhist philosophies and practice. It was founded in India. The origins of Mahayana are still not completely understood. Although the Mahayana movement traces its origin to Gautama Buddha, scholars believe that it originated in South India in the 1st century CE, or the 1st century BCE. Alternatively, some scholars say there is some evidence that Mahayana originated in north-west India in the 1st century CE. Some scholars say that Mahayana could have initially developed in the south-east of India as a non-monastic tradition and that later it underwent a process of monasticization and emerged in the north-west of India as a monastic movement. Mahayana was first propagated into China by Lokaksema, the first translator of Mahayana sutras into Chinese during the second century CE.

Mahayana Buddhism emerged in the first century CE as a more liberal, accessible interpretation of Buddhism. As the "Greater Vehicle" (literally, the "Greater Ox-Cart"), Mahayana is a path available to people from all walks of life - not just monks and ascetics. Mahayana Buddhism is the primary form of Buddhism in North Asia and the Far East, including China, Japan, Korea, Tibet and Mongolia, and is thus sometimes known as Northern Buddhism. Mahayana Buddhists accept the Pali Canon as sacred scripture with the Theravadas, but also many other works, the Sutras, which were written later and in Sanskrit.

Most Mahayana schools believe in a pantheon of quasidivine Bodhisattvas that devote themselves to personal excellence, ultimate knowledge, and the salvation of humanity and all other sentient beings (animals, ghosts, demigods, etc.). Zen Buddhism is a school of Mahayana which often deemphasizes the pantheon of Bodhisattvas and instead focuses on the meditative aspects of the religion. In Mahayana, the Buddha is seen as the ultimate, highest being, present in all times, in all beings, and in all places, and the Bodhisattvas come to represent the universal ideal of altruistic excellence.

The Mahayana form of Buddhism tends to be more religious in nature than its Theravada counterpart. It often includes veneration of celestial beings, Buddhas and bodhisattvas, ceremonies, religious rituals, magical rites, and the use of icons, images, and other sacred objects. The role of such religious elements varies, however; it is central to Tibetan/Tantric Buddhism, but is highly discouraged by Zen practitioners, who have been known to burn statues of the Buddha to demonstrate their unimportance.

I am very grateful to Mr. Pranav Gupta, Director of MD Publications Pvt Ltd, New Delhi, for his kind cooperation and support for this book.

K S Dwivedi

Contents

1

Mahayana Buddhism
An Introduction

Mahayana Buddhism is both a system of metaphysics dealing with the basic structure and principles of reality and, primarily, a theoretical propaedeutic to the achievement of a desired state. Arising in India in the 1st century CE, it spread to Central Asia, China, Japan, mainland Southeast Asia, Java, Sumatra, and even Sri Lanka. Its teachings involved basic shifts in doctrine and approach, though there were precedents in earlier schools. It taught that neither the self nor the *dharmas* exist. Moreover, for the elite arhat ideal, it substituted the bodhisattva, one who vows to become a Buddha and delays entry into nirvana to help others. In Mahayana, love for creatures is exalted to the highest; a bodhisattva is encouraged to offer the merit he derives from good deeds for the good of others.

The tension between morality and mysticism that agitated India also influenced the Mahayana. In the Mahayana tradition the Buddha is viewed as a supramundane being. He multiplies himself and is often reflected in a pentad of Buddhas-Vairocana, Aksobhya, Ratnasambhava, Amitābha, and Amoghasiddhi- who reveal various doctrines and elaborate liturgies and sometimes take the place of Shakyamuni. As the tradition developed, there emerged new texts that were considered by Mahayana adherents to be Buddhavacana ("the word or words of the Buddha"). This new literature went far beyond the ancient canons and was believed to be the highest revelation, superseding earlier texts. In this literature the teaching is thought to operate on various levels, each adapted to the intellectual capacity and karmic propensities of those who hear it.

THE BODHISATTVA IDEAL

The purpose of the bodhisattva is to achieve enlightenment and to fulfill the vow to become a Buddha. The bodhisattva also foregoes entrance into nirvana in order to remain in the world as long as there are creatures to be saved from suffering. Beginning with the vow to become a Buddha, the career of a bodhisattva, according to some texts, traverses 10 stages or spiritual levels (*bhumi*) and achieves purification through the practice of the 10 perfections (*paramitas*). These levels elevate the bodhisattva to Buddhahood. The first six levels are preliminary, representing the true practice of the six perfections (generosity, morality, patience, vigour, concentration, and wisdom).

Even though further purification and fortification must be achieved in the following stages, irreversibility occurs as soon as the seventh stage has been reached and the bodhisattva has assumed the true Buddha nature. This is the moment when he engages in activity aimed at fulfilling the obligations of a bodhisattva. The difference between this and the preceding six stages is that now the activity is explained as an innate and spontaneous impulse manifested with conscious constraint and therefore not subject to doubt. Everything is now uncreated, ungenerated; thus, the body of the bodhisattva becomes identified more and more completely with the essential body (*dharma- kaya*), with Buddhahood, and with omniscience.

THE THREE BUDDHA BODIES

The three bodies (*tri- kaya*; i.e., modes of being) of the Buddha are rooted in Hinayana teachings concerning the physical body, the mental body, and the body of the law. The theory of the three bodies was a subject of major discussion for the Mahayana, becoming part of the salvation process and assuming central significance in doctrine. The emanation body (*nirmana- kaya*) is the form of the Buddha that appears in the world to teach people the path to liberation. The enjoyment (or bliss) body (*sambhoga- kaya*) is the celestial body of the Buddha to which contemplation can ascend.

In the heavenly regions, or Pure Lands, the enjoyment body teaches the bodhisattva doctrines that are unintelligible to those who are unenlightened. The unmanifested body of the law (*dharma- kaya*) already appears in the *Saddharmapundarika*, or *Lotus Sutra*, a transitional text of great importance to Mahayana devotional schools. In many Mahayana texts Buddhas are infinite and share an identical nature- the *dharma- kaya*. As anticipated in ancient schools, the Buddha is the law (*dharma*) and is identified with an eternal *dharma*, enlightenment (*bodhi*), and nirvana.

In later schools real existence is opposed to the mere appearance of existence, and voidness, the "thingness of things," an undefinable condition, present and immutable within the Buddhas, is stressed. All is in the *dharma- kaya*, the third body and expression of ultimate reality; nothing is outside it, just as nothing is outside space; transcendence and immanence come together. Other schools posit a presence that is innate within all human beings, even if it is not perceived. It is like a gem hidden in dross, which shines in its purity as soon as the veil of ignorance has been removed.

NEW REVELATIONS

New revelations are made on earth and in heavenly paradises by Shakyamuni and other Buddhas. The teaching is expounded uninterruptedly in the universe because worlds and paradises are infinite and all Buddhas are consubstantial with the essential body. They speak to assemblies of *shravakas* (disciples), bodhisattvas, gods, and demons. The authors of the new doctrines revealed their religious enthusiasm in various highly expressive ways, filling their works with phantasmagoria of celestial choruses, fabulous visions in which shine flashes of new speculations, and trains of thought influenced by Indian speculative and mystical traditions.

Then there is the texts from which new trends springs with repetitions and modulate the same arguments with a variety of readings. Mahayana thinkers faced the daunting challenge of producing a completely logical arrangement of this prolix literature, some of which had legendary origins. The *Prajnaparamita* ("Perfection of Wisdom") and the *Avatamsaka-sutras* ("Flower Ornament Sutra"), for instance, are said to have been concealed by the *nagas*, demigods that live in miraculous palaces in an underground kingdom.

There are various *Prajnaparamita* texts, ranging from 100,000 verses (the *Shatasahasrika*) to only a few lines (the *Prajnaparamitahrdaya- sutra*, famous in English as the *Heart Sutra*). The fundamental assumption of the *Prajnaparamita* is expounded in a famous verse: "like light, a mirage, a lamp, an illusion, a drop of water, a dream, and a lightning flash; thus must all compounded things be considered." Not only is there no "self," but all things lack a real nature (*svabhava*) of their own. The *Prajnaparamita- sutras* announce that the world as it appears to us does not exist, that reality is the indefinable "thingness of things" (*tathata; dharmanam dharmata*), that voidness (*shunyata*) is an absolute "without signs or characteristics" (*animitta*).

THE MAHAYANA SCHOOLS AND THEIR TEXTS

The Mahayana tradition encompasses a great many different schools, including the Madhyamika; the Yogacara or Vijnanavada (Vijnaptamatrata); the Avatamsaka School, which recognized the special importance of the *Avatamsaka Sutra*; a number of different schools that recognized the special authority of the *Saddharmapundarika* (*Lotus Sutra*); various Pure Land devotional schools; and several Dhyana ("Meditation") schools.

MADHYAMIKA (SANLUN/SANRON)

The Madhyamika ("Doctrine of the Middle Way") system, also known as Shunyavada ("Theory of Negativity or Relativity"), held both subject and object to be unreal and systematized the doctrine of *shunyata* ("cosmic emptiness") contained in the *Prajnaparamita* literature. Along with his disciple Aryadeva, the Indian philosopher Nagarjuna (*c.* 150–250 CE) is recognized as the founder and principal exponent of the Madhyamika system. Nagarjuna is the presumed author of the voluminous *Mahaprajnaparamita- shastra* ("The Great Treatise on the Perfection of Wisdom"), preserved in its Chinese translation (402–405) by Kumarajia, and the *Mulamadhyamakakarika* (more commonly known as *Madhyamika Karika*; "Fundamentals of the Middle Way"), which is considered by many to be the Madhyamika work par excellence.

The main work of Aryadeva, the *Catuhshataka*, criticizes other forms of Buddhism and the classical Sanskrit philosophical systems. Nagarjuna and his followers sought a middle position, devoid of name and character and beyond all thought and words. They used rigorous logic to demonstrate the absurdity of various philosophical positions, including those of Hindus and other Buddhists. Assuming that contradiction is proof of error, Nagarjuna took any point of view that would reveal the error of his opponents. He did not, however, accept the opposing point of view but used it only as a means to expose the relativity of the system he was attacking. Because he was willing to refute his first position, he could claim adherence to no doctrine.

Moreover, Nagarjuna attempted to prove that all worldly thought is empty (*shunya*) or relative and that the true path is that of the middle, the path that is between or, more correctly, above extremes. This belief has been called the doctrine of emptiness of all things, which posits that all things lack essential characteristics and exist only in relation to conditions surrounding them. Nagarjuna presented this middle path above extremes in his statement of the Eightfold Path of Buddhism:

> Nothing comes into being, nor does anything disappear.
>
> Nothing is eternal, nor has anything an end.
>
> Nothing is identical, nor is anything differentiated.
>
> Nothing moves here, nor does anything move there.

In presenting these pairs of opposites, Nagarjuna taught that anything that can be conceptualized or put into words is relative. This led to the Madhyamika identification of nirvana and samsara, which are empty concepts with the truth lying somewhere beyond. After the world's emptiness or relativity has been proved, the question arises of how one is to go beyond this position. Nagarjuna answered with the doctrine of the two truths, explaining that humans can gain salvation and are not irreconcilably caught in this world, which can be used as a ladder leading to the absolute. In his doctrine the relative truth is of this existence.

This leads first to the realization that all things are empty of *subhava* ("own being") and then to the intuition of an absolute truth beyond all conceptions. The link between these two truths- the relative and the absolute- is the Buddha. He experienced the absolute truth, which is *nisprapanca*- i.e., inexplicable in speech and unrealizable in ordinary thought- and yet he returned to point to this truth in the phenomenal world. By following this path, one can be saved. Thus, Nagarjuna taught that through the middle path of Madhyamika, which is identified as the Buddha's true teachings, one is guided to an experience beyond affirmation and negation, being and nonbeing. Madhyamika is a philosophy that can rightly be called a doctrine of salvation, for it claims to present humans with a system that leads to rescue from their situation.

The Madhyamika School divided into two subtraditions in the 5th and 6th centuries. The Prasangika School, which emphasized a more negative form of argumentation, was founded by Buddhapalita (*c.* 470–540), who wrote many works, including a commentary on Nagarjuna's *Madhyamika Karika*. The school was continued by Candrakirti, a famous logician of the 7th century and author of a commentary on the *Madhyamika Karika*, and by Shantideva (*c.* 650–750), whose *Shiksa- samuccaya* ("Summary of Training") and *Bodhicaryavatara* ("The Coming of the Bodhisattva Way of Life") are among the most popular Mahayana literary works.

The Svatantrika School, which utilized a syllogistic mode of argumentation, was founded by Bhavaviveka, a contemporary of Buddhapalita and author of a commentary on the *Madhyamika Karika*. Santiraksita, a great scholar who wrote the *Tattvasamgraha* ("Summary of Essentials") and the *Madhyamikalankara Karika* ("Verses on the Ornament of the Madhyamika Teaching"), continued the school. Both the Svatantrika tradition and the Prasangika tradition strongly influenced Buddhist philosophy in Tibet. The missionary translator Kumarajiva took the Madhyamika School to China from India in the 5th century. Three of the texts that he translated from Sanskrit into Chinese- the *Madhyamika Karika* and the *Dvadashamukha- shastra* or *Dvadasha- dvara- shastra* ("The Twelve Topics or Gates Treatise") of Nagarjuna and the *Shata- shastra* ("One Hundred Verses Treatise") of Aryadeva- became the basic texts of the Chinese Sanlun (Japanese: Sanron), or "Three Treatise," school of Madhyamika.

Although this school was challenged by the Silun, or "Four Treatise," school, which also accepted the *Mahaprajnaparamita-shastra* as a basic text, Sanlun regained preeminence as a result of the teachings of Sengzhao, Kumarajiva's disciple, and later of Jizang. Both of these Chinese Madhyamika masters commented on Nagarjuna's thesis in numerous influential works. A Korean disciple of Jizang, Ekwan (Huiguan), then spread Sanlun (Korean: Samnon) to Japan in 625. This school was never popular among the masses and rarely formed an independent sect, though it remained the basis of logical and philosophical thought among the learned.

YOGACARA/VIJNANAVADA (FAXIANG/HOSSÔ)

The Yogacara (or Vijnanavada) school was founded, according to tradition, by the brothers Asanga and Vasubandhu (4th/5th century CE) and by Sthiramati (6th century), who systematized doctrines found in the *Lankavatara-sutra* and the *Mahayana- shraddhotpada- shastra* (attributed to Ashvaghosa but probably written in Central Asia or in China). Later Mahayana and Esoteric Buddhism include doctrines that were to be influenced by Yogacara teaching.

The special characteristics of Yogacara are its emphasis on meditation and a broadly psychological analysis, which contrasts with the other great Mahayana system, Madhyamika, where the emphasis is on logical analysis and dialectic. Its central doctrine, however, is that only consciousness (*vijnanamatra*; hence the name Vijnanavada) is real and that eternal things do not exist. Thought or mind is the ultimate reality, and nothing exists outside the mind, according to this school. The common view that external things exist is due to an error that can be removed by a meditative or yogic process that brings an inner concentration and tranquility and a complete withdrawal or "revulsion" from fictitious externalities.

Alaya- vijnana ("store" or "storehouse consciousness") is postulated as the receptacle of the imprint of thoughts and deeds, the *vasana* (literally, "dwelling") of various karmic seeds (*bijas*). The "seeds" develop into touch, mental activity, feeling, perception, and will, corresponding to the five *skandhas* ("aggregates"; parts of an individual personality). This is followed first by the emergence of ideation (*manas*), which sets off the self or mind from the world, and then by the realization that objects exist only through the sense perceptions and thought of subject.

The store consciousness must be purged of its subject-object duality and restored to its pure state. This pure state is equivalent to the absolute "suchness" (*tathata*), to Buddhahood, to the undifferentiated. Corresponding to false imagination (*vikalpa*), right knowledge, and suchness are the three modes of being: the mere fictions of false imagination; the relative existence of things, under certain conditions or aspects; and the perfect mode of being. Corresponding to this threefold version of the modes of being and awareness is the *tri- kaya* doctrine of the Buddha (the apparitional body, the enjoyment body, and the *dharma* body), a doctrine that was systematized by Yogacara thinkers.

The Yogacara school was represented in China primarily by the Faxiang (or Dharmalaksana; also Weishi) school, called Hossô in Japan. Paramartha, an Indian missionary- teacher, introduced the basic Yogacara teachings to China in the 6th century, and his translation of the *Mahayana- samparigraha-*

shastra provided the foundation for the Silun School. Silun was succeeded as the major vehicle of Yogacara thought in China by the Faxiang School, which was founded by Xuanzang, the 7th- century Chinese pilgrim- translator, and his main disciple, Kuiji. Xuanzang went to India, where he studied the works of Dharmapala (died 561) and taught at the Vijnanavada centre at Valabhi.

When he returned to China, he translated Dharmapala's *Vijnapti- matrata- siddhi* and many other works and taught doctrines that were based on those of Dharmapala and other Indian teachers. Xuanzang's teachings were expressed systematically in *Fayuanyilinzhang* and *Weishishuji*, the basic texts of the Faxiang School. *Faxiang*, the Chinese translation of *dharmalaksana* (Sanskrit: "characteristic of *dharma*"), refers to the school's basic emphasis on the peculiar characteristics (*dharmalaksana*) of the *dharmas* that make up the world that appears in human ideation.

According to Faxiang teaching, there are five categories of *dharmas*: 8 mental *dharmas* (*cittadharma*), comprising the 5 sense consciousnesses, cognition, the cognitive faculty, and the store consciousness; 51 mental functions or capacities, dispositions, and activities (*caitashikadharma*); 11 elements concerned with material forms or appearances (*rupa- dharma*); 24 things, situations, and processes not associated with the mind- e.g., time, becoming (*cittaviprayuktasamskara*); and 6 noncreated or nonconditioned elements (*asamskrtadharma*)- e.g., space or suchness (*tathata*). In *Chengweishilun* ("Treatise on the Establishment of the Doctrine Consciousness Only"), Xuanzang explained how there can be a common empirical world for different individuals who construct or ideate particular objects and who possess distinct bodies and sensory systems.

According to Xuanzang, the universal "seeds" in the store consciousness account for the common appearance of things, and particular "seeds" account for the differences. According to traditional accounts, Faxiang was first taken to Japan by Dôshô, a Japanese priest who visited China, studied under Xuanzang, and established the teaching (now called Hossô) at Gangô Monastery. It was also taken there by other priests, Japanese and Korean, who studied in China under Xuanzang, Kuiji, or their disciples. Thus, the Japanese claim to have received the Hossô teaching in a direct line from its originators, and it continues to have a living and significant role in Japanese Buddhism.

AVATAMSAKA (HUAYAN/KEGON)

Unlike the Faxiang (Hossô) school, which concentrated on the differentiating characteristics of things and the separation of facts and principles, the Avatamsaka School (called Huayan in China, Kegon in Japan) stressed the sameness of things, the presence of absolute reality in them, and the identity of facts and ultimate principles. It took its name from the *Mahavaipulya-Buddhavatamsaka- sutra* ("The Great and Vast Buddha Garland Sutra"), often called simply the *Avatamsaka- sutra* ("Wreath Sutra" or "Garland Sutra"). According to legend, the *Avatamsaka- sutra* was first preached by the Buddha Vairocana shortly after his enlightenment but was replaced with simpler doctrines because it proved incomprehensible to his hearers.

The sutra tells of the pilgrimage of a young man in a quest to realize *dharma- dhatu* ("totality" or "universal principle"). Three Chinese versions and one Sanskrit original (the *Gandavyuha*), which contains the last section only, are extant. There is no trace of an Indian sectarian development, and the school is known only in its Chinese and Japanese forms. The forerunner of the Avatamsaka or Huayan School in China was the Dilun School, which was based on the *Shiyidijinglun* or *Dilun*, an early 6th- century translation of the *Dashabhumika-sutra* ("Sutra on the Ten Stages"). Since this work, which concerns the path of a bodhisattva to Buddhahood, was part of the *Avatamsaka- sutra* (which came to circulate independently), Dilun adherents readily joined the Huayan School that was established in the late 6th century by Dushun (Fashun), and the first patriarch (died 640).

The real founder of the school, however, was the third patriarch, Fazang (also called Xianshou; died 712), who systematized its teachings; hence, it is sometimes called the

Xianshou school. The school developed further under Fazang's student Chengguan (died *c.* 820 or *c.* 838), who wrote important commentaries on the *Avatamsaka- sutra*. After the death of the fifth and final patriarch, Zongmi, in 841, Huayan declined because of the general suppression of Buddhism in China in 845. Despite its decline, the school greatly influenced the development of Neo- Confucianism (a significant movement in Chinese thought beginning in the 11th century) and is regarded by many as the most highly developed form of Chinese Buddhist thought.

The Avatamsaka School was introduced into Japan by pupils of Fazang and by an Avatamsaka missionary from central India during the period from about 725 to 740. Known in Japan as the Kegon School, it has exerted an important influence in Japanese Buddhism that has continued to the present day. The school's most significant doctrine is the theory of causation by *dharma- dhatu* ("totality" or "universal principle"), according to which all elements arise simultaneously, the whole of things creates itself, ultimate principles and concrete manifestations are interfused, and the manifestations are mutually identical. Thus, in Fazang's *Essay on the Golden Lion*, written for the empress Wu Hou, gold is the essential nature or principle (Chinese: *li*), and lion is the particular manifestation or form (Chinese: *shi*). Moreover, as gold, each part or particle expresses the whole lion and is identical with every other part or particle.

This model suggests that all phenomena in the universe are expressions of the ultimate suchness or voidness while at the same time retaining their phenomenal character; each phenomenon is both "all" and "one." All the constituents of the world (the *dharmas*) are interdependent and possess a sixfold nature: universality, speciality, similarity, diversity, integration, and differentiation. The ideal expressed in this doctrine is a harmonious totality of things leading to the perfectly enlightened Buddha. The Buddha nature is present potentially in all things. There are an infinite number of Buddhas and Buddha realms. There are myriads of Buddhas in every grain of sand and a Buddha realm at the tip of a hair.

The universe is fourfold: a world of factual, practical reality; a world of principle or theory; a world of principle and facts harmonized; and a world of factual realities interwoven and mutually identified. The first three aspects are the particular emphases of other Buddhist schools. The fourth aspect- emphasizing the harmonious whole- is the distinctive doctrine that represents the perfect knowledge that was attained by the Buddha Vairocana and is communicated in the *Avatamsaka- sutra.*

TIANTAI/TENDAI

The school known as Tiantai in China and Tendai in Japan is one of the most important schools in Chinese and Japanese Buddhism. It is significant for its doctrines, which in many respects are similar to those of the Huayan/ Kegon school, and for its influence on devotion. The school's doctrines and practices are focused on the Indian or Central Asian *Saddharmapundarika- sutra* ("Lotus of the True Law Sutra") as well as on the *Mahaparinirvana* and *Mahaprajnaparamita- sutras.* Sometimes called Lotus (Fahua in Chinese; Hokke in Japanese), this school, which apparently had no separate development in India, took its name from the mountain in southeastern China where the basic interpretation of the *Lotus Sutra* was first propounded in the 6th century.

The origins of the school, however, are to be found in the early 5th century when the original text of the Sanskrit sutra was translated into Chinese by Kumarajiva and was then taught in North China by the monks and first patriarchs, Huiwen and Huisi. The latter's student Zhiyi, who established a famous monastery on Mount Tiantai ("Heavenly Terrace"), is regarded as the true founder of the school because he propounded the systematic interpretation of Lotus doctrines that came to be widely accepted. His interpretation spread to Japan in the early 9th century, where Saichô (known posthumously as Dengyô Daishi), a Buddhist priest who studied the teachings first in Japan and then on Mount Tiantai, founded a Japanese Tendai school.

He also founded a monastery on Mount Hiei that became one of Japan's greatest centres of Buddhist learning. Along with the Esoteric Buddhist school of Shingon, with which it was closely connected, Tendai became one of the most important influences on Japanese religious culture. Tendai has been markedly syncretistic, incorporating the teachings of various Buddhist schools and those of Shintô, the indigenous Japanese religion, into its traditions. The *Lotus Sutra*, which is recognized by Tiantai and Tendai as the locus of the most exalted Buddhist teaching, emphasizes the notion of the one way (or "vehicle" or "career") for attaining salvation (Buddhahood).

It claims to be the definitive and complete teaching of the Buddha, who is depicted as a transcendent eternal being, preaching to arhats, gods, bodhisattvas, and other figures, using all sorts of sermons, lectures, imaginative parables, and miracles. The Lotus is an object of devotion in this school, and those who preach, recite, or hear it are believed to accrue religious merit. In the Lotus the three ways of salvation supposedly preached by the Buddha are adjusted to the level and situation of the hearers: *shravakayana*, the way of the disciples (*shravakas*), appropriate for becoming an arhat; *pratyeka- buddhayana*, the way of those who aim at salvation for themselves alone; and *bodhisattvayana*, the way of those (the bodhisattvas) who, on the point of attaining salvation, give it up to work for the salvation of all other beings.

All are forms of the one way, the *buddhayana*, and the aim for all is to become a Buddha. The Tiantai/Tendai tradition divides the Buddha's teachings into five periods. The first immediately followed the Buddha's enlightenment, when, without success, he preached the *Avatamsaka- sutra* (or *Huayan/Kegon Sutra*). The second is the so- called Deer Park period, when he preached the *Agamas* (Hinayana scriptures) to those with ordinary human capacities. In the third or Fangdeng ("broad and equal") period, he preached the *Vaipulya* or early Mahayana teachings, which were intended for all persons.

During the fourth period he preached the *Mahaprajnaparamita*, or Ta- pan- jo- po- lo- mi- to, doctrines concerning absolute voidness and the falsity of all distinctions. Finally, in the *Saddharmapundarika* and *Mahaparinirvana* ("Wisdom") period, he taught the identity of contrasts, the unity of the three "vehicles," and the ultimate authority of the *Lotus Sutra*. Central to Tiantai/Tendai doctrine is the threefold truth principle (following Nagarjuna's [?] commentary on the *Mahaprajnaparamita*), according to which all things are void, without substantial reality; all things have temporary existence; and all things are in the mean or middle state, synthesizing voidness and temporary existence, being both at once.

The three truths are a harmonious unity, mutually including one another, and the mean or middle truth is equivalent to the absolute suchness. The world of temporary appearances is thus the same as absolute reality. Tiantai/Tendai propounds an elaborate cosmology of 3,000 realms. There are 10 basic realms, respectively, of Buddhas, bodhisattvas, *pratyeka Buddhas*, *shravakas*, heavenly beings, fighting spirits (*asuras*), human beings, hungry spirits or ghosts (*pretas*), beasts, and depraved hellish beings. Each realm, however, includes the other 9 and their characteristics, and counting these together thus yields 100 realms.

Each of these in turn is characterized by the 10 features of suchness manifested through phenomena- form, nature, substance, power, action, cause, condition, effect, compensation, and ultimacy- which thus brings the total to 1,000 realms. Finally, each of these realms is divided into living beings, space, and the aggregates (*skandhas*); hence, the whole of things consists of 3,000 realms. These realms interpenetrate one another and are immanent in one moment of thought: "one thought is the three thousand worlds." The universe is not produced by thought or consciousness but is manifest in it, as is the absolute suchness: hence, the central importance of concentration (*chih*) and insight (*kuan*) that leads to a realization of the unity of things and their manifestation of the ultimate.

PURE LAND

The main text of the Pure Land schools is the *Sukhavativyuha- sutra* ("Pure Land Sutra"). Written in northwestern India probably before the beginning of the 2nd century CE, the *Sukhavativyuha* exists in two original versions, a longer one that emphasizes good works and a shorter version that emphasizes faith and devotion alone. This sutra tells of a monk, Dharmakara, who heard the preaching of Lokeshvararaja Buddha aeons ago and asked to become a Buddha. After millions of years of study, Dharmakara vowed, among other things, to establish a Pure or Happy Land (Sanskrit: Sukhavati; Chinese: Qingtu; Japanese: Jôdo), also known as the Western Paradise, if he achieved Buddhahood. In this Pure Land no evil would exist, the people would be long- lived, they would receive whatever they desired, and from there they might attain nirvana.

Dharmakara then revealed in a series of 48 vows the means by which this Pure Land can be reached. Several vows emphasize meditation and good works on earth as a prerequisite, but the 18th one (a famous vow in the later development of Pure Land schools) states that, if one merely calls the name of the Buddha at the moment of death, then one will be reborn in the Pure Land. Dharmakara, it is believed, attained Buddhahood and is known as the Buddha Amitabha (Sanskrit: "Infinite Light"; Chinese: Emituofo; Japanese: Amida) or the Buddha Amitayus (Sanskrit: "Infinite Lifespan"). He is flanked in the Pure Land he created in fulfillment of his vows by Avalokitesvara (Chinese: Guanyin; Japanese: Kannon) on his left and Mahasthamaprapta on his right, who assist Amitabha in bringing the faithful to salvation.

By the 3rd century CE, the Amitabhist doctrine had spread from India to China, where a school based on it gradually became the most popular form of Buddhism. Followers of the Tendai School took Amitabhist teachings to Japan, where they attempted to weld the many sects of Buddhism into one system. By the 13th century CE, the Pure Land sect had separated from the Tendai

School and spread among the common people of Japan through the work of two outstanding figures, Hônen and Shinran.

The basic doctrines of the Pure Land schools emphasize the importance of devotion. Pure Land leaders teach that a person reaches salvation not by individual effort or the accumulation of merit but through faith in the grace of the Buddha Amitabha. The main practice of those who follow the Pure Land teachings is not the study of the texts or meditation on the Buddha but rather the constant invocation of the name Amitabha, a practice based on the 18th vow of Dharmakara. Furthermore, in Pure Land Buddhism the attainment of nirvana is not the most prominent goal; it is rather to become reborn in the Pure Land of Amitabha.

These doctrines and the practice of invoking the name Amitabha- called *nembutsu* in Japanese and *nianfo* in Chinese- became popular in China and Japan, where it was believed that the world had reached the decadent age, the so- called "latter days of the law" in which Buddhist doctrines were unclear and humans lacked the purity of heart or determination to attain salvation by their efforts. Therefore, the only hope was to be saved by the grace of Amitabha. This doctrine of grace became more and more radical, until individual actions were said by some to play no part in the attainment of salvation. Tanluan and the other 6th–7th- century Chinese Pure Land patriarchs, Daochuo and Shandao, were among those who rejected the role of works in salvation. Originally a follower of Daoism, Tanluan, while searching for the elixir of immortality, was converted to the Pure Land doctrine by an Indian monk.

Dedicating his life to the spread of this doctrine, Tanluan preached the invocation of the name Amitabha and declared that even evil persons were eligible for the Pure Land if they sincerely uttered the *nembutsu*. He warned, however, that the lowest hell awaited those who reviled the Buddhist *dharma*. Tanluan was followed by Daochuo, who argued that, because his was the age of the final decline predicted in Buddhist scriptures, people must take the "easy path" to salvation. They must trust Amitabha completely, for they are no longer able to follow the more difficult path of the saints. His disciple Shandao, believed by some Japanese Pure Land adherents to be the incarnation of Amida, shaped the doctrines of the later forms of Pure Land Buddhism.

He distributed many copies of the *Pure Land Sutra* and wrote a commentary in which he taught that rebirth in the Western Paradise is made possible by invoking Amida. The *nembutsu* must be supplemented, however, by the chanting of sutras, meditation on the Buddha, worshiping of Buddha images, and singing his praises. The work of Shandao inspired Hônen, the founder of the Pure Land sect (Jôdo- shu) in Japan, to declare that in this evil period people must put complete faith in the saving grace of Amida and constantly invoke his name. Hônen expressed his beliefs in the treatise *Senchaku hongan nembutsu- shu* (1198), which was popular among the common people, as were his teachings generally.

The treatise was burned by the monks of Mount Hiei, and his teachings were vigorously opposed by the established Buddhist priesthood. Indeed, opposition to Hônen was so great that his rivals forced him into exile from 1206 to 1211. Hônen's disciple Shinran, who was exiled at the same time was the founder of True Pure Land (Jôdo Shinshu or Shin), a more radical Amida school. Shinran married with Hônen's consent, which thus suggests that one need not be a monk to attain the Pure Land. In Shinran's teachings, which he popularized by preaching in Japanese villages, he rejected all sutras except the *Pure Land Sutra*, as well as the vows of Dharmakara in that sutra that stress individual merit. Basing his doctrines on the 18th vow, Shinran discouraged any attempt to accumulate merit, for he felt that this stood in the way of absolute faith and dependence on Amida.

Furthermore, he rejected Hônen's practice of continual invocation of Amida, believing that the *nembutsu* need be said only once in order to attain salvation and that repetition of it should be regarded as praise of Amida and not as affecting one's salvation. Thus, Shinran established the total ascendancy of the doctrine of grace. He also founded what would become the Shin school, the largest single Buddhist school in contemporary Japan. Throughout its history the Shin school has actively promoted music, dance, and drama and, since the late 19th century, has engaged in extensive educational and social welfare programs. A third Pure Land sect grew up around the itinerant teacher Ippen. He traveled throughout Japan, advocating the chanting of Amida's name at set intervals throughout the day; hence, his school was called the Ji ("Times") school, or Jishû.

NICHIREN

Like the Lotus Sutra and Pure Land schools, the indigenous Japanese Nichiren School focuses on the "Lotus of the True Law Sutra" and emphasizes fervent faith and the repetition of a key phrase. Unlike other schools that were named after a book or doctrine, the Nichiren School is unique in that it is named after its founder, Nichiren (1222–82). The son of a poor fisherman, Nichiren became a monk at an early age and studied at Mount Hiei, the centre of the Tendai School. He was frustrated by the many paths of Buddhism promising salvation and left Mount Hiei to search for the true path.

When he emerged from his independent studies, he taught that the *Lotus Sutra* (*Saddharmapundarika- sutra*) contains the final and supreme teaching of the Buddha Shakyamuni and offers the only true way to salvation. According to Nichiren, the three forms of the Buddha- the universal or law body (*dharma- kaya*), the enjoyment body (*sambhoga- kaya*), and the phenomenal body (*nirmana- kaya*)- are important aspects of the Buddha Shakyamuni and should be granted equal respect. Following the teaching of Zhiyi, the Chinese founder of Tiantai/Tendai, that the *Lotus Sutra* is the essence of Buddhism, Nichiren held that this same Buddha nature was possessed by all people and could be realized only by proper worship of the *Lotus Sutra*.

Furthermore, like the Pure Land Buddhists, Nichiren felt that his time, which was marked by political upheaval and unrest, was the period of degeneration known in the *Lotus Sutra* as the time of the latter- day *dharma* (*mappô*), when the purity of Buddhist doctrines could be kept only by the bodhisattvas. Nichiren identified himself as an incarnation of several of them, especially Vishistacaritra (Japanese: Jôgyô), the bodhisattva of supreme conduct. Nichiren believed that his distinctive bodhisattva mission was to propagate the true teachings of the *Lotus Sutra* in Japan, where he believed the regeneration of the Buddhist *dharma* would occur.

In attempting to guide Japan to the Buddhist *dharma* as he interpreted it, Nichiren drew great criticism for his strong-willed and uncompromising attitude. In one treatise Nichiren wrote that the unrest in Japan was caused by the chaotic state of religious belief, a condition that could be corrected only by adopting the teachings of the *Lotus Sutra*. He taught that if people turned to this sutra, they would realize their true Buddha nature, perceive that suffering is illusion, and see that this world is a paradise. If human beings- i.e., the Japanese- did not follow the teachings of the *Lotus Sutra*, however, natural disasters and invasions would result.

Moreover, Nichiren, confident of the righteousness of his cause, attacked the Shingon and Amida Buddhist groups for neglecting Shakyamuni, the true Buddha of the *Lotus Sutra*; and he attacked Zen for placing stress only upon Shakyamuni's historical form. He went so far as to declare that "the *Nembutsu* is hell, Zen is a devil, and Shingon is the nation's ruin." These sharp criticisms led Nichiren to be exiled twice and almost brought his execution, from which he was- according to his own account and the belief of his adherents- miraculously saved. Nichiren advocated two main religious practices. The first is the worship of the *honzon* (or *gohonzon*), a mandala (symbolic diagram) designed by Nichiren, which represents both the Buddha nature that is in all humans and the three forms of the Buddha Shakyamuni.

The second is the *daimoku* (Japanese: "sacred title"), the repetition- both orally and in every action of the believer- of the phrase "Namu Myôhô renge kyô" (Japanese: "Salvation to the *Lotus Sutra*") to affirm belief in the teaching and efficacy of the *Lotus Sutra*. Nichiren also taught that there should be a sacred place of ordination (Japanese: *kaidan*) where the believer could receive training in the doctrines of the *Lotus Sutra*. This sacred place might be seen as wherever the believer in the *Lotus Sutra* lives, for there is the Buddhist truth. The *honzon, daimoku,* and *kaidan*, "the three great secret laws" (or "mysteries"), are regarded as the essential teaching of Nichiren.

Nichiren's fervent faith brought him wide fame and many devotees, and at his death he chose six disciples to continue his work. They developed the Nichiren- shu (Japanese: "School of Nichiren"), which still controls the main temple founded by Nichiren at Mount Minobu. One of his disciples, Nikkô, established the Nichiren shô- shû (Japanese: "True School of Nichiren"), which taught that Nichiren, not Shakyamuni, was the saviour and that the mandala painted by Nichiren was alone efficacious in saving mankind. In the 20th century these schools gained many devotees. Within the Nichiren- shû the Reiyû- kai (Japanese: "Association of the Friend of the Spirit") arose in 1925.

This group, which preaches a combination of ancestor worship and Nichiren's doctrines, places faith not in the Buddha or in bodhisattvas but in the mandala, in which all saving power is concentrated. The Risshô- Kôsei- kai (Japanese: "Society for Establishing Righteousness and Friendly Relations"), which split from Reiyû- kai in 1938, teaches the recitation of the *daimoku* as an affirmation of faith in the teaching of the *Lotus Sutra* and the worship of the Buddha Shakyamuni. Like Reiyû- kai, it also allows the veneration of ancestral spirits. Risshô- Kôsei- kai gained many converts after World War II, but its success was soon eclipsed by Sôka- gakkai (Japanese: "Value Creation Society"), the lay movement of Nichiren Shôshû.

Founded by Makiguchi Tsunesaburô (1871–1944) in 1930, Sôka- gakkai was dedicated to educational research and the extension of Nichiren Shôshû. Its founder insisted on the practical values of worldly gain and happiness as well as the attainment of goodness, beauty, and world peace; he taught that Nichiren was to be worshiped as the True Buddha predicted in the *Lotus Sutra*. The members also fervently practice *daimoku* and worship the *honzon* as the repository of the power of all Buddhas and bodhisattvas.

After World War II, Sôka- gakkai, under the leadership of Toda Jôsei (1900–58), grew rapidly through a technique of evangelism called *shakubuku* (Japanese: "break and subdue"), in which the resistance of the other person is destroyed by forceful argument. Although its practice of *shakubuku* was curtailed by Ikeda Daisaku, the society's third president, Sôka-gakkai continued to grow throughout the second half of the 20th century and expanded into other countries, including the United States. Thus, Nichiren's teaching and personality are still strong influences today.

DHYANA (CHAN/ZEN)

The Dhyana (Sanskrit: "Meditation"; Chinese: Chan; Japanese: Zen) school of Buddhism emphasizes meditation as the way to awareness of ultimate reality, an important practice of Buddhism from its origin in India and one found in other Indian schools, such as Yogacara. Chan, which was also influenced by Daoism, promotes special meditation training techniques and doctrines. Despite Indian influences, Chan is generally considered a specifically Chinese product, a view reinforced by the fact that 4th–5th- century Chinese Buddhist monks, such as Huiyuan and Sengzhao, taught beliefs and practices similar to those of the Chan School before the traditional date of its arrival in China. Most Chinese texts name a South Indian monk, Bodhidharma, who arrived in China about 520 CE, as the founder of the Chan School.

Bodhidharma is regarded as the first Chan patriarch and the 28th patriarch of the Indian meditation school. The Indian school began with the monk Kashyapa, who received Buddha Shakyamuni's supreme teaching, which is found in the *Lankavatara- sutra* ("Descent to the Island of Lanka"). The sutra teaches that all beings possess a Buddha nature, often equated with *shunya* (Sanskrit: "the void") in Chan, and that realization of this fact is enlightenment (Chinese: Wu; Japanese: satori). The truly enlightened one cannot explain this ultimate truth or reality, nor can books, words, concepts, or teachers, for it is beyond the ordinary duality of subject and object and must be realized in direct personal experience. Bodhidharma was succeeded as patriarch of the Chan school by Huike, and this line of transmission continued to the fifth patriarch, Hengren, in the 7th century.

After Hengren's death a schism occurred between the adherents of the Northern school of Shenxiu, which held that enlightenment must be attained gradually, and the Southern school of Huineng, which taught that true wisdom, as undifferentiated, must be attained suddenly and spontaneously. Huineng's Southern school claimed to de-emphasizes rituals and the study of texts and to rely on teaching passed from master to pupil. Some proponents of the Southern school also adopted an iconoclastic attitude toward the Buddha, maintaining that if all things contain the Buddha nature, then the Buddha could rightfully be equated with a dung heap. The Southern school overcame its rival, and standard Chinese Chan texts therefore name Huineng as the true and only sixth patriarch. Huineng's *Liuzu Tanching* (Chinese: "Platform Scripture of the Sixth Patriarch") became a key text of the Chan school.

In the 9th century, the Linzi (Japanese: Rinzai) and Caodong (Japanese: Sôtô) branches of the Southern school emerged. The former relied heavily on the *gong'an* (Japanese: *koan*), a paradoxical question or aphorism that was intended to reveal that all conceptualization is wrong and thus leads to enlightenment. The *gong'an* was often accompanied by shouts and slaps from the master to provoke anxiety in the student and, from this, an instant realization of the truth. The Caodong/Sôtô school emphasized the practice of "silent illumination" or "just sitting" (Chinese: *zuochan*; Japanese: *zazen*), which involved sitting in silent meditation under the direction of a master and purging the mind of all notions and concepts.

Both schools followed the doctrine of Huaihai, who taught that a monk who would not work should not eat and that work (as well as everything else) should be done spontaneously and naturally. The emphasis on work made the Chan schools self-sufficient and saved them from the worst effects of the government purge of supposedly parasitic Buddhist monks in 845. The emphasis on spontaneity and naturalness stimulated the development of a Chan aesthetic that profoundly influenced later Chinese painting and writing. The relative success of the Chan tradition in subsequent Chinese history is demonstrated by the fact that virtually all Chinese monks eventually came to belong to one of the two Chan lineages.

Chan (Zen) Buddhism was introduced into Japan as early as the 7th century but flowered only in the 12th and 13th centuries, most notably in the work of the monks Eisai and Dôgen. Eisai, founder of the Rinzai School in the 12th century and a Tendai monk, wished to restore pure Buddhism to Japan and with that aim visited China. When he returned, he taught a system of meditation based on the use of the *koan* phrases. Unlike the Chan schools, Eisai taught that Zen should defend the state and could observe ceremonial rules and offer prayers and incantations. These teachings influenced the warrior class and led to a Zen influence on the martial arts of archery and swordsmanship. Zen influence can also be seen in the Noh theatre, poetry, flower arrangement, and the tea ceremony, all of which stress grace and spontaneity.

Dôgen, who established the Sôtô school in Japan in the 13th century, joined the Tendai monastery of Mount Hiei at an early age, after the death of his mother and father taught him the transitoriness of life. Unfulfilled by his experience at Mount Tendai, Dôgen sought the true path of Buddhism and may have studied with Eisai for a time. Like Eisai, whom he held in high esteem, Dôgen went to China, where he fell under the influence of a Chinese Chan master. Upon his return to Japan, he taught the discipline of "sitting straight" (Japanese: *zazen*), the practice of meditation in the cross- legged (lotus) position.

For Dôgen, practice and enlightenment were intertwined; in *zazen* the Buddha nature in each person is discovered. Unlike many of his Chinese counterparts, however, Dôgen studied scriptures and criticized those who did not. The Zen sects of Eisai and Dôgen have deeply influenced Japanese culture and continue to play a significant role in contemporary Japan. By the mid- 20th century, Zen had become one of the best- known of the Buddhist schools in the Western world.

MAIN FEATURES OF THE MAHAYANA

The obscurest period in the history of Buddhism is that which follows the reign of Asoka, but the enquirer cannot grope for long in these dark ages without stumbling upon the word Mahayana. This is the name given to a movement which in its various phases may be regarded as a philosophical school, a sect and a church, and though it is not always easy to define its relationship to other schools and sects it certainly became a prominent aspect of Buddhism in India about the beginning of our era besides achieving enduring triumphs in the Far East.

The word signifies Great Vehicle or Carriage, that is a means of conveyance to salvation, and is contrasted with Hinayana, the Little Vehicle, a name bestowed on the more conservative party though not willingly accepted by them. The simplest description of the two Vehicles is that given by the Chinese traveller I- Ching (635- 713 A.D.) who saw them both as living realities in India. He says "Those who worship Bodhisattvas and read Mahayana Sutras are called Mahayanists, while those who do not do this are called Hinayanists." In other words, the Mahayanists have scriptures of their own, not included in the Hinayanist Canon and adore superhuman beings in the stage of existence immediately below Buddhahood and practically differing little from Indian deities.

Many characteristics could be added to I- Ching's description but they might not prove universally true of the Mahayana nor entirely absent from the Hinayana, for however divergent the two Vehicles may have become when separated geographically, for instance in Ceylon and Japan, it is clear that when they were in contact, as in India and China, the distinction was not always sharp. But in general the Mahayana was more popular, not in the sense of being simpler, for parts of its teaching were exceedingly abstruse, but in the sense of striving to invent or include doctrines agreeable to the masses.

It was less monastic than the older Buddhism, and more emotional; warmer in charity, more personal in devotion, more ornate in art, literature and ritual, more disposed to evolution and development, whereas the Hinayana was conservative and rigid, secluded in its cloisters and open to the plausible if unjust accusation of selfishness. The two sections are sometimes described as northern and southern Buddhism, but except as a rough description of their distribution at the present day, this distinction is not accurate, for the Mahayana penetrated to Java, while the Hinayana reached Central Asia and China. But it is true that the development of the Mahayana was due to influences prevalent in northern India and not equally prevalent in the South. The terms Pali and Sanskrit Buddhism are convenient and as accurate as can be expected of any nomenclature covering so large a field.

Though European writers usually talk of two Yânas or Vehicles- the great and the little- and though this is clearly the important distinction for historical purposes, yet Indian and Chinese Buddhists frequently enumerate three. These are the *Srâvakayâna*, the vehicle of the ordinary Bhikshu who hopes to become an Arhat, the *Pratyekabuddhayâna* for the rare beings who are able to become Buddhas but do not preach the law to others, and in contrast to both of these the *Mahayana* or vehicle of Buddhas and Bodhisattvas. As a rule these three Vehicles are not regarded as hostile or even incompatible. Thus the *Lotus sutra*, maintains that there is really but one vehicle though by a wise concession to human weakness the Buddha lets it appear that there are three to suit divers tastes.

And the Mahayana is not a single vehicle but rather a train comprising many carriages of different classes. It has an unfortunate but distinct later phase known in Sanskrit as Mantrayâna and Vajrayâna but generally described by Europeans as Tantrism. This phase took some of the worst features in Hinduism, such as spells, charms, and the worship of goddesses and with misplaced ingenuity fitted them into Buddhism.The silence of Hsüan Chuang and I- Ching implies that in the seventh century it was not a noticeable aspect of Indian Buddhism. Although the record of the Mahayana in literature and art is clear and even brilliant, it is not easy either to trace its rise or connect its development with other events in India.

Its annals are an interminable list of names and doctrines, but bring before us few living personalities and hence are dull. They are like a record of the Christian Church's fight against Arians, Monophysites and Nestorians with all the great figures of Byzantine history omitted or called in question. I can only urge that if the history of the Mahayana is uncertain, its teaching fanciful and its scriptures tedious, yet it has been a force of the first magnitude in the secular history and art of China, Japan and Tibet and even to- day the most metaphysical of its sacred books, the Diamond Cutter, has probably more readers than Kant and Hegel.

Since the early history of the Mahayana is a matter for argument rather than precise statement, it will perhaps be best to begin with some account of its doctrines and literature and proceed afterwards to chronology. I may, however, mention that general tradition connects it with King Kanishka and asserts that the great doctors Aœvaghosha and Nâgârjuna lived in and immediately after his reign. The attitude of Kanishka and of the Council which he summoned towards the Mahayana is far from clear and I shall say something about this difficult subject below. Unfortunately his date is not beyond dispute for while a considerable consensus of opinion fixes his accession at about 78 A.D., some scholars place it earlier and others in the second century A.D.

Apart from this, it appears established that the Sukhâvatî-vyûha which is definitely Mahayanist was translated into Chinese between 147 and 186 A.D. We may assume that it was then already well known and had been composed some time before, so that, whatever Kanishka's date may have been,

Mahayanist doctrines must have been in existence about the time of the Christian era, and perhaps considerably earlier. Naturally no one date like a reign or a council can be selected to mark the beginning of a great school.

Such a body of doctrine must have existed piecemeal and unauthorized before it was collected and recognized and some tenets are older than others. Enlarging I- Ching's definition we may find in the Mahayana seven lines of thought or practice. All are not found in all sects and some are shared with the Hinayana but probably none are found fully developed outside the Mahayana. Many of them have parallels in the contemporary phases of Hinduism.

1. A belief in Bodhisattvas and in the power of human beings to become Bodhisattvas.
2. A code of altruistic ethics which teaches that everyone must do good in the interest of the whole world and make over to others any merit he may acquire by his virtues. The aim of the religious life is to become a Bodhisattva, not to become an Arhat.
3. A doctrine that Buddhas are supernatural beings, distributed through infinite space and time, and innumerable. In the language of later theology a Buddha has three bodies and still later there is a group of five Buddhas.
4. Various systems of idealist metaphysics, which tend to regard the Buddha essence or Nirvana much as Brahman is regarded in the Vedanta.
5. A canon composed in Sanskrit and apparently later than the Pali Canon.
6. Habitual worship of images and elaboration of ritual. There is a dangerous tendency to rely on formulæ and charms.
7. A special doctrine of salvation by faith in a Buddha, usually Amitâbha, and invocation of his name. Mahayanism can exist without this doctrine but it is tolerated by most sects and considered essential by some.

BODHISATTVAS

Let us now consider these doctrines and take first the worship of Bodhisattvas. This word means one whose essence is knowledge but is used in the technical sense of a being that is in process of obtaining but has not yet obtained Buddhahood. The Pali Canon shows little interest in the personality of Bodhisattvas and regards them simply as the preliminary or larval form of a Buddha, either Sâkyamuni or some of his predecessors. It was incredible that a being so superior to ordinary humanity as a Buddha should not be suddenly produced in a human family nor could he be regarded as an incarnation in the strict sense. But it was both logical and edifying to suppose that he was the product of a long evolution of virtue, of good deeds and noble resolutions extending through countless ages and culminating in a being superior to the Devas.

Such a being awaited in the Tushita heaven the time fixed for his appearance on earth as a Buddha and his birth was accompanied by marvels. But though the Pali Canon thus recognizes the Bodhisattva as a type which, if rare, yet makes its appearance at certain intervals, it leaves the matter there. It is not suggested that saints should try to become Bodhisattvas and Buddhas, or that Bodhisattvas can be helpers of mankind. But both these trains of thought are natural developments of the older ideas and soon made themselves prominent. It is a characteristic doctrine of Mahayanism that men can try and should try to become Bodhisattvas. In the Pali Canon we hear of Arhats, Pacceka Buddhas, and perfect Buddhas. For all three the ultimate goal is the same, namely Nirvana, but a Pacceka Buddha is greater than an Arhat, because he has greater intellectual powers though he is not omniscient, and a perfect Buddha is greater still, partly because he is omniscient and partly because he saves others.

But if we admit that the career of the Buddha is better and nobler, and also that it is, as the Introduction to the Jâtaka recounts, simply the result of an earnest resolution to school himself and help others, kept firmly through the long chain of existences, there is nothing illogical or presumptuous in making our goal not the quest of personal salvation, but the attainment of Bodhisattvaship, that is the state of those who may aspire to become Buddhas. In fact the Arhat, engrossed in his own salvation, is excused only by his humility and is open to the charge of selfish desire, since the passion for Nirvana is an ambition like any other and the quest for salvation can be best followed by devoting oneself entirely to others. But though my object here is to render intelligible the Mahayanist point of view including its objections to Hinayanism, I must defend the latter from the accusation of selfishness.

The vigorous and authoritative character of Gotama led him to regard all mankind as patients requiring treatment and to emphasize the truth that they could cure themselves if they would try. But the Buddhism of the Pali Canon does not ignore the duties of loving and instructing others; it merely insists on man's power to save him if properly instructed and bids him do it at once: "sell all that thou hast and follow me." And the Mahayana, if less self- centred, has also less self- reliance, and self- discipline. It is more human and charitable, but also more easygoing: it teaches the believer to lean on external supports which if well chosen may be a help, but if trusted without discrimination become paralyzing abuses.

And if we look at the abuses of both systems the fossilized monk of the Hinayana will compare favourably with the tantric adept. It was to the corruptions of the Mahayana rather than of the Hinayana that the decay of Buddhism in India was due. The career of the Bodhisattva was early divided into stages (bhûmi) each marked by the acquisition of some virtue in his triumphant course. The stages are variously reckoned as five, seven and ten. The Mahâvastu, which is the earliest work where the progress is described, enumerates ten without distinguishing them very clearly. Later writers commonly look at the Bodhisattva's task from the humbler point of view of the beginner who wishes to learn the initiatory stages.

For them the Bodhisattva is primarily not a supernatural being or even a saint but simply a religious person who wishes to perform the duties and enjoy the privileges of the Church to the full, much like a communicant in the language of contemporary Christianity. We have a manual for those who would follow this path, in the Bodhicaryâvatâra of Sântideva, which in its humility, sweetness and fervent piety has been rightly compared with the De Imitatione Christi. In many respects the virtues of the Bodhisattva are those of the Arhat. His must be strenuous and concentrated; he must cultivate the strictest morality, patience, energy, meditation and knowledge. But he is also a devotee, a *bhakta*: he adores all the Buddhas of the past, present and future as well as sundry superhuman Bodhisattvas, and he confesses his sins, not after the fashion of the Pâtimokkha, but by accusing himself before these heavenly Protectors and vowing to sin no more.

Sântideva lived in the seventh century but tells us that he follows the scriptures and has nothing new to say. This seems to be true for, though his book being a manual of devotion presents its subject- matter in a dogmatic form; its main ideas are stated and even elaborated in the Lotus. Not only are eminent figures in the Church, such as Sâriputra and Ânanda, there designated as future Buddhas, but the same dignity is predicted wholesale for five hundred and again for two thousand monks. The chief difference is that the Bodhicaryâvatâra portrays a more spiritual life, it speaks more of devotion, less of the million shapes that compose the heavenly host: more of love and wisdom, less of the merits of reading particular sûtras.

While rendering to it and the faith that produced it all honour, we must remember that it is typical of the Mahayana only in the sense that the De Imitatione Christi is typical of Roman Catholicism, for both faiths have other sides. Sântideva's Bodhisattva, when conceiving the thought of Bodhi or eventual supreme enlightenment to be obtained, it may be, only after numberless births, feels first a sympathetic joy in the good actions of all living beings. He addresses to the Buddhas a prayer which is not a mere act of commemoration, but a request to preach the law and to defer their entrance into Nirvana. He then makes over to others whatever merit he may possess or acquire and offers himself and all his possessions, moral and material, as a sacrifice for the salvation of all beings.

This on the one hand does not much exceed the limits of *dânam* or the virtue of giving as practised by Sâkyamuni in previous births according to the Pali scriptures, but on the other it contains in embryo the doctrine of vicarious merit and salvation through a saviour. The older tradition admits that the future Buddha (*e.g.* in the Vessantara birth- story) gives all that is asked from him including life, wife and children. To consider the surrender and transfer of merit (pattidâna in Pali) as parallel is a natural though perhaps false analogy. But the transfer of *Karma* is not altogether foreign to Brahmanic thought, for it is held that a wife may share in her husband's *Karma* nor is it wholly unknown to Sinhalese Buddhism.

After thus deliberately rejecting all personal success and selfish aims, the neophyte makes a vow (pranòidhâna) to acquire enlightenment for the good of all beings and not to swerve from the rules of life and faith requisite for this end. He is then a "son of Buddha," a phrase which is merely a natural metaphor for saying that he is one of the household of faith but still paves the way to later ideas which make the celestial Bodhisattva an emanation or spiritual son of a celestial Buddha. Asanga gives a more technical and scholastic description of the ten *bhûmis* or stages which mark the Bodhisattva's progress towards complete enlightenment and culminate in a phase bearing the remarkable but ancient name of Dharmamegha known also to the Yoga philosophy.

The other stages are called: *muditâ* (joyful): *vimalâ* (immaculate): *prabhâkarî* (light giving): *arcismatî* (radiant): *durjaya* (hard to gain): *abhimukhî* (facing, because it faces both transmigration and Nirvana): *dûramgamâ* (far- going): *acalâ* (immovable): *sâdhumatî* (good minded). The incarnate Buddhas and Bodhisattvas of Tibet are a travesty of the Mahayana which on Indian soil adhered to the sound doctrine that saints are known by their achievements as men and cannot be selected among infant prodigies. It was the general though not universal opinion that one who had entered on the career of a Bodhisattva could not fall so low as to be reborn in any state of punishment, but the spirit of humility and self-effacement which has always marked the Buddhist ideal tended to represent his triumph as incalculably distant.

Meanwhile, although in the whirl of births he was on the upward grade, he yet had his ups and downs and there is no evidence that Indian or Far Eastern Buddhists arrogated to themselves special claims and powers on the ground that they were well advanced in the career of Buddhahood. The vow to suppress self and follow the light not only in this life but in all future births contains an element of faith or fantasy, but has any religion formed a nobler or even equivalent picture of the soul's destiny or built a better staircase from the world of men to the immeasurable spheres of the superhuman? One aspect of the story of Sâkyamuni and his antecedent births thus led to the idea that all may become Buddhas. An equally natural development in another direction created celestial and superhuman Bodhisattvas.

The Hinayana held that Gotama, before his last birth, dwelt in the Tushita heaven enjoying the power and splendour of an Indian god and it looked forward to the advent of Maitreya. But it admitted no other Bodhisattvas, a consequence apparently of the doctrine that there can only be one Buddha at a time. But the luxuriant fancy of India, which loves to multiply divinities, soon broke through this restriction and fashioned for itself beautiful images of benevolent beings that refuse the bliss of Nirvana that they may alleviate the sufferings of others. So far as we can judge, the figures of these Bodhisattvas took shape just about the same time that the personalities of Vishnu and Siva were acquiring consistency.

The impulse in both cases is the same, namely the desire to express in a form accessible to human prayer and sympathetic to human emotion the forces which rule the universe. But in this work of portraiture the Buddhists laid more emphasis on moral and spiritual law than did the Brahmans: they isolated in personification qualities not found isolated in nature. Siva is the law of change, of death and rebirth, with all the riot of slaughter and priapism which it entails: Vishnu is the protector and preserver, the type of good energy warring against evil, but the unity of the figure is smothered by mythology and broken up into various incarnations. But Avalokita and Mañjuœrî, though they had not such strong roots in Indian humanity as Siva and Vishnu, are genii of purer and brighter presence. They are the personifications of kindness and knowledge.

Though manifold in shape, they have little to do with mythology, and are analogous to the archangels of Christian and Jewish tradition and to the Amesha Spentas of Zoroastrianism. With these latter they may have some historical connection, for Persian ideas may well have influenced Buddhism about the time of the Christian era. However difficult it may be to prove the foreign origin of Bodhisattvas, few of them have a clear origin in India and all of them are much better known in Central Asia and China. But they are represented with the appearance and attributes of Indian Devas, as is natural, since even in the Pali Canon Devas form the Buddha's retinue.

The early Buddhists considered that these spirits, whether called Bodhisattvas or Devas, had attained their high position in the same way as Sâkyamuni himself, that is by the practice of moral and intellectual virtues through countless existences, but subsequently they came to be regarded as emanations or sons of superhuman Buddhas. Thus the Kâranòdòa- vyûha relates how the original Âdi- Buddha produced Avalokita by meditation and how he in his turn produced the universe with its gods. Millions of unnamed Bodhisattvas are freely mentioned and even in the older books copious lists of names are found, but two, Avalokita and Mañjuœrî, tower above the rest, among whom only few have a definite personality.

The tantric school counts eight of the first rank. Maitreya (who does not stand on the same footing as the others), Samantabhadra, Mahâsthâna- prâpta and above all Kshitigarbha, have some importance, especially in China and Japan. Avalokita in many forms and in many ages has been one of the principal deities of Asia but his origin is obscure. His main attributes are plain. He is the personification of divine mercy and pity but even the meaning of his name is doubtful. In its full form it is Avalokiteœvara, often rendered the Lord who looks down (from heaven).

This is an appropriate title for the God of Mercy, but the obvious meaning of the participle *avalokita* in Sanskrit is passive, the Lord who is looked at. Kern thinks it may mean the Lord who is everywhere visible as a very present help in trouble, or else the Lord of View, like the epithet Dròishtiguru applied to Siva. Another form of the name is Lokeœvara or Lord of the world and this suggests that *avalokita* may be a synonym of *loka,* meaning the visible universe. It has also been suggested that the name may refer to the small image of Amitâbha which is set in his diadem and thus looks down on him. But such small images set in the head of a larger figure are not distinctive of Avalokita: they are found in other Buddhist statues and paintings and also outside India, for instance at Palmyra.

The Tibetan translation of the name means he who sees with bright eyes. Hsüan Chuang's rendering Kwan- tzÔ- tsai expresses the same idea, but the more usual Chinese translation Kuan- yin or Kuan- shih- yin, the deity who looks upon voices or the region of voices, seems to imply a verbal misunderstanding. For the use of Yin or voice makes us suspect that the translator identified the last part of *Avalokiteœvara* not with *Îœvara* lord but with *svara* sound. Avalokiteœvara is unknown to the Pali Canon and the Milinda Pañha. So far as I can discover he is not mentioned in the Divyâvadâna, Jâtakamâlâ or any work attributed to Aœvaghosha. His name does not occur in the Lalita- vistara but a list of Bodhisattvas in its introductory chapter includes Mahâkarunòâcandin, suggesting Mahâkaruna, the Great Compassionate, which is one of his epithets.

In the Lotus he is placed second in the introductory list of Bodhisattvas after Mañjuœrî. In this section his character as the all- merciful saviour is fully developed. He saves those who call on him from shipwreck, and execution, from robbers and all violence and distress. He saves too from moral evils, such as passion, hatred and folly. He grants children to women who worship him. This power, which is commonly exercised by female deities, is worth remarking as a hint of his subsequent transformation into a goddess. For the better achievement of his merciful deeds, he assumes all manner of forms, and appears in the guise of a Buddha, a Bodhisattva, a Hindu deity, a goblin, or a Brahman and in fact in any shape.

This chapter was translated into Chinese before 417 A.D. and therefore can hardly be later than 350. He is also mentioned in the Sukhâvatî- vyûha. The records of the Chinese pilgrims Fa- Hsien and Hsüan Chuang indicate that his worship prevailed in India from the fourth till the seventh century and we are perhaps justified in dating its beginnings at least two centuries earlier. But the absence of any mention of it in the writings of Aœvaghosha is remarkable. Avalokita is connected with a mountain called Potala or Potalaka. The name is borne by the palace of the Grand Lama at Lhassa and by another Lamaistic establishment at Jehol in north China. It reappears in the sacred island of P´u- t´o near Ningpo. In all these cases the name of Avalokita's Indian residence has been transferred to foreign shrines.

In India there were at least two places called Potala or Potalaka- one at the mouth of the Indus and one in the south. No certain connection has been traced between the former and the Bodhisattva but in the seventh century the latter was regarded as his abode. Our information about it comes mainly from Hsüan Chuang who describes it when speaking of the Malakuta country and as near the Mo- lo- ya (Malaya) mountain. But apparently he did not visit it and this makes it probable that it was not a religious centre but a mountain in the south of which Buddhists in the north wrote with little precision. There is no evidence that Avalokita was first worshipped on this Potalaka, though he is often associated with mountains such as Kapota in Magadha and Valavatî in Katâha.

In fact the connection of Potala with Avalokita remains a mystery. Avalokita has, like most Bodhisattvas, many names. Among the principal are Mahâkaruna, the Great Compassionate one, Lokanâtha or Lokeœvara, the Lord of the world, and Padmapâni, or lotus- handed. This last refers to his appearance as portrayed in statues and miniatures. In the older works of art his figure is human, without redundant limbs, and represents a youth in the costume of an Indian prince with a high jewelled chignon, or sometimes a crown. The head- dress is usually surmounted by a small figure of Amitâbha. His right hand is extended in the position known as the gesture of charity.

In his left he carries a red lotus and he often stands on a larger blossom. His complexion is white or red. Sometimes he has four arms and in later images a great number. He then carries besides the lotus such objects as a book, a rosary and a jug of nectar. The images with many eyes and arms seem an attempt to represent him as looking after the unhappy in all quarters and stretching out his hands in help. It is doubtful if the Bodhisattvas of the Gandhara sculptures, though approaching the type of Avalokita, represent him rather than any other, but nearly all the Buddhist sites of India contain representations of him which date from the early centuries of our era and others are preserved in the miniatures of manuscripts.

He is not a mere adaptation of any one Hindu god. Some of his attributes are also those of Brahmâ. Though in some late texts he is said to have evolved the world from himself, his characteristic function is not to create but, like Vishnu, to save and like Vishnu he holds a lotus. But also he has the title of Îœvara, which is specially applied to Siva. Thus he does not issue from any local cult and has no single mythological pedigree but is the idea of divine compassion represented with such materials as the art and mythology of the day offered.

He is often accompanied by a female figure Târâ. In the tantric period she is recognized as his spouse and her images, common in northern India from the seventh century onwards, show that she was adored as a female Bodhisattva. In Tibet Târâ is an important deity who assumes many forms and even before the tantric influence had become prominent she seems to have been associated with Avalokita. In the Dharmasangraha she is named as one of the four Devîs, and she is mentioned twice under the name of To- lo Pu- sa by Hsüan Chuang, who saw a statue of her in Vaisali and another at Tiladhaka in Magadha. This last stood on the right of a gigantic figure of Buddha, Avalokita being on his left.

Hsüan Chuang distinguishes To- lo (Târâ) and Kuan- tzÔ-tsai. The latter under the name of Kuan- yin or Kwannon has become the most popular goddess of China and Japan, but is apparently a form of Avalokita. The god in his desire to help mankind assumes many shapes and, among these, divine womanhood has by the suffrage of millions been judged the most appropriate. But Târâ was not originally the same as Kuan- yin, though the fact that she accompanies Avalokita and shares his attributes may have made it easier to think of him in female form.

The circumstances in which Avalokita became a goddess are obscure. The Indian images of him are not feminine, although his sex is hardly noticed before the tantric period. He is not a male deity like Krishna, but a strong, bright spirit and like the Christian archangels above sexual distinctions. No female form of him is reported from Tibet and this confirms the idea that none was known in India, and that the change was made in China. It was probably facilitated by the worship of Târâ and of Hâritî, an ogress who was converted by the Buddha and is frequently represented in her regenerate state caressing a child. She is mentioned by Hsüan Chuang and by I- Ching who adds that her image was already known in China. The Chinese also worshipped a native goddess called T'ien-hou or T'ou- mu. Kuan- yin was also identified with an ancient Chinese heroine called Miao- shên.

This is parallel to the legend of Ti- tsang (Kshitigarbha) who, though a male Bodhisattva, was a virtuous maiden in two of his previous existences. Evidently Chinese religious sentiment required a Madonna and it is not unnatural if the god of mercy, who was reputed to assume many shapes and to give sons to the childless, came to be thought of chiefly in a feminine form. The artists of the T'ang dynasty usually represented Avalokita as a youth with a slight moustache and the evidence as to early female figures does not seem to me strong, though *a priori* I see no reason for doubting their existence. In 1102 a Chinese monk named P'u- ming published a romantic legend of Kuan- yin's earthly life which helped to popularize her worship. In this and many other cases the later developments of Buddhism are due to Chinese fancy and have no connection with Indian tradition.

Târâ is a goddess of north India, Nepal and the Lamaist Church and almost unknown in China and Japan. Her name means she who causes to cross, that is who saves, life and its troubles being by a common metaphor described as a sea. Târâ also means a star and in Puranic mythology is the name given to the mother of Buddha, the planet Mercury. Whether the name was first used by Buddhists or Brahmans is unknown, but after the seventh century there was a decided tendency to give Târâ the epithets bestowed on the Saktis of Siva and assimilate her to those goddesses. Thus in the list of her 108 names she is described among other more amiable attributes as terrible, furious, the slayer of evil beings, the destroyer, and Kâlî: also as carrying skulls and being the mother of the Vedas. Here we have if not the borrowing by Buddhists of a Saiva deity, at least the grafting of Saiva conceptions on a Bodhisattva.

The second great Bodhisattva Mañjuœrî has other similar names, such as Mañjunâtha and Mañjughosha, the word Mañju meaning sweet or pleasant. He is also Vagîœvara, the Lord of Speech, and Kumârabhûta, the Prince, which possibly implies that he is the Buddha's eldest son, charged with the government under his direction. He has much the same literary history as Avalokita, not being mentioned in the Pali Canon or in the earlier Sanskrit works such as the Lalita- vistara and Divyâvadâna. But his name occurs in the Sukhâvatî- vyûha: he is the principal interlocutor in the Lankâvatâra sûtra and is extolled in the Ratna- karanòdòaka- vyûha- sûtra.

In the greater part of the Lotus he is the principal Bodhisattva and instructs Maitreya, because, though his youth is eternal, he has known many Buddhas through innumerable ages. The Lotus also recounts how he visited the depths of the sea and converted the inhabitants thereof and how the Lord taught him what are the duties of a Bodhisattva after the Buddha has entered finally into Nirvana. As a rule he has no consort and appears as a male Athene, all intellect and chastity, but sometimes Lakshmî or Sarasvatî or both are described as his consorts. His worship prevailed not only in India but in Nepal, Tibet, China, Japan and Java. Fa- Hsien states that he was honoured in Central India and Hsüan Chuang that there were stupas dedicated to him at Muttra.

He is also said to have been incarnate in Atîsa, the Tibetan reformer, and in Vairocana who introduced Buddhism to Khotan, but, great as is his benevolence, he is not so much the helper of human beings, which is Avalokita's special function, as the personification of thought, knowledge, and meditation. It is for this that he has in his hands the sword of knowledge and a book. A beautiful figure from Java bearing these emblems is in the Berlin Museum. Miniatures represent him as of a yellow colour with the hands (when they do not carry emblems) set in the position known as teaching the law. Other signs which distinguish his images are the blue lotus and the lion on which he sits.

An interesting fact about Mañjuœrî is his association with China, not only in Chinese but in late Indian legends. The mountain Wu- t'ai- shan in the province of Shan- si is sacred to him and is covered with temples erected in his honour. The name (mountain of five terraces) is rendered in Sanskrit as Pancaœîrsha, or Pancaœikha, and occurs both in the Svayambhû Purânòa and in the text appended to miniatures representing Mañjuœrî. The principal temple is said to have been erected between 471 and.500 A.D. I have not seen any statement that the locality was sacred in pre- Buddhist times, but it was probably regarded as the haunt of deities, one of whom- perhaps some spirit of divination- was identified with the wise Mañjuœrî.

It is possible that during the various inroads of Græco-Bactrians, Yüeh- Chih, and other Central Asian tribes into India, Mañjuœrî was somehow imported into the pantheon of the Mahayana from China or Central Asia, and he has, especially in the earlier descriptions, a certain pure and abstract quality which recalls the Amesha- Spentas of Persia. But still his attributes are Indian, and there is little positive evidence of a foreign origin. I- Ching is the first to tell us that the Hindus believed he came from China. Hsüan Chuang does not mention this belief, and probably did not hear of it, for it is an interesting detail which no one writing for a Chinese audience would have omitted. We may therefore suppose that the idea arose in India about 650 A.D.

By that date the temples of Wu- t'ai- Shan would have had time to become celebrated, and the visits paid to India by distinguished Chinese Buddhists would be likely to create the impression that China was a centre of the faith and frequented by Bodhisattvas. We hear that Vajrabodhi (about 700) and Prajña (782) both went to China to adore Mañjuœrî. In 824 a Tibetan envoy arrived at the Chinese Court to ask for an image of Mañjuœrî, and later the Grand Lamas officially recognized that he was incarnate in the Emperor. Another legend relates that Mañjuœrî came from Wu- t'ai- Shan to adore a miraculous lotus that appeared on the lake which then filled Nepal. With a blow of his sword he cleft the mountain barrier and thus drained the valley and introduced civilization.

There may be hidden in this some tradition of the introduction of culture into Nepal but the Nepalese legends are late and in their collected form do not go back beyond the sixteenth century. After Avalokita and Mañjuœrî the most important Bodhisattva is Maitreya, also called Ajita or unconquered, who is the only one recognized by the Pali Canon. This is because he does not stand on the same footing as the others. They are superhuman in their origin as well as in their career, whereas Maitreya is simply a being who like Gotama has lived innumerable lives and ultimately made himself worthy of Buddhahood which he awaits in heaven.

There is no reason to doubt that Gotama regarded himself as one in a series of Buddhas: the Pali scriptures relate that he mentioned his predecessors by name, and also spoke of unnumbered Buddhas to come. Nevertheless Maitreya or

Metteyya is rarely mentioned in the Pali Canon. He is, however, frequently eluded to in the exegetical Pali literature, in the Anâgata- vamòsa and in the earlier Sanskrit works such as the Lalita- vistara, the Divyâvadâna and Mahâvastu. In the Lotus he plays a prominent part, but still is subordinate to Mañjuœrî. Ultimately he was eclipsed by the two great Bodhisattvas but in the early centuries of our era he received much respect. His images are frequent in all parts of the Buddhist world: he was believed to watch over the propagation of the Faith, and to have made special revelations to Asanga.

In paintings he is usually of a golden colour: his statues, which are often gigantic, show him standing or sitting in the European fashion and not cross- legged. He appears to be represented in the earliest Gandharan sculptures and there was a famous image of him in Udyâna of which Fa- Hsien (399-414 A.D.) speaks as if it were already ancient. Hsüan Chuang describes it as well as a stupa erected to commemorate Sâkyamuni's prediction that Maitreya would be his successor. On attaining Buddhahood he will become lord of a terrestrial paradise and hold three assemblies under a dragon flower tree, at which all who have been good Buddhists in previous births will become Arhats. I- Ching speaks of meditating on the advent of Maitreya in language like that which Christian piety uses of the second coming of Christ and concludes a poem which is incorporated in his work with the aspiration

"Deep as the depth of a lake, be my pure and calm meditation. Let me look for the first meeting under the Tree of the Dragon Flower when I hear the deep rippling voice of the Buddha Maitreya." But messianic ideas were not much developed in either Buddhism or Hinduism and perhaps the figures of both Maitreya and Kalkî owe something to Persian legends about Saoshyant the Saviour. The other Bodhisattvas, though lauded in special treatises, have left little impression on Indian Buddhism and have obtained in the Far East most of whatever importance they possess. The makers of images and miniatures assign to each his proper shape and colour, but when we read about them we feel that we are dealing not with the objects of real worship or even the products of a lively imagination, but with names and figures which have a value for picturesque but conventional art.

Among the best known is Samantabhadra, the all gracious, who is still a popular deity in Tibet and the patron saint of the sacred mountain Omei in China, with which he is associated as Mañjuœrî with Wu- tiai- shan. He is represented as green and riding on an elephant. In Indian Buddhism he has a moderately prominent position. He is mentioned in the Dharmasangraha and in one chapter of the Lotus he is charged with the special duty of protecting those who follow the law. But the Chinese pilgrims do not mention his worship.

Mahâsthâmaprâpta is a somewhat similar figure. A chapter of the Lotus (XIX) is dedicated to him without however giving any clear idea of his personality and he is extolled in several descriptions of Sukhâvatî or Paradise, especially in the Amitâyurdhyâna- sûtra. Together with Amitâbha and Avalokita he forms a triad who rule this Happy Land and are often represented by three images in Chinese temples. Vajrapânòi is mentioned in many lists of Bodhisattvas (*e.g.* in the Dharmasangraha) but is of somewhat doubtful position as Hsüan Chuang calls him a deva. Historically his recognition as a Bodhisattva is interesting for he is merely Indra transformed into a Buddhist. The mysterious personages called Vajradhara and Vajrasattva, who in later times are even identified with the original Buddha spirit, are further developments of Vajrapânòi. He owes his elevation to the fact that *Vajra*, originally meaning simply thunderbolt, came to be used as a mystical expression for the highest truth.

More important than these is Kshitigarbha, Ti- tsang or Jizô who in China and Japan ranks second only to Kuan- yin. Visser has consecrated to him an interesting monograph which shows what strange changes and chances may attend spirits and how ideal figures may alter as century after century they travel from land to land. We know little about the origin of Kshitigarbha. The name seems to mean Earth- womb and he has a shadowy counterpart in Akâœagarbha, a similar deity of the air, who it seems never had a hold on human hearts.

The Earth is generally personified as a goddess and Kshitigarbha has some slight feminine traits, though on the whole decidedly masculine.

The stories of his previous births relate how he was twice a woman: in Japan he was identified with the mountain goddess of Kamado, and he helps women in labour, a boon generally accorded by goddesses. In the pantheon of India he played an inconspicuous part, though reckoned one of the eight great Bodhisattvas, but met with more general esteem in Turkestan, where he began to collect the attributes afterwards defined in the Far East. It is there that his history and transformations become clear. He is primarily a deity of the nether world, but like Amitâbha and Avalokita he made a vow to help all living creatures and specially to deliver them from hell. The Taoists pictured hell as divided into ten departments ruled over by as many kings, and Chinese fancy made Ti- tsang the superintendent of these functionaries.

He thus becomes not so much a Saviour as the kindly superintendent of a prison who preaches to the inmates and willingly procures their release. Then we hear of six Ti- tsangs, corresponding to the six worlds of sentient beings, the gracious spirit being supposed to multiply his personality in order to minister to the wants of all. He is often represented as a monk, staff in hand and with shaven head. The origin of this guise is not clear and it perhaps refers to his previous births. But in the eighth century a monk of Chiu Hua was regarded as an incarnation of Ti- tsang and after death his body was gilded and enshrined as an object of worship. In later times the Bodhisattva was confused with the incarnation, in the same way as the portly figure of Pu- tai, commonly known as the laughing Buddha, has been substituted for Maitreya in Chinese iconography.

In Japan the cult of the six Jizôs became very popular. They were regarded as the deities of roads and their effigies ultimately superseded the ancient phallic gods of the crossways. In this martial country the Bodhisattva assumed yet another character as Shôgun Jizô, a militant priest riding on horseback and wearing a helmet that became the patron saint of warriors and was even identified with the Japanese war god, Hachiman. Until the seventeenth century Jizô was worshipped principally by soldiers and priests, but subsequently his cult spread among all classes and in all districts. His benevolent activities as a guide and saviour were more and more emphasized: he heals sickness, he lengthens life, he leads to heaven, and he saves from hell: he even suffers as a substitute in hell and is the special protector of the souls of children amid the perils of the underworld. Though this modern figure of Jizô is wrought with ancient materials, it is in the main a work of Japanese sentiment.

2

The Origins of Mahayana

Mahâyâna is a field of Buddhism accepted widely throughout northern and eastern Asia. Much of the western adepts and practitioners also perceive its significance. This chapter, therefore, is written and aimed to elaborate the origin of Mahâyâna Buddhism by means of "Dharma" analysis. It is an efficient way to demonstrate the historical movement that affected Buddhist cognition of the Three Jewels (The Buddha, his doctrine and the monk's order). I enlist three main interpretations of the word "Dharma" and link them to the new conjecture on Buddhism. At the shift in the level of wisdom, Nâgârjuna and his treatises of the middle way played the dominant role in forming Mahâyâna philosophy. But to put stress on the aspect of compassion, the concepts of "the Buddha's Triple Bodies" and "Bodhisattva" bestowed the Buddhist embodiment with Mahâyâna proliferation.

Mahâyâna means the great way or path. What is the great way? It is the way to help infinite sentient beings cross the ocean of birth and death to the shore of liberation. It was like a vast ship floating under the cruel wind of ignorance just to pick innumerable beings up and bring to the shore of eternal bliss. Led by vowing bodhisattvas, every potential mind would be encouraged to be free from suffering. The concept of Mahâyâna first originated from different attitudes toward Buddhism in all aspects. If we discuss Buddhism, most of us surely think of the three jewels – Buddha: the Lord, Dharma (Pâli: Dhamma): the doctrine, and *Sangha*: the monk's order.

These three jewels had been reinterpreted (or redefined) throughout history and brought about conflicts. Conflicts expanded when time passed by. The process of reinterpretation was not merely change, but like a conceptual revolution. I prefer to call it a movement. The movement could be summarized into three stages as follows:

Firstly, conflicts occurred on the level of "*Sangha*". Since the time of the Lord's passing away, the community of monks was divided into two groups. The First Group consisted of friends and followers of venerated monks. They generated the first Council. The concern of these Buddhist disciples was mainly the purification of the doctrine and discipline. In order to keep the discipline acceptable and universal, having the same standards at all times and all places, monks should not add, delete or adjust any part of the discipline regardless of major or minor ones. They believed this was the only way to sustain Buddhism in the long run. Hence, they chose to be conservative rather than flexible. The other group thought in the contrary. They wanted the discipline to be flexible due to their concern for the safety and welfare of monks.

As we know, some places of ancient India were lands of calamity. There was either human- based or natural disasters around the year - famine, drought, flood, war and so on. In order that monks might survive in these lands, we should be able to add, delete or adjust some parts of discipline especially those included in the minor section. They insisted that the Lord made allowances before them to adjust minor parts of the discipline to suit various circumstances and situations. Buddhism could not be broadly propagated and sustained if the monk's order was too strict on minor parts of the discipline. The case of Vajjian monks is the best example to show the conflict between these two groups. Since those monks had added ten minor precepts for their group, i.e., monks could keep salt to eat with food in another meal, monks could drink mild alcoholic beverages, or monks could get, keep and use money.

In the Second Council they were called "Pâpa bhikkhus" (the sinful monks). Their behavior was unacceptable from the view of the traditional Buddhist adherents. Thus, the movement called for an entire dissolution of the monk's order. They established their own tradition and called them "Mahâsaghikas" (The Great Assembly) The conflict on discipline paved a way for schism. From the very minor points of disagreement, Buddhist disciples evoked a sense of hostility against each other. Without taking into consideration the concern of both sides, they adhered to their own beliefs. While a group paid attention only to the purification of the doctrine and the discipline, the other concerned of self too much on the welfare of monks. There is no need to be enemies if they understood that both the doctrine and the monk's order were equally important to the establishment of Buddhism.

Since the Lord was so benevolent, he did not assign anyone to have full power over the monk's order. No one could arbitrarily claim to be the supreme leader. But his hospitality caused weakness on the other hand. In Buddhism we had no authoritative person to justify what was right or wrong. We had no human leader to make a final conclusion in times of conflict, so disciples relied on views of their teachers as final. Teachers became leaders with full power and authority. The situation worsened deplorably at the wider range. Next, the conflict occurred on the level of "Dharma". Before the Lord's passing away, he once declared before the assembly that monks (also including lay disciples) would have the doctrine and the discipline as their leaders in the future. But the conflict on account of the discipline turned out to be fractured. It seemed that no one wanted to compromise. Some Buddhist disciples, mostly monks of the Great Assembly, found themselves having no shelter left except the doctrine. So they went on searching for the true Dharma.

Amazingly, the statement of the Lord found somewhere else states that "who sees Dharma, that one sees me; who sees me, that one sees Dharma." also supported their struggle. If we use logical implications to judge this sentence, we would find an interesting argument. The argument could be pitched through these questions. What should be the true doctrine so that when we saw it, we might be able to see the Lord? How should we see the doctrine so that we could also see the Lord? Or what should be the best interpretation of Dharma so as to make it valid and approachable to the Lord? For some Buddhist scholars, Dharma had no longer been the teaching messages of the Lord. It contained more latent meanings of which we did not realize. Dharma in their comprehension was something more and wider than the speech of the Lord. The speech was merely a part of him, not the totality. These disciples had shifted the ethical facet of Buddhism to a metaphysical focus. And what they had done was to seek out the truest doctrine.

The true doctrine also revealed the status of the Lord after death. Simultaneously, the assumption that the Lord still existed pervaded and caught the disciples' faithful minds. Unenlightened disciples made an effort to see the Lord through the right understanding of the doctrine. So many interpretations were given to this word. As aforementioned, many Buddhist scholars give priority to the metaphysical rather than moral achievement. By having the Lord as the final goal, they strived to reach the destination through the doctrine. Dharma turned to be a means to reach (the state of) Buddhahood. And this was a new trend within the Buddhist community. It was a conceptual revolution that Dharma was no longer the message, but something real- in- itself. And its truth was, in fact, the truth of the Lord.

Moreover, this word was widely used in the history of Buddhism. It was not only equally significant and pointed to the Lord, but it also pointed to every available entity. Entity herein implied the existence of radical elements either transient or permanent. Dharma meant things when examined fundamentally; had their existence in the form of flowing energy. The existence of such and such appeared and disappeared momentarily. Some called them instantaneous beings. Difficulties to explain, nevertheless, those beings were real and real- in- itself. From the brief explanation to this word, it might be easier if we classify the bulk of definitions into groups in accordance with differing assumptions. Each group represented unique beliefs toward the three jewels. Some of them had a direct impact on the emergence of Mahâyâna Buddhism.

Firstly, there were groups that defined "Dharma" as the Buddhist scriptures; Dharma implied the doctrine or discourse of the Lord recited by disciples. It was no other than the teaching messages. These groups placed emphasis on the moral and practical meanings explicitly found in the doctrine. They paid no attention to any metaphysical views. For them, whether the Lord existed or not was less important than the liberation from all kinds of suffering. To meditate and purify our minds should be the main functions of humans. The chain of birth was too tedious so we should not prolong our destiny in vanity. The Lord taught us to help ourselves, and all of what he had taught was relevant only to suffering and liberation from it. Liberation was their aim, not the truth of the Lord.

The reason was simple and easy. Despite finding him, we were still bound and fluctuated by subtle defilements like greed, hatred or delusion. To see Dharma meant to practice and trust the Lord's wisdom. Dharma was not a means for us to see the Lord, but it was the perfect guideline for self- help. Dharma had its final destination at the liberation of learners, not the realization of the Lord. The Lord had gone far away. It was no use to ponder his existence after death. These groups had rarely influenced the emergence of Mahâyâna Buddhism. Most Thai Theravâda monks belonged to these groups or, at least, shared their beliefs. Secondly, there were groups that defined "Dharma" as the ultimate truth underlying phenomena.

Dharma was in some classes like instantaneous beings as mentioned earlier. Adherents of these groups were titled realists, either being Substantialists or Essentialists. For them, Dharma covered every radical element at both mundane and supramundane levels. Elements hereafter did not merely mean the fundamental materialistic atoms, but included psychic force of consciousness and also the state of emancipation. So it might be clear to equalize elements with entities existing on their own. In the mundane level, Dharma implied an infinite process of evanescent elements. It means that separate elements are linked together by causal laws. There were many categories of elements, but I focus here on the human mind. Of course, our minds are sets of truth. They existed ultimately and objectively. No matter of being caught at sight by anyone, they automatically remained and functioned at normal.

Despite we could never catch our minds by sense organs, the fact that it existed could not be denied. Like other mundane elements, our minds appeared and disappeared spontaneously. Change and impermanence were their attributes. Our minds changed every moment, not day by day, but second by second. All of us were changing, both physically and mentally. Change is a common and natural process of the mind. In the supramundane level, it was quite different in explanations of truth. If we talked about supramundane entities, the state of liberation was included and focused. Like those of mundane elements, the state of liberation was a set of truth. It existed somewhere and somehow regardless of the viewer.

We could never touch it by ordinary sense, but it still existed and was true always. The truth of it was not in the practical but the ontological sense. It was real and real- in-itself. That state was pure and perfect, unique and independent. Permanence was its existence while eternity was its duration. All of these were attributes of that transcendent state. The state of liberation never changed. Since it was so perfect and self- sufficient, no more causation would be required to explain it. As it was unconditioned, it would remain eternal and endless. It is our hope and is still waiting for us. Dharma in the definition of these groups might look far from the Lord. They seemed not relative to the existence of him. In fact, these disciples viewed Dharma as a natural composition of real elements. If viewed from life's framework, Dharma was phenomena and their relations to each other.

It was not the Lord's leaving messages. All messages were just a part of Dharma. Since their viewpoint was centered on metaphysical interest, they gave a high rank of interest to the topic of truth or falsehood. Fact got more significance and left inferior position to the value of practice. Logic took part into the movement. It provided a better method to investigate and specify what should be true. Seeing Dharma for them signified the realization of natural process. If we realized the ultimate truth of all things, it was sure that we would be free from all types of bondage. To see Dharma was to see the truth of phenomena. When we saw the truth of phenomena, the wisdom of the Lord was fulfilled within us. That was the reason why one saw Dharma; he would also see the Lord. A big problem happened from this explanation. Due to the assumption that truth is classified into levels, the question of how could we transmigrate to the pure level might be raised.

As we know, the human mind was defiled, transient and changeable. But the state of liberation remained fixed at all times. The polemical argument lied under the acceptance that both mind and the state of liberation were real (true in the ontological sense). If so, how could the mind meet that state? It was impossible for any human mind to approach the state of liberation. It was such a paradox in saying that we would liberate in the self- sufficient state. If the state of liberation was the objective truth, being permanent and independent on its own, no one could transmigrate. Since transmigration meant change, and change implied non- substantiality but that state of bliss was not open to any kind of change. It remained still. Causation and change could never affect its essence.

And it was futile for us to talk about liberation. Furthermore, the fact that the human mind and the state of liberation existed in severance would restrain humans from their potentiality to liberate. So long as the perfect state abided in its own purification, independence and transcendence beyond all worldly conditions, all mental practices of humans were hopeless. No achievement would be attained and no liberation could be reached. How should the doctrine of the four noble truths (Âryasatya/ Pâli: Ariyasacca) which is the core of Buddhism be comprehensive and fulfilled, if the suffering (Dukkha/ Pâli: Dukkha) implied the transient attachment of ordinary minds but the cessation of it (Nirodha/ Pâli: Nirodha) belonged to the fixed and absolute type of truth? If both were real entities, the four noble truths would represent double standards of opposite truth and cause self-contradiction.

It was irrational that the enlightened one had ever taught such a meaningless doctrine to liberate people. Since the state of liberation had never welcomed our transmigration, all of our hard endeavors would end up in vain and no liberation was really approached. Pioneering was Nâgârjuna in his attempt to evoke his contemporaries of this unintentional disaster. Unless those adherents stopped their propagation of stray views, Buddhism would turn to be dogmatism and fail to help anybody. The principle of interdependence and thus the emptiness of Dharma were declared to break down any absolute concepts. The state of the mind and liberation were no longer two separate truths. But the existence of one depended on the existence of the other. Both existed in relativity. Without one, the other could not be illustrated and approached.

We could not say that either mind or the state of liberation was real- in- itself. In fact, there was no truth in such a manner at all. Truth would be mentioned when the value of practices was evaluated in advance. It meant efficiency rather than objectivity, or the effectiveness of natural law than its being. Truth was no other than the capacity to bring about an effect. By this explanation, truth of liberation was the state of mind when it is pure and devoid of defilement. Mind and the state of liberation need not be apart. The state of liberation was the same as the unconditioned mind. The proclamation of interdependence and emptiness led to the development of sophisticated philosophy among Buddhist scholars. The situation indicated a movement to dissolve from all kinds of realistic traditions that were title "Abhidharma".

And Mahâyâna partly occurred as a result of this struggle. One of the major differences between traditional Buddhism and Mahâyâna was the attitude of disciples toward the state of liberation. At the time of Nâgârjuna, the state of liberation was not real any more. Any attempt to explore and reveal its truth was a sign of ignorance. The state of liberation was empty in the practical sense and entirely imaginative in the metaphysical sense. In the practical sense, it was empty or non-substantial due to its dependence on the mind's existence and vice versa. When the human mind was pure and detached from all types of impurities, such a state is called liberation. So, the state of liberation was possibly obtained within the process of life, not beyond.

As Nâgârjuna stated in his prominent work titled "*Mûlamadhyamakakârikâ*" (*MMK*) that "the life process has no thing that distinguishes it from freedom. Freedom has no thing that distinguishes it from the life- process." Nirvâžna was not something other than Samsâra and Samsâra was not something other than Nirvâžna. Both were empty and relative. Thirdly, there were groups that defined "Dharma" as the ultimate truth of the Lord. Adherents of these groups pressed overwhelmingly to the story of the Lord. More they investigated his life; the less and less they believed he had gone away.

For them, it was unacceptable for the great man who had made infinite vows through aeons of ages would easily pass away without residue. It was hard to admit that he no longer existed. We could not affirm his power if nothing left for us to affirm. How could we make sure that all sentient beings, especially humans, were capable to liberate if his potentiality did not still rest hidden within us. Hence, the Lord's wisdom, compassion and purity coalesced into a flux of energy pervading around the universe. These groups tended to relate Dharma with the Lord's compassion. To see Dharma was to see the Lord's power penetrated through all things. Or to see Dharma was to see the nature of Buddha (Buddhahood) within us.

No matter of phenomena was real on their own, or the state of liberation included some fixed essence, the fact was that the Lord existed somewhere and somehow. Their concern was to search for him through the realization of his power. Only by this explanation of seeing Dharma, would we really see the Lord. Similar to those of the second groups, they regarded Dharma as the means to reach the Lord. But to reach the Lord had a peculiar meaning for they adhered to the linguistic hint of the messages. While the realists understood that to see Dharma was to understand natural process of things. If we realized the ultimate truth of all phenomena, we would certainly perceive the Lord's wisdom. When every attachment was discerned, and the state of liberation was fulfilled, we would, then, derive within us the transcendent intuition like the Lord had once obtained.

But adherents of these groups viewed Dharma as equally important to the Lord. Not equivalent in the sense of having two identical truths, but Dharma was in complete identity with the Lord. No dualism dichotomized from the truth of the Lord. Dharma was his energy illuminating in three aspects: wisdom, purity and compassion. We could absorb this energy by faith and meditation. Especially, his love tied up all sentient beings together under the sphere of potentiality to liberate. Everyone was nourishing in the realm of his radiance. It was like an embryo, the inner sanctum or seed of Buddhahood waiting for attainment within us. His compassion was immense and infinite that the energy formed a potential seed called Buddha's Mind inherently hidden in us. Although liberation had not yet been realized, still we were fully aware of our capacity and freewill to choose what we wanted to. Thus, the Lord exists all times and his energy permeates in all directions.

These groups seemed to uphold the superiority of the Lord over all things. Truth was the Lord or the Lord was truth. The principle of interpenetration and mutual identity came into consideration, but its conceptual fabrication was only at the incipient stage. He was once human, capable of all sciences, at present he has gone away but he left his best inner qualifications available in humans. One really important, duty of man, was to live and spend his life in accordance with the Lord's intention. His intention was to liberate sentient beings from suffering, if unsuccessful, other preliminary helps would be provided without hesitation. So, in order to approach the Buddhahood within us, it was crucial and inevitable that we had to help other sentient beings too. And the best of assistance was to take them with us on the way to liberation.

The notion of Bodhisattva and Mahâyâna sprang up from this attitude. Bodhisattvas were ones who had seriously taken a vow to follow the path to Buddhahood aimed at being fully enlightened and powerful. Metaphorically speaking, Bodhisattvas incessantly trained and exerted themselves at hardiness till they achieved the state of Omniscience and Omnipresence was quite similar to the concept of God in theistic cultures. However, in Buddhism we had no idea of God as the creator. Buddha or the Lord was utterly freed from life's circle, but with his compassion, flourishing out of infinite vows and perfections performed through aeons, his abstract composition in the form of pure energy still existed and functioned in guidance of beings to the right way. The Lord herein was not the same as God. Instead of being the supreme God, Buddha performed the role of kind leader and supporter.

The viewpoint on the topic of Bodhisattva in the Mahâyâna tradition led to the exaltation of Bodhisattvas over Arahants. Despite Arahants seeing appellations of those who had attained the extinction of all defilements and suffering, some Buddhist scholars suspected their fulfillment of the final holiness. In comparison with the concept of Bodhisattva, the latter seemed by all means superior either examined from the scope of wisdom or compassion. While the traditional Buddhism (dominant was Theravâda) confined the explanation of this concept to the previous lives of the Lord. They related the notion of Bodhisattva mainly to the historical human Buddha called Sâkyamunî Buddha. The cult of Mahâyâna did things differently. The latter preferred to use this word in reflection to the seed of the Lord illumined within us.

The dimension of the Lord's benevolence was focused on so intensely that everyone had equal intrinsic value to become a bodhisattva. Not restricted to only extraordinary persons in the past and no random beings to possess Buddhahood, the seed of the Lord had been distributed in equity. Thus, all sentient beings possessed the potentiality to be saviors (bodhisattvas), or received an opportunity to be saved by other bodhisattvas. No one would be discarded by any excuse. And vows to help others would be made for whoever aspired to this career. By this elucidation, it was not surprising if someone called the inculcated pattern of Bodhisattva in the traditional doctrines as descripted in the past, while in Mahâyâna sources the pattern was like a prescription for the present and future.

Apart from these three dominant interpretations of Dharma, still there were varieties of expositions given to this word. For some disciples who were attracted to the monistic philosophical view, the meaning of Dharma would be extended to cover all illusive elements constructed by the human mind. But for Buddhist folks unfamiliar to all sorts of intellectual methodology, Dharma was easily understood as merely virtue or good deeds. In the midst of available assumptions, the three aforesaid groups of cognition reserved the high rank of significance in the history of Buddhism. The other meanings were associations or complements in the sense that they could be accrued to one or more prevailing groups. Mahâyâna sub- sects or schools developed out of these movements. Some created their system of thought based on the adoption of two or more philosophical hints found in those meanings. Some synthesized or compromised groups of definitions together and formed a holistic theory of totality in oneness (or mutual identity).

An interesting standpoint was the belief that the Lord remained as one in all things. Thirdly, conflicts occurred on the level of "Buddha". When the doctrine and the discipline fully split up, the only way for novices and unenlightened disciples to prolong their faith was to go back to the Lord. Without him, no refuge could be leant on. Differences and oppositions on views could no longer merge into unity. Each school concentrated on their own instruction. Apathy to the Lord's intention, they regarded their doctrines as higher or truer, while rebutting others as inferior and phenomenal based. The way to Buddhahood was taught, but its practical suggestions to achieve that state were scattered and disordered due to variances of beliefs. At that time, must Buddhist disciples, especially monks of the Great Assembly admitted the existence of the Lord in the transcendent state.

The real Lord returned to his universal transparency. He still existed but no more in human shape and thought. His human compositions dissipated and turned back to be the natural principle or force that propelled the universe since the beginningless time. There was neither concrete form for us to adhere, nor worldly knowledge able to classify. The Lord after death became the abstract foundation or principle of the universe. This principle was identical and completely relevant to the meaning of Dharma in the third category. The Lord contained within himself the Triple Bodies (Trîkâya). The language was used conventionally and merely signified to aspect than numerical quantity. The first and most fundamental body is called the Cosmic Body (Dharmakâya). This idea could never be comprehensive through human dualistic patterns of thought.

It looked like wisdom, purity and compassion of the Lord since the beginningless time had been gathered up and condensed into the source of pure energy illuminated all around. It was beyond rational analysis in the sense that no kind of thought construction appeared and worked in discrimination. The Cosmic Body penetrated and functioned in radiance. When meditating firmly in a trance we are entitled to that state of the Lord as the Blissful Body (Sambhogakâya). The Blissful Body was such a body of communal enjoyment in some interpretations. Perhaps this cognition derived from the image of the celestial beings beyond the wheel of mundane life. The Blissful Body was also radiance. It functioned around the intersection of defiled and pure level.

While the Cosmic Body permeated his energy from the immaculate core of virtue to cherish universes in all directions, the glistered Blissful Body shone up and down in accord to the Lord's intuition and intelligence. The function of this body mainly aimed at leading celestial bodhisattvas and beings to the path of Mahâyâna. It meant that in order that these beings might realize the Lord's wisdom and compassion, it was impossible not to help other sentient beings. Since all beings possessed the seed of the Lord, to perform oneself for the benefit of others meant to realize the identity of all things. All phenomena were empty, thus they reflected similar Buddhahood. To help others, hence, was to cherish our own Buddhahood.

The third body called Nirmâakâya – the Body of transformation. It was human in shape and form like us but extraordinary in the way of explanation. In fact, this body signified the historical Buddha of this period; Sâkyamunî Buddha. He had born and died two thousand five hundred years ago. The special attentions to which monks of the Great Assembly called were his manifestation out of the first two Bodies. The human Body was just a phenomenon. He had come and gone under the will of radiant Bodies. His life in ancient India was real, but transient and non- substantial so it could not be accepted as the ultimate refuge. Sâkyamunî Buddha once born fulfilled his human functions in leading particular kinds of beings to liberation.

When he finished his short- termed duty, his physical body perished. His death taught us of the three common characteristics of life, impermanence, suffering from attachment and egolessness. So, it was a means or expedient to express Dharma in the preliminary stage. When the human mind detached all substantial views from subtle defilements, the ontological doctrine of Buddha Nature would be taught. The truth of him persisted in eternity but finite human had no capacity to absorb his transcendent body. His radiance was still there but masked by the lack of knowledge (ignorance). So long as humans did not realize the true Dharma, anguish of departure from the Lord still happened. The concept of the Lord's Triple Bodies was very significant in the later Mahâyâna tradition. The Cosmic and Blissful Body were quite weird if viewed from the standpoint of the old sect.

Due to the perpetual existence of transcendent Bodies in the form of universal law and endless radiance, opponents always referred to this recognition as the impact of Hinduism.

Since later Hinduism (especially Vedanta) accepted the authenticity of the Absolute called Brahman despite of being refused to get in part of Buddhism by some scholars, many offshoots of Mahâyâna concepts and schools had yet evolved and preserved in the history. Mahâyâna Buddhism was one of the best systems that advocated the optimistic glance of emotion through reason. Logic had been used to facilitate the role of intellectual wisdom, while the role of intellectual wisdom served and functioned under the call of universal love. These were the enchantments of the Mahâyâna attitude.

DECADENCE OF BUDDHISM IN INDIA

The theme of this chapter is sad for it is the decadence, degradation and ultimate disappearance of Buddhism in India. The other great religions offer no precise parallel to this phenomenon but they also do not offer a parallel to the circumstances of Buddhism at the time when it flourished in its native land. Mohammedanism has been able to maintain itself in comparative isolation: up to the present day Moslims and Christians share the same cities rather than the same thoughts, especially when (as often) they belong to different races.

European Christianity after a few centuries of existence had to contend with no rival of approximately equal strength, for the struggle with Mohammedanism was chiefly military and hardly concerned the merits of the faiths. But Buddhism never had a similarly paramount and unchallenged position. It never attempted to extirpate its rivals. It coexisted with a mass of popular superstition which it only gently reprobated and with a powerful hereditary priesthood, intellectual and pliant, tenacious of their own ideas and yet ready to countenance almost any other ideas as the price of ruling. Neither Islam nor Christianity had such an adversary, and both of them and even Judaism resemble Buddhism in having won greater success outside their native lands than in them. Jerusalem is not an altogether satisfactory spectacle to either Christians or Jews.

Still all this does not completely explain the disappearance of Buddhism from India. Before attempting to assign reasons, we shall do well to review some facts and dates relating to the period of decadence. If we take all India into consideration the period is long, but in many, indeed in most, districts the process of decay was rapid. The latter frankly deplores the decay of the faith which he had witnessed in his own life (*i.e.* about 650- 700 A.D.) but his travels in India were of relatively small extent and he gives less local information than previous pilgrims.

Hsüan Chuang describing India in 629- 645 A.D. is unwilling to admit the decay but his truthful narrative lets it be seen. It is only of Bengal and the present United Provinces that he can be said to give a favourable account, and the prosperity of Buddhism there was largely due to the personal influence of Harsha. In central and southern India, he tells us of little but deserted monasteries. It is clear that Buddhism was dying out but it is not so clear that it had ever been the real religion of this region. In many parts it did not conquer the population but so to speak built fortresses and left garrisons. It is probable that the Buddhism of Andhra, Kalinga and the south was represented by little more than such outposts. They included Amarâvati, where portions of the ruins seem assignable to about 150 A.D., and Ajantâ, where some of the cave paintings are thought to be as late as the sixth century. But of neither site can we give any continuous history.

In southern India the introduction of Buddhism took place under the auspices of Asoka himself, though his inscriptions have as yet been found only in northern Mysore and not in the Tamil country. The Tamil poems Manimêgalei and Silappadigaram, especially the former, represent it as prevalent and still preserving much of its ancient simplicity. Even in later times when it had almost completely disappeared from southern India, occasional Buddhist temples were founded. Rajaraja endowed one at Negapatam about 1000 A.D. In 1055 a monastery was erected at Belgami in Mysore and a Buddhist town named Kalavati is mentioned as existing in that state in 1533. But in spite of such survivals, even in the sixth century

Buddhism could not compete in southern India with either Jainism or Hinduism and there are no traces of its existence in the Deccan after 1150.

For the Konkan, Maharashtra and Gujarat, Hsüan Chuang's statistics are fairly satisfactory. But in this entire region the Sammitîya sect who apparently was nearer to Ḥinduism than the others was the most important. In Ujjain Buddhism was almost extinct but in many of the western states it lingered on, perhaps only in isolated monasteries, until the twelfth century. Inscriptions found at Kanheri (843 and 851 A.D.), Dambal (1095 A.D.) and in Miraj (1110 A.D.) testify that grants were made to monasteries at these late dates. But further north the faith had to endure the violence of strangers. Sind was conquered by the Arabs in 712; Gujarat and the surrounding country were invaded by northern tribes and such invasions were always inimical to the prosperity of monasteries.

This is even truer of the Panjab, the frontier provinces and Kashmir. The older invaders such as the Yüeh- chih had been favourably disposed to Buddhism, but those who came later, such as the Huns, were predaceous barbarians with little religion of any sort. In Hsüan Chuang's time it was only in Udyana that Buddhism could be said to be the religion of the people and the torrent of Mohammedan invasion which swept continuously through these countries during the middle ages overwhelmed all earlier religions and even Hinduism had to yield. In Kashmir Buddhism soon became corrupt and according to the Râjatarangini the monks began to marry as early as the sixth century. King Lâlitâditya (733- 769) is credited with having built monasteries as well as temples to the Sun, but his successors were Sivaites.

Bengal, especially western Bengal and Bihar, was the stronghold of decadent Buddhism, though even here hostile influences were not absent. But about 730 A.D. a pious Buddhist named Gopâla founded the Pâla dynasty and extended his power over Magadha. The Pâlas ruled for about 450 years and supplied a long and devout line of defenders of the faith. But to the east of their dominions lay the principality of Kanauj, a state of varying size and fortunes and from the eighth century onwards a stronghold of Brahmanic learning. The revolution in Hinduism which definitely defeated, though it did not annihilate Buddhism, is generally connected with the names of Kumârilòa Bhatta (*c.* 750) and Sankara (*c.* 800).

We know the doctrines of these teachers, for many of their works have come down to us, but when we enquire what was their political importance, or the scope and extent of the movement which they chàmpioned we are conscious (as so often) of the extraordinary vagueness of Indian records even when the subject might appeal to religious and philosophic minds. Kumârilòa is said to have been a Brahman of Bihar who abjured Buddhism for Hinduism and raged with the ardour of a proselyte against his ancient faith. Tradition represents him as instigating King Sudhanvan to exterminate the Buddhists. But nothing is known of this king and he cannot have had the extensive empire with which he is credited. Sankara was a Brahman of the south who in a short life found time to write numerous works, to wander over India, to found a monastic order and build four monasteries.

In doctrine and discipline he was more pliant than Kumârilòa and he assimilated many strong points of Buddhism. Both these teachers are depicted as the successful heroes of public disputations in which the interest at stake was considerable. The vanquished had to become a disciple of the vanquisher or to forfeit his life and,. if he was the head of an institution, to surrender its property. These accounts, though exaggerated, are probably a florid version of what occurred and we may surmise that the popular faith of the day was generally victorious. What violence the rising tide of Hinduism may have wrought, it is hard to say.

There is no evidence of any general persecution of Buddhism in the sense in which one Christian sect persecuted another in Europe. But at a rather later date we hear that Jains were persecuted and tortured by Saiva princes both in southern India and Gujarat, and if there were any detailed account, epigraphic or literary, of such persecutions in the eighth and ninth centuries, there would be no reason for doubting it. But no details are forthcoming. Without resorting to massacre, an anti- Buddhist king had in his power many effective methods of hostility. He might confiscate or transfer monastic property, or forbid his subjects to support monks. Considering the state of Buddhism as represented by Hsüan Chuang and I-Ching it is probable that such measures would suffice to ensure the triumph of the Brahmans in most parts of India.

After the epoch of Sankara, the history of Indian Buddhism is confined to the Pâla kingdom. Elsewhere we hear only of isolated grants to monasteries and similar acts of piety, often striking but hardly worthy of mention in comparison with the enormous number of Brahmanic inscriptions. But in the Pâla kingdom Buddhism, though corrupt, was flourishing so far as the number of its adherents and royal favour were concerned. Gopâla founded the monastery of Odontapuri or Udandapura, which according to some authorities was in the town of Bihar. Dharmapâla the second king of the dynasty (*c.* 800 A.D.) built on the north bank of the Ganges the even more celebrated University of Vikramaœila, where many commentaries were composed. It was a centre not only of tantric learning but of logic and grammar, and is interesting as showing the connection between Bengal and Tibet.

Tibetans studied there and Sanskrit books were translated into Tibetan within its cloisters. Dharmapâla is said to have reigned sixty- four years and to have held his court at Patna, which had fallen into decay but now began to revive. According to Târanâtha his successor Devapâla built Somapuri, conquered Orissa and waged war with the unbelievers who had become numerous, no doubt as a result of the preaching of Sanskara. But as a rule the Pâlas, though they favoured Buddhism, did not actively discourage Hinduism. They even gave grants to Hindu temples and their prime ministers were generally Brahmans who used to erect non- Buddhist images in Buddhist shrines.

The dynasty continued through the eleventh century and in this period some information as to the condition of Indian Buddhism is afforded by the relations between Bengal and

Tibet. After the persecution of the tenth century Tibetan Buddhism was revived by the preaching of monks from Bengal. Mahîpâla then occupied the throne (*c.* 978- 1030) and during his reign various learned men accepted invitations to Tibet. More celebrated is the mission of Atîsa, a monk of the Vikramaœila monastery, which took place about 1038.

These two missions should have been invited and despatched shows that in the eleventh century Bengal was a centre of Buddhist learning. Probably the numerous Sanskrit works preserved in Tibetan translations then existed in its monasteries. But about the same time the power of the Pâla dynasty, and with it the influence of Buddhism, were curtailed by the establishment of the rival Sena dynasty in the eastern provinces. Still, under Râmapâla, who reigned about 1100, the great teacher Abhayakara was an ornament of the Mahayana. Târanâtha says that he corrected the text of the scriptures and that in his time there were many Pandits and resident Bhikshus in the monasteries of Vikramasîla, Bodh Gaya and Odontapuri.

There is thus every reason to suppose that in the twelfth century Buddhism still nourished in Bihar that its clergy numbered several thousands and its learning was held in esteem. The blow which destroyed its power was struck by a Mohammedan invasion in 1193. In that year Ikhtiyar- ud- Din Muhammad, a general of Kutb- ud- Din, invaded Bihar with a band of only two hundred men and with amazing audacity seized the capital, which, consisting chiefly of palaces and monasteries, collapsed without a blow. The monks were massacred to a man, and when the victors, who appear not to have understood what manner of place they had captured, asked the meaning of the libraries which they saw, no one was found capable of reading the books.

It was in 1193 also that Benares was conquered by the Mohammedans. There is no record of the sack of the monastery at Sarnath but the ruins are said to show traces of fire and other indications that it was overwhelmed by some sudden disaster. The Mohammedans had no special animus against Buddhism. They were iconoclasts who saw merit in the destruction of images and the slaughter of idolaters. But whereas Hinduism was spread over the country, Buddhism was concentrated in the great monasteries and when these were destroyed there remained nothing outside them capable of withstanding either the violence of the Moslims or the assimilative influence of the Brahmans. Hence Buddhism suffered far more from these invasions than Hinduism but still vestiges of it lingered long and exist even now in Orissa.

Târanâtha says that the immediate result of the Moslim conquest was the dispersal of the surviving teachers and this may explain the sporadic occurrence of late Buddhist inscriptions in other parts of India. He also tells us that a king named Cangalarâja restored the ruined Buddhist temples of Bengal about 1450. Elsewhere he gives a not discouraging picture of Buddhism in the Deccan, Gujarat and Rajputana after the Moslim conquest of Magadha but adds that the study of magic became more and more prevalent. In the life of Caitanya it is stated that when travelling in southern India (about 1510 A.D.) he argued with Buddhists and confuted them, apparently somewhere in Arcot.

Manuscripts preserved in Nepal indicate that as late as the fifteenth or sixteenth century Bengali copyists wrote out Buddhist works, and there is evidence that Bodh- Gaya continued to be a place of pilgrimage. In 1585 it was visited by a Nepalese named Abhaya Râjâ who on his return erected in Patan a monastery imitated from what he had seen in Bengal, and in 1777 the Tashi Lama sent an embassy. But such instances prove little as to the religion of the surrounding Hindu population, for at the present day numerous Buddhist pilgrims, especially Burmese, frequent the shrine. The control of the temple passed into the hands of the Brahmans and for the ordinary Bengali Buddha became a member of India's numerous pantheons.

Pandit Harapraœad Sastri mentions a singular poem called Buddhacaritra, completed in 1711 and celebrating an incarnation of Buddha which apparently commenced in 1699 and was to end in the reappearance of the golden age. But the being called Buddha is a form of Vishnòu and the work is as strange a jumble of religion as it is of languages, being written in "a curious medley of bad Sanskrit, bad Hindi and bad Bihari." It is chiefly in Orissa that traces of Buddhism can still be found within the limits of India proper. The Saraks of Baramba, Tigaria and the adjoining parts of Cuttack describe themselves as Buddhists.

Their name is the modern equivalent of Srâvaka and they apparently represent an ancient Buddhist community which has become a sectarian caste. They have little knowledge of their religion but meet once a year in the cave temples of Khandagiri, to worship a deity called Buddhadeva or Caturbhuja. All their ceremonies commence with the formula *Ahimòsâ parama dharma* and they respect the temple of Puri, which is suspected of having a Buddhist origin. Nagendranâth Vasu has published some interesting details as to the survival of Buddhist ideas in Orissa. He traces the origin of this hardy though degraded form of Mahayanism to Râmâi Pandit, a tantric Âcârya of Magadha who wrote a work called Sûnya Purânòa which became popular.

Orissa was one of the regions which offered the longest resistance to Islam, for it did not succumb until 1568. A period of Sivaism in the tenth and eleventh centuries is indicated by the temples of Bhuvaneshwar and other monuments. But in the twelfth and thirteenth centuries the reigning dynasty were worshippers of Vishnu and built the great temples at Puri and Konârak, dedicated to Jagannâtha and Sûrya- nârâyanòa respectively. We do not however hear that they persecuted Buddhism and there are reasons for thinking that Jagannâtha is a form of the Buddha and that the temple at Puri was originally a Buddhist site.

It is said that it contains a gigantic statue of the Buddha before which a wall has been built and also that the image of Jagannâtha, which is little more than a log of wood, is really a case enclosing a Buddhist relic. King Pratâparudra persecuted Buddhism, which implies that at this late date its adherents were sufficiently numerous to attract attention. Either at the beginning of his reign or before it there flourished a group of six poets of whom the principal were Acyutânanda Dâsa and Caitanya Dâsa. Their works are nominally devoted to the celebration of Kròishnòa's praises and form the chief vernacular scripture of the Vaishnòavas in Orissa but in them Kròishnòa, or the highest form of the deity by whatever name he is called, is constantly identified with Sûnya or the Void, that favourite term of Mahayanist philosophy.

Passages from them are also quoted stating that in the Kali age the followers of the Buddha must disguise themselves; that there are 3000 crypto- Buddhists hidden in various parts of Orissa, that Hari has been incarnate in many Buddhas and that the Buddha will appear again on earth. The phrase "I take refuge in the Buddha, in Mâtâ Âdiœakti (= Dharma) and in the Sangha" is also quoted from these works and Caitanya Dâsa describes five Vishnus, who are apparently identical with the five Dhyâni Buddhas. Târanâtha states that the last king of Orissa, Mukunda Deva, who was overthrown by the Mohammedans in 1568, was a Buddhist and founded some temples and monasteries.

In the seventeenth century, there flourished a Buddhist poet named Mahâdevadâsa, and the Tibetan pilgrim Buddhagupta visited among other sites the old capital of Mayurabhanja and saw a stupa there. It is claimed that the tribe known as Bâthuris or Bâuris have always been crypto-Buddhists and have preserved their ancient customs. They are however no credit to their religion, for one of their principal ceremonies is hook- swinging. The doctrine of the Bâthuris is called Mahimâ Dharma and experienced an interesting revival in 1875.

A blind man named Bhîma Bhoi had a vision of the Buddha who restored his sight and bade him preach the law. He attracted some thousands of adherents and led a band to Puri proclaiming that his mission was to bring to light the statue of Buddha concealed in the temple. The Raja resisted the attempt and the followers of Bhîma Bhoi were worsted in a sanguinary encounter. Since that time they have retired to the more remote districts of Orissa and are said to hold that the Buddha will appear again in a new incarnation. They are also called Kumbhipatias and according to the last census of India (1911) are hostile to Brahmans and probably number about 25,000.

Traces of Buddhism also survive in the worship of a deity called Dharma- Râjâ or Dharma- Thakur which still prevails in western and southern Bengal. Priests of this worship are usually not Brahmans but of low caste, and Haraprasad thinks that the laity who follow it may number "several millions." Though Dharma has come to be associated with the goddess of smallpox and is believed even by his adorers to be a form of Vishnu or of Siva, yet Dhyâna, or meditation, forms a part of his worship and the prayers and literature of the sect retain some traces of his origin. Thus he is said to be highly honoured in Ceylon and receives the epithet Sûnyamûrti.

A corrupt form of Buddhism still exists in Nepal. This country when first heard of was in the hands of the Nevars who have preserved some traditions of a migration from the north and are akin to the Tibetans in race and language, though like many non- Aryan tribes they have endeavoured to invent for themselves a Hindu pedigree. Buddhism was introduced under Asoka. As Indian influence was strong and communication with Tirhut and Bengal easy, it is probable that Buddhism in Nepal reflected the phases which it underwent in Bengal. A Nepalese inscription of the seventh century gives a list of shrines of which seven are Sivaite, six Buddhist and four Vishnuite.

After that date it was more successful in maintaining itself, for it did not suffer from Mohammedan attacks and was less exposed to the assimilative influence of Brahmanism. That influence however, though operating in a foreign country and on people not bred among Brahmanic traditions, was nevertheless strong. In 1324 the king of Tirhut, being expelled thence by Mohammedans, seized the throne of Nepal and brought with him many learned Brahmans. His dynasty was not permanent but later in the fourteenth century a subsequent ruler, Jayasthiti, organized society and religion in consultation with the Brahman immigrants.

The followers of the two religions were arranged in parallel divisions, a group of Buddhists classified according to occupation corresponding to each Hindu caste, and appropriate rules and ceremonies were prescribed for the different sections.

The code then established is still in force in essentials and Nepal, being intellectually the pupil of India, has continued to receive such new ideas as appeared in the plains of Bengal. When these ascended to the mountain valleys they were adopted, with free modification of old and new material alike, by both Buddhists and Hindus, but as both sects were geographically isolated, each tended to resemble the other more than either resembled normal Buddhism or Hinduism.

Naturally the new ideas were mainly Brahmanic and Buddhism had no chance of being fortified by an importation of even moderately orthodox doctrine. In the fourteenth century arose the community of wandering ascetics called Nâthas who were reverenced by Hindus and Buddhists alike. They rejected the observances of both creeds but often combined their doctrines and, though disavowed by the Brahmans, exercised a considerable influence among the lower castes. Some of the peculiar deities of Nepal, such as Matsyendranâth, have attributes traceable to these wanderers. In 1769 Nepal was conquered by the Gurkhas. This tribe seems related to the Tibetan stock, as are the Nevars, but it had long been Hinduized and claimed a Rajput ancestry. Thus Gurkha rule has favoured and accelerated the hinduizing of Nepalese Buddhism.

Since the time of Hodgson the worship of the Âdi-Buddha, or an original divine Buddha practically equivalent to God, has been often described as characteristic of Nepalese religion and such worship undoubtedly exists. But recent accounts indicate that it is not prominent and also that it can hardly be considered a distinct type of monotheistic Buddhism. The idea that the five Dhyâni- Buddhas are emanations or manifestations of a single primordial Buddha-spirit is a natural development of Mahayanist ideas, but no definite statement of it earlier than the Kâlacakra literature is forthcoming, though many earlier works point towards it.

In modern Nepal the chief temple of the Âdi- Buddha is on the hill of Svayambhû (the self- existent) near Katmandu.

According to a legend preserved in the Svayambhû Purânòa, a special divine manifestation occurred in ancient times on an adjoining lake; a miraculous lotus arose on its surface, bearing an image, over which a Caitya was subsequently erected. The shrine is greatly venerated but this Âdi- Buddha, or Svayambhû, does not differ essentially from other miraculous images in India which are said not to consist of ordinary matter but to embody in some special way the nature of a deity. The religion of Nepal is less remarkable for new developments of Buddhism than for the singular fusion of Buddhism with Hinduism which it presents and which helps us to understand what must have been the last phase in Bengal.

The Nepalese Brahmans tolerate Buddhism. The Nepâlamâhâtmya says that to worship Buddha is to worship Siva, and the Svayambhû Purâna returns the compliment by recommending the worship of Paœupati. The official itinerary of the Hindu pilgrim includes Svayambhû, where he adores Buddha under that name. More often the two religions adore the same image under different names: what is Avalokita to the one is Mahâkâla to the other. Durgâ is explained as being the incarnation of the Prajñâ- pâramitâ and she is even identified with the Âdi- Buddha. The Nepalese pantheon like the Tibetan contains three elements, often united in modern legends: firstly aboriginal deities, such as Nagas and other nature spirits: secondly definitely Buddhist deities or Bodhisattvas of whom Mañjuœrî receives the most honour: thirdly Hindu deities such as Ganòeœa and Kròishnòa. The popular deity Matsyendranath appears to combine all three elements in his own person.

Modern accounts of Nepal leave the impression that even corrupt Buddhism is in a bad way, yet the number of religious establishments is considerable. Celibacy is not observed by their inmates, who are called banras (bandyas). On entering the order the novice takes the ancient vows but after four days he returns to his tutor, confesses that they are too hard for him and is absolved from his obligations. The classes known as Bhikshus and Gubhârjus officiate as priests, the latter being the higher order. The principal ceremony is the offering of melted butter. The more learned Gubhârjus receive the title of Vajrâcârya and have the sole right of officiating at marriages and funerals.

There is little learning. The oldest scriptures in use are the so- called nine Dharmas. Hodgson describes these works as much venerated and Rajendralal Mitra has analysed them, but Sylvain Lévi heard little of them in 1898, though he mentions the recitation of the Prajñâ- pâramitâ. The Svayambhû Purânòa is an account of the manifestation of the Âdi- Buddha written in the style of those portions of the Brahmanic Purânòas which treat of the glories of some sacred place. In its present form it can hardly be earlier than the sixteenth century A.D. The Nepâla- mâhâtmya is a similar work which, though of Brahmanic origin, puts Buddha, Vishnu and Siva on the same footing and identifies the first with Krishna.

The Vâgvatî- mâhâtmya on the other hand is strictly Sivaite and ignores Buddha's claims to worship. The Vâmœâvali, or Chronicle of Nepal, written in the Gurkha language (Parbatiya) is also largely occupied with an account of sacred sites and buildings and exists in two versions, one Buddhist, the other Brahmanical. But let us return to the decadence of Buddhism in India. It is plain that persecution was not its main cause nor even very important among the accessory causes. The available records contain clearer statements about the persecution of Jainism than of Buddhism but no doubt the latter came in for some rough handling, though not enough to annihilate a vigorous sect.

Great numbers of monasteries in the north were demolished by the Huns and a similar catastrophe brought about the collapse of the Church in Bihar. But this last incident cannot be called religious persecution, for Muhammad did not even know what he was destroying. Buddhism did not arouse more animosity than other Indian religions: the significant feature is that when its temples and monasteries were demolished it did not live on in the hearts of the people, as did Hinduism with all its faults. The relation between the laity and the Church in Buddhism is curious and has had serious consequences for both good and evil. The layman "takes refuge" in the Buddha, his law and his church but does not swear exclusive allegiance: to follow supplementary observances is not treasonable, provided they are not in themselves objectionable.

The Buddha prescribed no ceremonies for births, deaths and marriages and apparently expected the laity to continue in the observance of such rites as were in use. Today in China and Japan the good layman is little more than one who pays more attention to Buddhism than to other faiths. This charitable pliancy had much to do with the victories of Buddhism in the Far East, where it had to struggle against strong prejudices and could hardly have made its way if it had been intolerant of local deities. But in India we see the disadvantages of the omission to make the laity members of a special corporation and the survival of the Jains, who do form such a corporation, is a clear object lesson.

Social life in India tends to combine men in castes or in communities which if not castes in the technical sense have much the same character. Such communities have great vitality so long as they maintain their peculiar usages, but when they cease to do so they soon disintegrate and are reabsorbed. Buddhism from the first never took the form of a corporation. The special community which it instituted was the sangha or body of monks. Otherwise, it aimed not at founding a sect but at including the entire world as lay believers on easy terms. This principle worked well so long as the faith was in the ascendent but its effect was disastrous when decline began. The line dividing Buddhist laymen from ordinary Hindus became less and less marked: distinctive teaching was found only in the monasteries: these became poorly recruited and as they were gradually deserted or destroyed by Mohammedans the religion of the Buddha disappeared from his native land.

Even in the monasteries the doctrine taught bore a closer resemblance to Hinduism than to the preaching of Gotama and it is this absence of the protestant spirit, this pliant adaptability to the ideas of each age, which caused Indian Buddhism to lose its individuality and separate existence. In some localities its disappearance and absorption were preceded by a monstrous phase, known as Tantrism or Sâktism, in which the worst elements of Hinduism, those which would have been most repulsive to Gotama, made an unnatural alliance with his church.

The original meaning of Tantra as applied to literary compositions is a simplified manual. Thus we hear of Vishnuite Tantras and in this sense there is a real similarity between Buddhist and tantric teaching, for both set aside Brahmanic tradition as needlessly complicated and both profess to preach a simple and practical road to salvation. But in Hinduism and Buddhism alike such words as Tantra and tantric acquire a special sense and imply the worship of the divine energy in a female form called by many names such as Kâlî in the former, Târâ in the latter.

This worship which in my opinion should be called Sâktism rather than Tantrism combines many elements: ancient, savage superstitions as well as ingenious but fanciful speculation, but its essence is always magic. It attempts to attain by magical or sacramental formulæ and acts not only prosperity and power but salvation, nirvana and union with the supreme spirit. Some of its sects practise secret immoral rites. It is sad to confess that degenerate Buddhism did not remain uncorrupted by such abuses. It is always a difficult and speculative task to trace the early stages of new movements in Indian religion, but it is clear that by the eighth century and perhaps earlier the Buddhism of Bihar and Bengal had fallen a prey to this influence.

Apparently the public ritual in the Vihâras remained unchanged and the usual language about *nirvâṇa* and *œûnyatâ* was not discarded, but it was taught that those who followed a certain curriculum could obtain salvation by magical methods. To enter this curriculum it was necessary to have a qualified teacher and to receive from him initiation or baptism (abhisheka). Of the subsequent rites the most important is to evoke one of the many Buddhas or Bodhisattvas recognized by the Mahayana and identify oneself with him. He who wishes to do this is often called a sâdhaka or magician but his achievements, like many Indian miracles, are due to self-hypnotization. He is directed to repair to a lonely place and offer worship there with flowers and prayers.

To this office succeed prolonged exercises in meditation which do not depart much from the ancient canon since they include the four Brahmâ- vihâras. Their object is to suppress thought and leave the mind empty. Then the sâdhaka fills this void with the image of some Bodhisattva, for instance Avalokita. This he does by uttering mystic syllables called bîja or seed, because they are supposed to germinate and grow into the figures which he wishes to produce. In this way he imagines that he sees the emblems of the Bodhisattva spring up round him one by one and finally he himself assumes the shape of Avalokita and becomes one with him. Something similar still exists in Tibet where every Lama chooses a tutelary deity or Yi- dam whom he summons in visible form after meditation and fasting.

Though this procedure when set forth methodically in a mediæval manual seems an absurd travesty of Buddhism, yet it has links with the early faith. It is admitted in the Pitakas that certain forms of meditation lead to union with Brahmâ and it is no great change to make them lead to union with other supernatural beings. Still we are not here breathing the atmosphere of the Pitakas. The object is not to share Brahmâ's heaven but to become temporarily identified with a deity, and this is not a byway of religion but the high road.

But there is a further stage of degradation. I have already mentioned that various Bodhisattvas are represented as accompanied by a female deity, particularly Avalokita by Târâ.

The mythological and metaphysical ideas which have grown up round Siva and Durgâ also attached themselves to these couples. The Buddha or Bodhisattva is represented as enjoying nirvana because he is united to his spouse, and to the three bodies already enumerated is added a fourth, the body of perfect bliss. Sometimes this idea merely leads to further developments of the practices described above. Thus the devotee may imagine that he enters into Târâ as an embryo and is born of her as a Buddha. More often the argument is that since the bliss of the Buddha consists in union with Târâ, nirvana can be obtained by sexual union here, and we find many of the tantric wizards represented as accompanied by female companions.

The adept should avoid all action but he is beyond good and evil and the dangerous doctrine that he can do evil with impunity, which the more respectable sects repudiate, is expressly taught. The sage is not defiled by passion but conquers passion by passion: he should commit every infamy: he should rob, lie and kill Buddhas. These crazy precepts are probably little more than a speculative application to the moral sphere of the doctrine that all things are non- existent and hence equivalent. But though tantrists did not go about robbing and murdering so freely as their principles allowed, there is some evidence that in the period of decadence the morality of the Bhikshus had fallen into great discredit. Thus in the allegorical Vishnuite drama called Prabodhacandrodaya and written at Kalanjar near the end of the eleventh century Buddhists and Jains are represented as succumbing to the temptations of inebriety and voluptuousness.

It is necessary to mention this phase of decadence but no good purpose would be served by dwelling further on the absurd and often disgusting prescriptions of such works as the Tathâgata- guhyaka. If the European reader is inclined to condemn unreservedly a religion which even in decrepitude could find place for such monstrosities, he should remember that the aberrations of Indian religion are due not to its inherent depravity, but to its universality. In Europe those who follow disreputable occupations rarely suppose that they have anything to do with the Church. In India, robbers, murderers, gamblers, prostitutes, and maniacs all have their appropriate gods, and had the Marquis de Sade been a Hindu he would probably have founded a new tantric sect. But though the details of Sâktism are an unprofitable study, it is of some importance to ascertain when it first invaded Buddhism and to what extent it superseded older ideas.

Some critics seem to imply- for their statements are not very explicit- that Sâktism formed part if not of the teaching of the Buddha, at least of the medley of beliefs held by his disciples. But I see no proof that Sâktist beliefs- that is to say erotic mysticism founded on the worship of goddesses- were prevalent in Magadha or Kosala before the Christian era. Although Siri, the goddess of luck, is mentioned in the Pitakas, the popular deities whom they bring on the scene are almost exclusively masculine. And though in the older Brahmanic books there are passages which might easily become tantric, yet the transition is not made and the important truths of religion are kept distinct from unclean rites and thoughts.

The Bròihad- âranòyaka contains a chapter which hardly admits of translation but the object of the practices inculcated is simply to ensure the birth of a son. The same work (not without analogies in the ecstatic utterances of Christian saints) boldly compares union with the Âtman to the bliss of one, who is embraced by a beloved wife, but this is a mere illustration and there is no hint of the doctrine that the goal of the religious life is obtainable by *maithuna*. Still such passages, though innocent in themselves, make it easy to see how degrading superstitions found an easy entrance into the noblest edifices of Indian thought and possibly some heresies condemned in the Kathâvatthu indicate that even at this early date the Buddhist Church was contaminated by erotic fancies. But, if so, there is no evidence that such malpractices were widespread.

The appendices to the Lotus show that the worship of a many- named goddess, invoked as a defender of the faith, was beginning to be a recognized feature of Buddhism. But they contain no indications of left- handed Tantrism and the best proof that it did not become prevalent until much later is afforded by the narratives of the three Chinese pilgrims who all describe the condition of religion in India and notice anything which they thought singular or reprehensible. Fa- Hsien does not mention the worship of any female deity, nor does the Life of Vasubandhu, but Asanga appears to allude to Sâktism in one passage. Hsüan Chuang mentions images of Târâ but without hinting at tantric ritual, nor do I- Ching allude to it, nor does the evidence of art and inscriptions attest its existence.

It may have been known as a form of popular superstition and even have been practised by individual Bhikshus, but the silence of I- Ching makes it improbable that it was then countenanced in the schools of Magadha. He complains of those who neglect the Vinaya and "devote their whole attention to the doctrine of nothingness," but he says not a word about tantric abuses. The change probably occurred in the next half century for Padma- Sambhava, the founder of Lamaism who is said to have resided in Gaya and Nalanda and to have arrived in Tibet in 747 A.D., is represented by tradition as a tantric wizard, and about the same time translations of Tantras begin to appear in Chinese.

The translations of the sixth and seventh centuries, including those of I- Ching, comprise a considerable though not preponderant number of Dhâranòîs. After the seventh century these became very numerous and several Tantras were also translated. The inference seems to be that early in the eighth century Indian Buddhists officially recognized Tantrism. Tantric Buddhism was due to the mixture of Mahayanist teaching with aboriginal superstitions absorbed through the medium of Hinduism, though in some cases there may have been direct contact and mutual influence between Mahayanism and aboriginal beliefs.

But as a rule what happened was that aboriginal deities were identified with Hindu deities and Buddhism had not sufficient independence to keep its own pantheon distinct, so that Vairocana and Târâ received most of the attributes, Brahmanic or barbarous, given to Siva or Kâli. The worship of the goddesses, described in their Hinduized form as Durgâ, Kâlî, etc., though found in most parts of India was especially prevalent in the sub- himalayan districts both east and west. Now Padma- Sambhava was a native of Udyâna or Swat and Târanâtha represents the chief Tantrists as coming from there or visiting it. Hsüan Chuang tells us that the inhabitants were devout Mahayanists but specially expert in magic and exorcism.

He also describes no less than four sacred places in it where the Buddha in previous births gave his flesh, blood or bones for the good of others. Have we here in a Buddhist form some ancient legend of dismemberment like that told of Satî in Assam? Of Kashmir he says that its religion was a mixture of Buddhism with other beliefs. These are precisely the conditions most favourable to the growth of Tantrism and though the bulk of the population are now Mohammedans, witchcraft and sorcery are still rampant. Among the Hindu Kashmîris the most prevalent religion has always been the worship of Siva, especially in the form representing him as half male, half female. This cult is not far from Sâktism and many allusions in the Râjataranginî indicate that left- hand worship was known, though the author satirizes it as a corruption. He also several times mentions Mâtri- cakras that is circles sacred to the Mothers or tantric goddesses.

In Nepal and Tibet tantric Buddhism is fully developed but these countries have received so much from India that they exhibit not a parallel growth, but late Indian Tantrism as imported ready- made from Bengal. It is here that we come nearest to the origins of Tantrism, for though the same beliefs may have flourished in Udyâna and Kashmir they did not spread much in the Panjab or Hindustan, where their progress was hindered at first by a healthy and vigorous Hinduism and subsequently by Mohammedan invasions. But from 700 to 1197 A.D. Bengal was remote alike from the main currents of Indian religion and from foreign raids: little Aryan thought or learning leavened the local superstitions which were infecting and stifling decadent Buddhism.

Hsüan Chuang informs us that Bhaskaravarma king of Kâmarûpa attended the fêtes celebrated by Harsha in 644 A.D. and inscriptions found at Tezpur indicate that kings with Hindu names reigned in Assam about 800 A.D. This is agreeable to the supposition that an amalgamation of Sivaism and aboriginal religion may have been in formation about 700 A.D. and have influenced Buddhism. In Bihar from the eighth century onwards the influence of Tantrism was powerful and disastrous. The best information about this epoch is still to be found in Târanâtha, in spite of his defects. He makes the interesting statement that in the reign of Gopâla who was a Buddhist, although his ministers were not (730- 740 A.D.), the Buddhists wished their religious buildings to be kept separate from Hindu temples but that, in spite of protests, life- sized images of Hindu deities were erected in them.

The ritual too was affected, for we hear several times of burnt offerings and how Bodhibhadra, one of the later professors of Vikramaœila, was learned in the mystic lore of both Buddhists and Brahmans. Nalanda and the other viharas continued to be seats of learning and not merely monasteries, and for some time there was a regular succession of teachers. Târanâtha gives us to understand that there were many students and authors but that sorcery occupied an increasingly important position. Of most teachers we are told that they saw some deity, such as Avalokita or Târâ. The deity was summoned by the rites already described and the object of the performer was to obtain magical powers or siddhi.

The successful sorcerer was known as siddha, and we hear of 84 mahâsiddhas, still celebrated in Tibet, who extend from Rahulabhadra Nâgârjuna to the thirteenth century. Many of them bear names which appear not to be Indian. The topics treated of in the Tantras are divided into Kriyâ (ritual), Caryâ (apparently corresponding to Vinaya), Yoga, and Anuttara-yoga. Sometimes the first three are contrasted with the fourth and sometimes the first two are described as lower, the third and fourth as higher. But the Anuttara- yoga is always considered the highest and most mysterious. Târanâtha says that the Tantras began to appear simultaneously with the Mahayana sûtras but adds that the Anuttara- yoga tantras appeared gradually.

He also observes that the Âcârya Ânanda- garbha did much to spread them in Magadha. It is not until a late period of the Pâla dynasty that he mentions the Kâlacakra which is the most extravagant form of Buddhist Tantrism. This accords with other statements to the effect that the Kâlacakra tantra was introduced in 965 A.D. from Sambhala, a mysterious country in Central Asia. This system is said to be Vishnuite rather than Sivaite. It specially patronizes the cult of the mystic Buddhas such as Kâlacakra and Heruka, all of whom appear to be regarded as forms of Âdi- Buddha or the primordial Buddha essence. The Siddha named Pito is also described as the author of this doctrine, which had less importance in India than in Tibet.

On the other hand Târanâtha gives us the names of several doctors of the Vinaya who flourished under the Pâla dynasty. Even as late as the reign of Râmapâla (1080- 1120) we hear that the Hinayanists were numerous. In the reign of Dharmapâla (*c.* 800 A.D.) some of them broke up the great silver image of Heruka at Bodh- Gaya and burnt the books of Mantras. These instances show that the older Buddhism was not entirely overwhelmed by Tantrism though perhaps it was kept alive more by pilgrims than by local sentiment. Thus the Chinese inscriptions of Bodh- Gaya though they speak at length of the three bodies of Buddha show no signs of Tantrism. It would appear that the worship celebrated in the holy places of Magadha preserved a respectable side until the end.

In the same way although Tantrism is strong in the literature of the Lamas, none of the many descriptions of Tibet indicate that there is anything scandalous in the externals of religion. Probably in Tibet, Nepal and mediæval Magadha alike the existence of disgraceful tantric literature does not indicate such widespread depravity as might be supposed. But of its putrefying influence in corrupting the minds of those who ought to have preserved the pure faith there can be no doubt. More than any other form of mixed belief it obliterated essential differences,, for Buddhist Tantrism and Sivaite Tantrism are merely two varieties of Tantrism.

What is happening at Bodh Gaya at present illustrates how Buddhism disappeared from India. The abbot of a neighbouring Sivaite monastery who claims the temple and grounds does not wish, as a Mohammedan might, to destroy the building or even to efface Buddhist emblems. He wishes to supervise the whole establishment and the visits of pilgrims, as well as to place on the images of Buddha Hindu sectarian marks and other ornaments. Hindu pilgrims are still taken by their guides to venerate the Bodhi tree and, but for the presence of foreign pilgrims, no casual observer would suppose the spot to be anything but a Hindu temple of unusual construction. The same process went a step further in many shrines which had not the same celebrity and effaced all traces and memory of Buddhism.

At the present day the Buddha is recognized by the Brahmans as an incarnation of Vishnu, though the recognition is often qualified by the statement that Vishnu assumed this form in order to mislead the wicked who threatened to become too powerful if they knew the true method of attaining superhuman powers. But he is rarely worshipped *in propriâ personâ.* As a rule Buddhist images and emblems are ascribed to Vishnu or Siva, according to sectarian preferences, but in spite of fusion some lingering sense of original animosity prevents Gotama from receiving even such respect as is accorded to incarnations like Paraœu râma. At Bodh Gaya I have been told that Hindu pilgrims are taken by their guides to venerate the Bodhi- tree but not the images of Buddha.

Yet in reviewing the disappearance of Buddhism from India we must remember that it was absorbed not expelled. The result of the mixture is justly called Hinduism, yet both in usages and beliefs it has taken over much that is Buddhist and without Buddhism it would never have assumed its present shape. To Buddhist influence is due for instance the rejection by most sects of animal sacrifices: the doctrine of the sanctity of animal life: monastic institutions and the ecclesiastical discipline found in the Dravidian regions. We may trace the same influence with more or less certainty in the philosophy of Sanskara and outside the purely religious sphere in the development of Indian logic.

3

The Buddhas in Mahayanism

The extraordinary changes of meaning both mythological and metaphysical which the word Buddha undergoes in Mahayanist theology we must keep in mind not the personality of Gotama but the idea that he is one of several successive Buddhas who for convenience may be counted as four, seven or twenty- four but who really form an infinite series extending without limit backwards into the past and forwards into the future. This belief in a series of Buddhas produced a plentiful crop of imaginary personalities and also of speculations as to their connection with one another, with the phenomena of the world and with the human soul.

In the Pali Canon the Buddhas antecedent to Gotama are introduced much like ancient kings as part of the legendary history of this world. But in the Lalita- vistara (Chap. XX) and the Lotus (Chap. VII) we hear of Buddhas, usually described as Tathâgatas, who apparently do not belong to this world at all, but rule various points of the compass, or regions described as Buddha- fields (Buddha- kshetra). Their names are not the same in the different accounts and we remain dazzled by an endless panorama of infinity of universes with infinity of shining Buddhas, illuminating infinite space. Somewhat later five of these unearthly Buddhas were formed into a pentad and described as Jinas or Dhyâni Buddhas (Buddhas of contemplation), namely, Vairocana, Akshobhya, Ratnasambhava, Amitâbha and Amoghasiddhi.

In the fully developed form of this doctrine these five personages are produced by contemplation from the Âdi-Buddha or original Buddha spirit and themselves produce various reflexes, including Bodhisattvas, human Buddhas and goddesses like Târâ. The date when these beliefs first became part of the accepted Mahayana creed cannot be fixed but probably the symmetrical arrangement of five Buddhas is not anterior to the tantric period of Buddhism. The most important of the five are Vairocana and Amitâbha. Akshobhya is mentioned in both the Lotus and Smaller Sukhâvatî- vyûha as the chief Buddha of the eastern quarter, and a work purporting to be a description of his paradise still extant in Chinese is said to have been translated in the time of the Eastern Han dynasty.

But even in the Far East he did not find many worshippers. More enduring has been the glory of Vairocana who is the chief deity of the Shingon sect in Japan and is represented by the gigantic image in the temple at Nara. In Java he seems to have been regarded as the principal and supreme Buddha. The name occurs in the Mahâvastu as the designation of an otherwise unknown Buddha of luminous attributes and in the Lotus we hear of a distant Buddha- world called Vairocana-rasmi- pratimandita, embellished by the rays of the sun.

Vairocana is clearly a derivative of Virocana, a recognized title of the sun in Sanskrit, and is rendered in Chinese by Ta-jih meaning great Sun. How this solar deity first came to be regarded as a Buddha is not known but the connection between a Buddha and light has always been recognized. Even the Pali texts represent Gotama as being luminous on some occasions and in the Mahayanist scriptures Buddhas are radiant and light- giving beings, surrounded by halos of prodigious extent and emitting flashes which illuminate the depths of space. The visions of innumerable paradises in all quarters containing jewelled stupas and lighted by refulgent Buddhas which are frequent in these works seem founded on astronomy vaporized under the influence of the idea that there are millions of universes all equally transitory and unsubstantial.

There is no reason, to regard Gotama as a mythical solar hero, but the celestial Buddhas clearly have many solar attributes. This is natural. Solar deities are so abundant in Vedic mythology that it is hardly possible to be a benevolent god without having something of the character of the sun. The stream of foreign religions which flowed into India from Bactria and Persia about the time of the Christian era brought new aspects of sun worship such as Mithra, Helios and Apollo and strengthened the tendency to connect divinity and light. And this connection was peculiarly appropriate and obvious in the case of a Buddha, for Buddhas are clearly revealers and light- givers, conquerors of darkness and dispellers of ignorance.

Amitâbha (or the Buddha of measureless light), rising suddenly from an obscure origin, has like Avalokita and Vishnu become one of the great gods of Asia. He is also known as Amitâyus or measureless life, and is therefore a god of light and immortality. According to both the Lotus and the Smaller Sukhâvatî- vyûha he is the lord of the western quarter but he is unknown to the Lalita- vistara. It gives the ruler of the west a lengthy title, which suggests a land of gardens. Now Paradise, which has biblical authority as a name for the place of departed spirits, appears to mean in Persian a park or enclosed garden and the Avesta speaks of four heavens, the good thought Paradise, the good word Paradise, the good deed Paradise and the Endless Lights.

This last expression bears a remarkable resemblance to the name of Amitâbha and we can understand that he should rule the west, because it is the home to which the sun and departed spirits go. Amitâbha's Paradise is called Sukhâvatî or Happy Land. In the Puranas the city of Varunòa (who is suspected of having a non- Indian origin) is said to be situated in the west and is called Sukha (Linga P. and Vayu P.) or Mukhya (so Vishnu P. and others). The name Amitâbha also occurs in the Vishnu Purana as the name of a class of gods and it is curious that they are in one place associated with other deities called the Mukhyas. The worship of Amitâbha, so far as its history can be traced, goes back to Saraha, the teacher of

Nâgârjuna. He is said to have been a Sudra and his name seems un- Indian. This supports the theory that this worship was foreign and imported into India.

This worship and the doctrine on which it is based are an almost complete contradiction of Gotama's teaching, for they amount to this, that religion consists in faith in Amitâbha and prayer to him, in return for which he will receive his followers after death in his paradise. Yet this is not a late travesty of Buddhism but a relatively early development which must have begun about the Christian era. The principal works in which it is preached are the Greater Sukhâvatî- vyûha or Description of the Happy Land, translated into Chinese between 147 and 186 A.D., the lesser work of the same name translated in 402 A.D. and the Sûtra of meditation on Amitâyus translated in 424. The first of these works purports to be a discourse of Sâkyamuni himself, delivered on the Vulture's Peak in answer to the questions of Ânanda. He relates how innumerable ages ago there was a monk called Dharmâkara who, with the help of the Buddha of that period, made a vow or vows to become a Buddha but on conditions.

That is to say he rejected the Buddhahood to which he might become entitled unless his merits obtained certain advantages for others, and having obtained Buddhahood on these conditions he can now cause them to be fulfilled. In other words he can apportion his vast store of accumulated merit to such persons and in such manner as he chooses. The gist of the conditions is that he should when he obtained Buddhahood be lord of a paradise whose inhabitants live in unbroken happiness until they obtain Nirvana. All who have thought of this paradise ten times are to be admitted therein, unless they have committed grievous sin, and Amitâbha will appear to them at the moment of death so that their thoughts may not be troubled.

The Buddha shows Ânanda a miraculous vision of this paradise and its joys are described in language recalling the account of the New Jerusalem in the book of Revelation and, though coarser pleasures are excluded, all the delights of the eye and ear, such as jewels, gardens, flowers, rivers and the songs of birds await the faithful. The smaller Sukhâvatî- vyûha, represented as preached by Sâkyamuni at Srâvasti, is occupied almost entirely with a description of the paradise. It marks a new departure in definitely preaching salvation by faith only, not by works, whereas the previous treatise, though dwelling on the efficacy of faith, also makes merit a requisite for life in heaven. But the shorter discourse says dogmatically "Beings are not born in that Buddha country as a reward and result of good works performed in this present life. No, all men or women who hear and bear in mind for one, two, three, four, five, six or seven nights the name of Amitâyus, when they come to die, Amitâyus will stand before them in the hour of death, they will depart this life with quiet minds and after death they will be born in Paradise."

The Amitâyur- dhyâna- sûtra also purports to be the teaching of Sâkyamuni and has an historical introduction connecting it with Queen Vaidehî and King Bimbisâra. In theology it is more advanced than the other treatises: it is familiar with the doctrine of Dharma- kâya (which will be discussed below) and it represents the rulers of paradise as a triad, Amitâyus being assisted by Avalokita and Mahasthâmaprâpta. Admission to the paradise can be obtained in various ways, but the method recommended is the practice of a series of meditations which are described in detail. The system is comprehensive, for salvation can be obtained by mere virtue with little or no prayer but also by a single invocation of Amitâyus, which suffices to free from deadly sins.

Strange as such doctrines appear when set beside the Pali texts, it is clear that in their origin and even in the form which they assume in the larger Sukhâvatî- vyûha they are simply an exaggeration of ordinary Mahayanist teaching. Amitâbha is merely a monk who devotes himself to the religious life, namely seeking *bodhi* for the good of others. He differs from every day devotees only in the degree of sanctity and success obtained by his exertions. The operations which he performs are nothing but examples on a stupendous scale of parinòâmanâ or the assignment of one's own merits to others.

His paradise, though in popular esteem equivalent to the Persian or Christian heaven, is not really so: strictly speaking it is not an ultimate ideal but a blessed region in which Nirvana may be obtained without toil or care.

Though this teaching had brilliant success in China and Japan, where it still flourishes, the worship of Amitâbha was never predominant in India. In Nepal and Tibet he is one among many deities: the Chinese pilgrims hardly mention him: his figure is not particularly frequent in Indian iconography and, except in the works composed specially in his honour; he appears as an incidental rather than as a necessary figure. The whole doctrine is hardly strenuous enough for Indians. To pray to the Buddha at the end of a sinful life, enter his paradise and obtain ultimate Nirvana in comfort is not only open to the same charge of egoism as the Hinayana scheme of salvation but is much easier and may lead to the abandonment of religious effort. And the Hindu, who above all things likes to busy himself with his own salvation, does not take kindly to these expedients.

Numerous deities promise a long spell of heaven as a reward for the mere utterance of their names, yet the believer continues to labour earnestly in ceremonies or meditation. It would be interesting to know whether this doctrine of salvation by the utterance of a single name or prayer originated among Buddhists or Brahmans. In any case it is closely related to old ideas about the magic power of Vedic verses. The five Jinas and other supernatural personages are often regarded as manifestations of a single Buddha- force and at last this force is personified as Âdi- Buddha. This admittedly theistic form of Buddhism is late and is recorded from Nepal, Tibet (in the Kâlacakra system) and Java, a distribution which implies that it was exported from Bengal.

But another form in which the Buddha- force is impersonal and analogous to the Parabrahma of the Vedânta is much older. Yet when this philosophic idea is expressed in popular language it comes very near to Theism. As Kern has pointed out, Buddha is not called Deva or Îœvara in the Lotus simply because he is above such beings. He declares that he has existed and will exist for incalculable ages and has preached and will preach in innumerable millions of worlds. His birth here and his nirvana are illusory, kindly devices which may help weak disciples but do not mark the real beginning and end of his activity. This implies a view of Buddha's personality which is more precisely defined in the doctrine known as Tòrikâya or the three bodies and expounded in the Mahâyâna- sûtrâlankâra, the Awakening of Faith, the Suvarnòa- prabhâsa sûtra and many other works.

It may be stated dogmatically as follows, but it assumes somewhat divergent forms according as it is treated theologically or metaphysically. A Buddha has three bodies or forms of existence. The first is the Dharma- kâya, which is the essence of all Buddhas. It is true knowledge or Bodhi. It may also be described as Nirvana and also as the one permanent reality underlying all phenomena and all individuals. The second is the Sambhoga- kâya, or body of enjoyment, that is to say the radiant and superhuman form in which Buddhas appear in their paradises or when otherwise manifesting themselves in celestial splendour. The third is the Nirmâna- kâya, or the body of transformation, that is to say the human form worn by Sâkyamuni or any other Buddha and regarded as a transformation of his true nature and almost a distortion, because it is so partial and inadequate an expression of it.

Later theology regards Amitâbha, Amitâyus and Sâkyamuni as a series corresponding to the three bodies. Amitâbha does not really express the whole Dharma- kâya, which is incapable of personification, but when he is accurately distinguished from Amitâyus (and frequently they are regarded as synonyms) he is made the more remote and ethereal of the two. Amitâyus with his rich ornaments and his flask containing the water of eternal life is the ideal of a splendidly beneficent saviour and represents the Sambhoga-kâya. Sâkyamuni is the same beneficent being shrunk into human form. But this is only one aspect, and not the most important, of the doctrine of the three bodies. We can easily understand the Sambhoga- kâya and Nirmâna- kâya: they correspond to a deity such as Vishnu and his incarnation Krishna, and they are puzzling in Buddhism simply because we think naturally of the older view (not entirely discarded by the Mahayana) which makes the human Buddha the crown and apex of a series of lives that find in him their fulfilment. But it is less easy to understand the Dharma- kâya.

The word should perhaps be translated as body of the law and the thought originally underlying it may have been that the essential nature of a Buddha, that which makes him a Buddha, is the law which he preaches. As we might say, the teacher lives in his teaching: while it survives, he is active and not dead. The change from metaphor to theology is illustrated by Hsüan Chuang when he states (no doubt quoting from his edition of the Pitakas) that Gotama when dying said to those around him "Say not that the Tathâgata is undergoing final extinction: his spiritual presence abides for ever unchangeable." This apparently corresponds to the passage in the Pali Canon, which runs "It may be that in some of you the thought may arise, the word of the Master is ended: we have no more a teacher. But it is not thus that you should regard it.

The truths and the rules which I have set forth, let them, after I am gone, be the Teacher to you." But in Buddhist writings, including the oldest Pali texts, Dharma or Dhamma has another important meaning. It signifies phenomenon or mental state (the two being identical for an idealistic philosophy) and comprises both the external and the internal world. Now the Dharma- kâya is emphatically not a phenomenon but it may be regarded as the substratum or totality of phenomena or as that which gives phenomena whatever reality they possess and the double use of the word dharma rendered such divagations of meaning easier. Hindus have a tendency to identify being and knowledge.

According to the Vedânta philosophy he who knows Brahman, knows that he himself is Brahman and therefore he actually is Brahman. In the same way the true body of the Buddha is prajñâ or knowledge. By this is meant a knowledge which transcends the distinction between subject and object and which sees that neither animate beings nor inanimate things have individuality or separate existence. Thus the Dharma- kâya being an intelligence which sees the illusory quality of the world and also how the illusion originates may be regarded as the origin and ground of all phenomena. As such it is also called Tathâgatagarbha and Dharma- dhâtu, the matrix or store- house of all phenomena. On the other hand, inasmuch as it is beyond them and implies their unreality, it may also be regarded as the annihilation of all phenomena, in other words as Nirvana.

In fact the Dharma- kâya (or Bhûta- tathatâ) is sometimes defined in words similar to those which the Pali Canon makes the Buddha use when asked if the Perfect Saint exists after death- "it is neither that which is existence nor that which is non- existence, nor that which is at once existence and non-existence nor that which is neither existence nor non-existence." In more theological language it may be said that according to the general opinion of the Mahayanists a Buddha attains to Nirvana by the very act of becoming a Buddha and is therefore beyond everything which we call existence. Yet the compassion which he feels for mankind and the good *Karma* which he has accumulated cause a human image of him (Nirmâna- kâya) to appear among men for their instruction and a superhuman image, perceptible yet not material, to appear in Paradise.

MAHAYANIST METAPHYSICS

Thus the theory of the three bodies, especially of the Dharma- kâya, is bound up with a theory of ontology. Metaphysics became a passion among the travellers of the Great Vehicle as psychology had been in earlier times. They may indeed be reproached with being bad Buddhists since they insisted on speculating on those questions which Gotama had declared to be unprofitable and incapable of an answer in human language. He refused to pronounce on the whence, the whither and the nature of things, but bade his disciples walk in the eightfold path and analyse the human mind, because such analysis conduces to spiritual progress. India was the last country in the world where such restrictions were likely to be observed. Much Mahayanist literature is not religious at all but simply metaphysics treated in an authoritative and ecclesiastical manner.

The nature and origin of the world are discussed as freely as in the Vedânta and with similar results: the old ethics and psychology receive scant attention. Yet the difference is less than might be supposed. Anyone who reads these treatises and notices the number of apparently eternal beings and the talk about the universal mind is likely to think the old doctrine that nothing has an âtman or soul, has been forgotten. But this impression is not correct; the doctrine of *Nairâtmyam* is asserted so uncompromisingly that from one point of view it may be said that even Buddhas do not exist. The meaning of this doctrine is that no being or object contains an unchangeable permanent self, which lives unaltered in the same or in different bodies. On the contrary individual existences consist of nothing but a collection of skandhas or a *santâna,* a succession or series of mental phenomena. In the Pali books this doctrine is applied chiefly to the soul and psychological enquiries.

The Mahayana applied it to the external world and proved by ingenious arguments that nothing at all exists. Similarly the doctrine of *Karma* is maintained; though it is seriously modified by the admission that merit can be transferred from one personality to another. The Mahayana continued to teach that an act once performed affects a particular series of mental states until its effect is exhausted, or in popular language that an individual enjoys or suffers through a series of births the consequences of previous acts. Even the instance of Amitâbha's paradise, though it strains the doctrine of *Karma* to the utmost, does not repudiate it. For the believer performs an act- to wit, the invocation of Amitâbha- to which has been attached the wonderful result that the performer is reborn in a blessed state.

This is not essentially different from the idea found in the Pali Canon that attentions paid to a Buddha may be rewarded by a happy rebirth in heaven. Mahayanist metaphysics, like all other departments of this theology, are beset by the difficulty that the authorities who treat of them are not always in accord and do not pretend to be in accord. The idea that variety is permissible in belief and conduct is deeply rooted in later Buddhism: there are many vehicles, some better than others no doubt and some very ramshackle, but all are capable of conveying their passengers to salvation. Nominally the Mahayana was divided into only two schools of philosophy: practically every important treatise propounds a system with features of its own.

The two schools are the Yogâcâras and Mâdhyamikas. Both are idealists and deny the reality of the external world, but whereas the Yogâcâras (also called Vijñânavâdins) admit that Vijñâna or consciousness and the series of states of which it consists are real, the Mâdhyamikas refuse the title of reality to both the subjective and the objective world and hence gained a reputation of being complete nihilists. Probably the Mâdhyamikas are the older school. Both schools attach importance to the distinction between relative and absolute knowledge. Relative knowledge is true for human beings living in the world: that is to say it is not more false than the world of appearance in which they live. The Hinayanist doctrines are true in this sense. Absolute knowledge rises above the world of appearance and is altogether true but difficult to express in words.

The Yogâcâra makes three divisions, dividing the inferior knowledge into two. It distinguishes first illusory knowledge (*parikalpita*) such as mistaking a piece of rope for a snake or belief in the existence of individual souls. Secondly knowledge which depends on the relations of things (*paratantra*) and which though not absolutely wrong is necessarily limited, such as belief in the real existence of ropes and snakes and thirdly, the absolute knowledge (*parinishpanna*) which understands all things as the manifestation of an underlying principle. The Mâdhyamikas more simply divide knowledge into *samvròiti-satya* and *paramârtha- satya,* that is the truth of every day life and transcendental truth. The world and ordinary religion with its doctrines and injunctions about good works are real and true as *samvròiti* but in absolute truth (*paramârtham*) we attain Nirvana and then the world with its human Buddhas and its gods exists no more.

The word *œûnyam* or *œûnyatâ*, that is *void*, is often used as the equivalent of *paramârtham*. Void must be understood as meaning not an abyss of nothingness but that which is found to be devoid of all the attributes which we try to ascribe to it. The world of ordinary experience is not void, for a great number of statements can be made about it, but absolute truth is void, because nothing whatever can be predicated of it. Yet even this colourless designation is not perfectly accurate, because neither being nor not- being can be predicated of absolute truth. It is for this reason, namely that they admit neither being nor not- being but something between the two, that the followers of Nâgârjuna are known as the Mâdhyamikas or school of the middle doctrine, though the European reader is tempted to say that their theories are extreme to the point of being a *reductio ad absurdum* of the whole system. Yet though much of their logic seems late and useless sophistry, its affinity to early Buddhism cannot be denied.

The fourfold proposition that the answer to certain questions cannot be any of the statements "is," "is not," "both is and is not," "neither is nor is not," is part of the earliest known stratum of Buddhism. The Buddha himself is represented as saying that most people hold either to a belief in being or to a belief in not being. But neither belief is possible for one who considers the question with full knowledge. "That things have being is one extreme: that things have no being is the other extreme. These extremes have been avoided by the Tathâgata and it is a middle doctrine that he teaches," namely, dependent origination as explained in the chain of twelve links. The Mâdhyamika theory that objects have no absolute and independent existence but appear to exist in virtue of their relations is a restatement of this ancient dictum.

The Mahayanist doctors find an ethical meaning in their negations. If things possessed *svabhâva*, real, absolute, self-determined existence, and then the four truths and especially the cessation of suffering and attainment of sanctity would be impossible. For if things were due not to causation but to their own self- determining nature (and the Hindus always seem to understand real existence in this sense) cessation of evil and attainment of the good would be alike impossible: the four Noble Truths imply a world which is in a state of constant becoming, that is a world which is not really existent. But for all that the doctrine of *œûnyatâ* as stated in the Mâdhyamika aphorisms ascribed to Nâgârjuna leaves an impression of audacious and ingenious sophistry.

After laying down that every object in the world exists only in relation to every other object and has no self- existence, the treatise proceeds to prove that rest and motion are alike impossible. We speak about the path along which we are passing but there is really no such thing, for if we divide the path accurately, it always proves separable into the part which has been passed over and the part which will be passed over. There is no part which is being passed over. This of course amounts to a denial of the existence of present time. Time consists of past and future separated by an indivisible and immeasurable instant. The minimum of time which has any meaning for us implies a change, and two elements, a former and a subsequent. The present minute or the present hours are fallacious expressions.

Therefore no one ever is passing along a path. Again you cannot logically say that the passer is passing, for the sentence is redundant: the verb adds nothing to the noun and *vice versa*: but on the other hand you clearly cannot say that the non-passer is passing. Again if you say that the passer and the passing are identical, you overlook the distinction between the agent and the act and both become unreal. But you cannot maintain that the passer is different from the passing, for a passer as distinct from passing and passing as distinct from a passer have no meaning. "But how can two entities exist at all, if they exist neither as identical with one another nor as different from one another?" The above, though much abridged, gives an idea of the logic of these sûtras. They proceed to show that all manner of things, such as the five skandhas, the elements, contact, attachment, fire and fuel, origination, continuation and extinction have no real existence.

Similar reasoning is then applied to religious topics: the world of transmigration as well as bondage and liberation are declared non- existent. In reality no soul is in bondage and none is released. Similarly *Karma*, the Buddha himself, the four truths, Nirvana and the twelve links in the chain of causation are all unreal. This is not a declaration of scepticism. It means that the Buddha as a human or celestial being and Nirvana as a state attainable in this world are conceivable only in connection with this world and therefore, like the world, unreal. No religious idea can enter into the unreal (that is the practical) life of the world unless it is itself unreal. This sounds a topsy turvy argument but it is really the same as the Advaita doctrine. The Vedânta is on the one hand a scheme of salvation for liberating souls which transmigrate unceasingly in a world ruled by a personal God.

But when true knowledge is attained, the soul sees that it is identical with the Highest Brahman and that souls which are in bondage and God who rules the world are illusions like the world itself. But the Advaita has at least a verbal superiority over the Mâdhyamika philosophy, for in its terminology Brahman is the real and the existent contrasted with the world of illusion. The result of giving to what the Advaita calls the real and existent the name of œûnyatâ or void is disconcerting. To say that everything without distinction is non- existent is much the same as saying that everything is existent. It only means that a wrong sense is habitually given to the word exist, as if it meant to be self- contained and without relation to other objects. Unless we can make a verbal contrast and assert that there is something which does exist, it seems futile to insist on the unreality of the world. Yet this mode of thought is not confined to text- books on logic.

It invades the scriptures, and appears (for instance) in the Diamond Cutter which is still one of the most venerated books of devotion in China and Japan. In this work the Buddha explains that a Bodhisattva must resolve to deliver all living beings and yet must understand that after he has thus delivered innumerable beings, no one has been delivered. And why? Because no one is to be called a Bodhisattva for whom there exists the idea of a being, or person. Similarly a saint does not think that he is a saint, for if he did so think, he would believe in a self, and a person. There occur continually in this work phrases cast in the following form: "what was preached as a store of merit, that was preached as no store of merit by the Tathâgata and therefore it is called a store of merit. If there exist a store of merit, the Tathâgata would not have preached a store of merit."

That is to say, if I understand this dark language rightly, accumulated merit is part of the world of illusion which we live in and by speaking of it as he did the Buddha implied that it, like everything else in the world, is really non- existent. Did it belong to the sphere of absolute truth; he would not have spoken of it as if it were one of the things commonly but erroneously supposed to exist. Finally we are told of the highest knowledge "Even the smallest thing is not known or perceived there; therefore it is called the highest perfect knowledge." That is to say perfect knowledge transcends all distinctions; it recognises the illusory nature of all individuality and the truth of sameness, the never- changing one behind the ever- changing many. In this sense it is said to perceive nothing and know nothing.

One might expect that a philosophy thus prone to use the language of extreme nihilism would slip into a destructive or at least negative system. But Mahayanism was pulled equally strongly in the opposite direction by the popular and mythological elements which it contained and was on the whole inclined to theism and even polytheism quite as much as to atheism and acosmism. A modern Japanese writer says that Dharma- kâya "may be considered to be equivalent to the Christian conception of the Godhead." This is excessive as a historical statement of the view current in India during the early centuries of our era, but it does seem true that Dharma- kâya was made the equivalent of the Hindu conception of Param Brahma and also that it is very nearly equivalent to the Chinese Tao. The work called *Awakening of Faith* and ascribed to Aœvaghosha is not extant in Sanskrit but was translated into Chinese in 553 A.D.

Its doctrine is practically that of the Yogâcâra School and this makes the ascription doubtful, but it is a most important treatise. It is regarded as authoritative in China and Japan at the present day and it illustrates the triple tendency of the Mahayana towards metaphysics, mythology, and devotional piety. It declares that faith has four aspects. Three of these are the three Jewels, or Buddha, the Law and the Church, and cover between them the whole field of religion and morality as generally understood. The exposition is tinged with a fine unselfish emotion and tells the believer that though he should strive not for his own emancipation but for the salvation of others yet he himself receives unselfish and supernatural assistance. He is remembered and guarded by Buddhas and Bodhisattvas in all quarters of the Universe who are eternally trying to liberate mankind by various expedients (upâya). By expedient is meant a modified presentment of the truth, which is easier of comprehension and, if not the goal, at least on the road to it, such as the Paradise of Amitâbha. But the remaining aspect of faith, which is the one that the author puts first in his enumeration, and treats at great length, is "to believe in the fundamental truth that is to think joyfully of suchness."

By suchness (in Sanskrit *bhûta- tathatâ*, in Chinese *Chên ju*) is meant absolute truth as contrasted with the relative truth of ordinary experience. The word is not illuminating or likely to excite religious emotion and the most that can be said for it is that it is less dreary than the void of Nâgârjuna. Another and more positive synonym is *dharma- dhâtu*, the all- embracing totality of things. It is only through cur ignorance and subjectivity that things appear distinct and individuate. Could we transcend this subjectivity, isolated objects would cease to exist. Things in their fundamental nature cannot be named or explained: they are beyond the range of language and perception: they have no signs of distinction but possess absolute sameness (samatâ). From this totality of things nothing can be excluded and to it nothing can be added. Yet it is also œûnyatâ, negation or the void, because it cannot be said to possess any of the attributes of the world we live in: neither existence nor non- existence, nor unity nor plurality can be predicted of it.

According to the celebrated formula of Nâgârjuna known as the eight Nos there is in it "neither production (*utpâda*) nor destruction (*uccheda*) nor annihilation (*nirodha*) nor persistence (*sasvatâ*) nor unity (*ekârtha*) nor plurality (*nânârtha*) nor coming in (*âgamana*) nor going out (*nirgama*)." But when we perceive that both subject and object are unreal we also see that suchness is the one reality and from that point of view it may be regarded as the Dharma- kâya of all Buddhas. It is also called Tathâgatagarbha, the womb or store house of the Buddha, from which all individual existences are evolved under the law of causation, but this aspect of it is already affected by ignorance, for in Bhûta- tathatâ as known in the light of the highest truth there is neither causation nor production. The Yogâcâra employs the word *œûnyatâ* (void), though not so much as its sister school, but it makes special use of the term *âlaya- vijñâna*, the receptacle or store of consciousness.

This in so far as it is superindividual is an aspect of suchness, but when it affirms and particularises itself it becomes *citta*, that is the human mind, or to be more accurate the substratum of the human mind from which is developed *manas*, or the principle of will, self- consciousness and self- affirmation. Similarly the Vedânta philosophy, though it has no term corresponding to *âlaya- vijñâna*, is familiar with the idea that Brahman is in one aspect immeasurable and all- embracing but in another is infinitesimal and dwells in the human heart: or that Brahman after creating the world entered into it. Again another aspect of suchness is enlightenment (*bodhi*) that is absolute knowledge free from the limitations of subject and object. This "is the universal Dharma- kâya of the Tathâgatas" and on account of this all Tathâgatas are spoken of as abiding in enlightenment *a priori*.

This enlightenment may be negative (as *œûnyata*) in the sense that it transcends all relations but it may also be affirmative and then "it transforms and unfolds itself, whenever conditions are favourable, in the form of a Tathâgata or some other form in order that all beings may be induced to bring their store of merit to maturity." It will be seen from the above that the absolute truth of the Mahayanists varies from a severely metaphysical conception, the indescribable thing in itself, to something very like an all- pervading benevolent essence which from time to time takes shape in a Buddha. And here we see how easy the transition from the old Buddhism to a form of pantheism is. For if we admit that the Buddha is a superhuman intelligence appearing from time to time according to a certain law, we add little to this statement by saying that the essence or spirit of the cosmos manifests itself from time to time as a Buddha. Only, such words as essence or spirit are not really correct.

The world of individuals is the same as the highest truth, the same as the Dharma- kâya, and the same as Nirvana. It is only through ignorance that it appears to be different and particularized. Ignorance, the essence of which consists in believing in the distinction between subject and object, is also called defilement and the highest truth passes through various stages of defilement ending with that where under the influence of egoism and passion the external world of particulars is believed to be everything. But the various stages may influence one another so that under a higher influence the mind which is involved in subjectivity begins to long for Nirvana. Yet Nirvana is not something different from or beyond the world of experience; it does not really involve annihilation of the skandhas.

Just as in the Advaita he who has the true knowledge sees that he himself and everything else is Brahman, so for the Mahayanist all things are seen *to be* Nirvana, *to be* the Dharma-kâya. It is sometimes said that there are four kinds of Nirvana

(*a*) absolute Nirvana, which is a synonym of the Dharma-kâya and in that sense universally present in all beings,

(*b*) upadhiœesha- nirvânòa, the state of enlightenment which can be attained during life, while the body with its limitations still remains,

(*c*) anupadhiœesha- nirvânòa, a higher degree of the same state attained after death when the hindrances of the body are removed, (*d*) Nirvana without abode or apratishtòhita- nirvânòa.

Those who attain to this understand that there is no real antithesis between Samsâra and Nirvana: they do not seek for rest or emancipation but devote themselves to beneficent activity and to leading their fellows to salvation. Although these statements that Nirvana and Samsâra is the same are not at all in the manner of the older Buddhism, yet this ideal of disinterested activity combined with Nirvana is not inconsistent with the portrait of Gotama preserved in the Pali Canon. The Mahayanist Buddhism of the Far East makes free use of such phrases as the Buddha in the heart, the Buddha mind and the Buddha nature. These seem to represent such Sanskrit terms as Buddhatva and Bodhicitta which can receive either an ethical or a metaphysical emphasis. The former line of thought is well shown in Sântideva who treats Bodhicitta as the initial impulse and motive power of the religious life, combining intellectual illumination and unselfish devotion to the good of others. Thus regarded it is a guiding and stimulating principle somewhat analogous to the Holy Spirit in Christianity.

But the Bodhicitta is also the essential quality of a Buddha (and the Holy Spirit too is a member of the Trinity) and in so far as a man has the Bodhicitta he is one with all Buddhas. This conception is perhaps secondary in Buddhism but it is also as old as the Upanishads and only another form of the doctrine that the spirit in every man (antaryâmin) is identical with the Supreme Spirit. It is developed in many works still popular in the Far East and was the fundamental thesis of Bodhidharma, the founder of the Zen school. But the practical character of the Chinese and Japanese has led them to attach more importance to the moral and intellectual side of this doctrine than to the metaphysical and pantheistic side.

MAHAYANIST SCRIPTURES

The Mahayanist scriptures are the largest body of sacred writings extant in the world, but it is not easy either to define the limits of the Canon or to say when it was put together. According to a common tradition Kanishka played for the

Church of the Great Vehicle much the same part as Asoka for the Theravâdins and summoned a Council which wrote commentaries on the Tripitaka. This may be reasonably held to include a recension of the text commented on but we do not know what that text was, and the brief and perplexing accounts of the Council which we possess indicate not that it gave its imprimatur to Mahayanist sutras but that it was especially concerned with the Abhidharma works of the Sarvâstivâdin School. In any case no Canon formed in the time of Kanishka can have been equivalent to the collections of writings accepted to day in China and Tibet, for they contain works later than any date which can be assigned to his reign, as do also the nine sacred books revered in Nepal.

It was agreed among Indian Buddhists that the scriptures were divided among the three Pitakas or baskets, but we may surmise that there was no unanimity as to the precise contents of each basket. In India the need for unanimity in such matters is not felt. The Brahmans always recognized that the most holy and most jealously preserved scriptures could exist in various recensions and the *Mahabharata* shows how generations of respectful and uncritical hearers may allow adventitious matter of all sorts to be incorporated in a work. Something of the same kind happened with the Pitakas. We know that the Pali recension which we possess was not the only one, for fragments of a Sanskrit version have been discovered. There was probably a large floating literature of sutras, often presenting several recensions of the same document worked up in different ways.

Just as additions were made to the list of Upanishads up to the middle ages, although the character of the later works was different from that of the earlier, so new sutras, modern in date and in tone, were received in the capacious basket. And just as the Puranas were accepted as sacred books without undermining the authority of the Vedas, so new Buddhist scriptures superseded without condemning the old ones. Various Mahayanist schools had their own versions of the Vinaya which apparently contain the same rules as the Pali text but also much additional narrative, and Asanga quotes from works corresponding to the Pali Nikâyas, though his doctrine belongs to another age. The Abhidharma section of the Pali Canon seems however to have been peculiar to the Theravâda school. The Sarvâstivâdin Pitaka of the same name was entirely different and, judging from the Chinese Canon, the Mahayanists gave the title to philosophic works by such authors as Asanga and Vasubandhu, some of which were described as revelations from Maitreya.

Special characteristic of Mahayanist Buddhism are the Vaipulya sutras that is sutras of great extension or development. These works, of which the Lotus is an example, follow the same scheme as the older sutras but are of wider scope and on a much larger scale, for they often consist of twenty or more chapters. They usually attempt to give a general exposition of the whole Dharma, or at least of some aspect of it which is extolled as sufficient for the right conduct of life. The chief speaker is usually the Buddha, who is introduced as teaching on the Vulture Peak, or some other well- known locality, and surrounded by a great assemblage many of whom are superhuman beings. The occasion of the discourse is commonly signalized by his sending forth rays of light which illuminate the universe until the scene includes other worlds.

As early as the Anguttara Nikâya we find references to the danger of a taste for ornate and poetic sutras and these compositions seem to be the outcome of that taste. The literary ideas and methods which produced them are illustrated by the Sûtrâlankâra of Aœvaghosha, a collection of edifying tales, many of which use the materials supplied by the Pali Nikâyas and Vinaya but present them in a more effective and artistic form. It was thought a pious task to amplify and embellish the simple narratives handed down by tradition. The Mahayanist scriptures are composed in Sanskrit not in Pali, but it is only rarely- for instance in the works of Aœvaghosha- that Buddhist Sanskrit conforms to the rules of the classical language. Usually the words deviate from this standard both in form and meaning and often suggest that the text as we have it is a Sanskritized version of an older work in some popular dialect, brought into partial conformity with literary usage.

In the poetical portions, this process of sanskritization encountered greater difficulties than in prose, because metre and prosody often refused to admit the changes required by grammar, so that this poetical dialect cannot be called Sanskrit, Pali or Magadhi but remains a mixture of learned and popular speech. But Sanskrit did not become a sacred language for the Mahayanists like Latin for Roman Catholics. It is rather Pali which has assumed this position among the Hinayanists, for Burmese and Sinhalese translations of the Pitakas acquired no authority. But in the north the principle that every man might read the Buddha's word in his own vernacular was usually respected: and the populations of Central Asia, the Chinese, the Tibetans, and the Mongols translated the scriptures into their own languages without attaching any superstitious importance to the original words, unless they were Dhâranòîs or spells.

About the time of the Christian era or perhaps rather earlier, greater use began to be made of writing for religious purposes. The old practice of reciting the scriptures was not discontinued but no objection was made to preserving and reading them in written copies. According to tradition, the Pali scriptures were committed to writing in Ceylon during the reign of Vatòtòagâmanòi, that is according to the most recent chronology about 20 B.C., and Kanishka caused to be engraved on copper plates the commentaries composed by the council which he summoned. In Aœvaghosha we find the story of a Brahman who casually taking up a book to pass the time lights on a copy of the Sutra of the Twelve Causes and is converted. But though the Buddhists remained on the whole true to the old view that the important thing was to understand and disseminate the substance of the Master's teaching and not merely to preserve the text as if it were a sacred formula, still we see growing up in Mahayanist works ideas about the sanctity and efficacy of scripture which are foreign to the Pali Canon.

Many sutras (for instance the Diamond Cutter) extol themselves as all- sufficient for salvation: the Prajñâ- pâramitâ commences with a salutation addressed not as usual to the

Buddha but to the work itself, as if it were a deity and Hodgson states that the Buddhists of Nepal worship their nine sacred books. Nor was the idea excluded that certain words, especially formulæ or spells called Dhâranòî, have in themselves a mysterious efficacy and potency. Some of these are cited and recommended in the Lotus. In so far as the repetition of sacred words or spells is regarded as an integral part of the religious life, the doctrine has no warrant in the earlier teaching.

It obviously becomes more and more prominent in later works. But the idea itself is old, for it is clearly the same that produced a belief in the Brahmanic mantras, particularly the mantras of the Atharva Veda, and early Buddhism did not reject mantras in their proper place. Thus the deities present themselves to the Buddha and offer to teach him a formula which will protect his disciples from the attacks of evil spirits. Hsüan Chuang even states that the council which sat at Râjagròiha after the Buddha's death compiled five Pitakas, one of which consisted of Dhâranòîs, and it may be that the collection of such texts was begun as early as the collection of discourses and rules. But for many centuries there is no evidence that they were in any way confounded with the Dharma. The Mahayanist scriptures are so voluminous that not even the clergy were expected to master any considerable part of them.

Indeed they make no claim to be a connected whole. The theory was rather that there were many vehicles plying on the road to salvation and many guide books. No traveller thought of taking the whole library but only a few volumes which suited him. Most of the Chinese and Japanese sects avowedly base themselves upon three sutras, selected according to the taste of each school from the hundreds quoted in catalogues. Thus the T'ien- t'ai sect has for its scriptures the Lotus, the Nirvânòa- sûtra and the Prajñâ- pâramitâ, while the Shin- shu sect admits only the three Amidist sutras. The following are the names of some of the principal Mahayanist scriptures. Comparatively few of them have been published in Europe and some exist only in Chinese or Japanese translations.

1. *Prajñâ- pâramitâ* or transcendental knowledge is a generic name given to a whole literature consisting of treatises on the doctrine of œûnyatâ, which vary greatly in length. They are classed as sutras, being described as discourses delivered by the Buddha on the Vulture Peak. At least ten are known, besides excerpts which are sometimes described as substantive works. The great collection translated into Chinese by Hsüan Chuang is said to consist of 200,000 verses and to comprise sixteen different sutras. The earliest translation of one of these treatises into Chinese (Nanjio, 5) was made about 170 A.D. and everything indicates that portions of the Prajñâ- pâramitâ are among the earliest Mahayanist works and date from about the first century of our era.

   Prajñâ not only means knowledge of the absolute truth that is to say of œûnyatâ or the void, but is regarded as an ontological principle synonymous with Bodhi and Dharma- kâya. Thus Buddhas not only possess this knowledge in the ordinary sense but they *are* the knowledge manifest in human form, and Prajñâ is often personified as a goddess. All these works lay great stress on the doctrine of œûnyatâ, and the non- existence of the world of experience. The longest recension is said to contain a polemic against the Hinayana. The Diamond Cutter is one of the best known of these transcendental treatises and the two short works called Heart of the Prajñâ- pâramitâ, which are widely read in Japan, appear to be brief abstracts of the essence of this teaching.

2. The *Saddharma- Punòdòarîka*, or Lotus of the Good Law, is one of the best known Mahayanist sutras and is highly esteemed in China and Japan. It purports to be a discourse delivered by Sâkyamuni on the Vulture Peak to an assemblage of Bodhisattvas. The Lotus clearly affirms the multiplicity of vehicles, or various ways of teaching the law, and also the eternity of the Buddha, but it does not emphasize, although it mentions, the doctrine of œûnyatâ. The work consists of two parts of which the second is a later addition. This second part contains spells and many

mythological narratives, including one of an ancient Bodhisattva who burnt himself alive in honour of a former Buddha. Portions of the Lotus were translated into Chinese under the Western Tsin Dynasty 265- 316 A.D. and it is quoted in the Mahâ- prajñâ- pâramitâ- œâstra ascribed to Nâgârjuna. The first part is probably not later than the first century A.D. The Lotus is unfortunately accessible to English readers only in a most unpoetic translation by the late Professor Kern, but it is a great religious poem which starting from humanity regards religion as cosmic and universal, rather than something mainly concerned with our earth. The discourses of Sâkyamuni are accompanied in it by stupendous miracles culminating in a grand cosmic phantasmagoria in which is evoked the stupa containing the body of a departed Buddha, that is a shrine containing the eternal truth.

3. The *Lalita- vistara* is a life of Sâkyamuni up to the commencement of his mission. Though the setting of the story is miraculous and Buddhas and Bodhisattvas innumerable are freely spoken of, yet the work does not enunciate the characteristic Mahayanist doctrines so definitely as the other treatises here enumerated. It is said to have originally belonged to the school of the Sarvâstivâdins and to have been subsequently accepted by the Mahayanists, and though it is not an epic but a collection of ballads and legends, yet it often reads as if it were a preliminary study for Aœvaghosha's Buddhacarita. It contains Sanskrit versions of old legends, which are almost verbal renderings of the Pali text, but also new material and seems to be conscious of relating novelties which may arouse scepticism for it interrupts the narrative to anathematize those who do not believe in the miracles of the Nativity and to extol the merits of faith (*œraddhâ* not *bhakti*). It is probably coeval with the earlier Gandharan art but there are no facts to fix its date.
4. The *Lankâvatâra* gives an account of the revelation of the good Law by Sâkyamuni when visiting Lanka. It is presumably subsequent to the period when Ceylon had

become a centre of Buddhism, but the story is pure fancy and unconnected with history or with older legends. It relates how the Buddha alighted on Mt. Malaya in Lanka. Ravana came to pay his respects and asked for definitions of virtue and vice which were given. The Bodhisattva Mahâmati (apparently Mañjuœrî) proceeded to propound a series of more abstruse questions which are answered at considerable length.

The Lankâvatâra represents a mature phase of speculation and not only criticizes the Sânkhya, Pâsupata and other Hindu schools, but is conscious of the growing resemblance of Mahayanism to Brahmanic philosophy and tries to explain it. It contains a prophecy about Nâgârjuna and another which mentions the Guptas, and it appears to allude to the domination of the Huns. This allusion would make its date as late as the sixth century but a translation into Chinese which is said to correspond with the Sanskrit text was made in 513. If so the barbarians referred to cannot be the Huns. An earlier translation made in 443 does not agree with our Sanskrit text and perhaps the work existed in several recensions.

5. The *Suvarnòa- prabhâsa* or Glitter of Gold is a Vaipulya sûtra in many ways resembling the Lotus. It insists on the supernatural character of the Buddha. He was never really born or entered into Nirvana but is the Dharma-kâya. The scene is laid at Râjagròiha and many Brahmanic deities are among the interlocutors. It was translated into Chinese about 420 A.D. and fragments of a translation into Uigur have been discovered in Turkestan. The contents comprise philosophy, legends and spells.
6. *Ganòdòa- vyûha* or the Structure of the World, which is compared to a bubble. The name is not found in the catalogue of the Chinese Tripitaka but the work is said to be the same as the Avatamòsaka sûtra which is popular in the Far East under the name of Hua- yên in China or Ke- gon in Japan. The identity of the two books could not have been guessed from the extracts and analyses which have been published but is guaranteed by high

authorities.It is possible however that the Ganòdòa- vyûha is only a portion of the larger work called Avatamòsaka. So far as can be judged from the extracts, this text preaches in a fully developed form, the doctrines of Sûnyatâ, Dharma- kâya, the omnipresence of the Buddha and the redemption of the world by the exertions of Bodhisattvas. Yet it seems to be early, for a portion of it was translated into Chinese about 170 A.D. and about 405 Kumârajîva translated a commentary on it ascribed to Nâgârjuna.

7. *Tathâgata- guhyaka-* This work is known by the analysis of Rajendralala Mitra from which it appears to be a Tantra of the worst class and probably late. Its proper title is said to be Srîguhyasamaja. Watanabe states that the work catalogued by Nanjio under No. 1027 and translated into Chinese about 1000 A.D. is an expurgated version of it. The Sikshâsamuccaya cites the Tathâgata- guhya- sûtra several times. The relations of these works to one another are not quite clear.
8. *Samâdhirâja* is a Vyâkaranòa or narrative describing different forms of meditation of which the Samâdhirâja is the greatest and best. The scene is laid on the Vulture's Peak and the principal interlocutors are Sâkyamuni and Candraprabha, a rich man of Râjagròiha. It appears to be the same as the Candrapradîpa- sûtra and is a complete and copious treatise, which not only expounds the topic from which it takes its name but incidentally enumerates the chief principles of Mahayanism. Watanabe states that it is the Yüeh- têng- san- mei- ching (Nanjio, 191) translated about 450 and again in 557 A.D.
9. *Daœabhûmiîœvara* - An account of the ten stages in the career of a Bodhisattva before he can attain to Buddhahood. The scene is laid in the paradise of Indra where Sâkyamuni was temporarily sojourning and the principal interlocutor is a Bodhisattva named Vajragarbha. It is said to be the same as the Daœabhûmika- sûtra first translated into Chinese about 300 A.D. but this work appears to be merely a portion of the Ganòdòa- vyûha or Avatamòsaka mentioned above.

These nine works are all extant in Sanskrit and are known in Nepal as the nine Dharmas, the word Dharma being an abbreviation for *Dharmaparyâya*, revolution or exposition of the law, a term frequently used in the works themselves to describe a comprehensive discourse delivered by the Buddha. They are all quoted in the Sikshâsamuccaya, supposed to have been written about 650 A.D. No similar collection of nine seems to be known in Tibet or the Far East and the origin of the selection is obscure. As however the list does not include the Svayambhû Purânòa, the principal indigenous scripture of Nepal, it may go back to an Indian source and represent an old tradition. Besides the nine Dharmas, numerous other sûtras exist in Sanskrit, Chinese, Tibetan and the languages of Central Asia. Few have been edited or translated and even when something is known of their character detailed information as to their contents is usually wanting. Among the better known are the following.

10. One of the sûtras most read in China and admired because its style has a literary quality unusual in Buddhist works is commonly known as the *Lêng- yen- ching*. The full title is Shou- lêng- yen- san- mei- ching which is the Chinese transliteration of Sûrangama Samâdhi. This sutra is quoted by name in the Sikshâsamuccaya and fragments of the Sanskrit text have been found in Turkestan. The Sûrangama- Samâdhi Sûtra has been conjectured to be the same as the Samâdhirâja, but the accounts of Rajendralala Mitra and Beal do not support this theory. Beal's translation leaves the impression that it resembles a Pali sutta. The scene is laid in the Jetavana with few miraculous accessories. The Buddha discusses with Ânanda the location of the soul and after confuting his theories expounds the doctrine of the Dharma- kâya. The fragments found in Turkestan recommend a particular form of meditation.
11. Târanâtha informs us that among the many Mahayanist works which appeared in the reign of Kanishka's son

was the Ratnakûtòa- dharma- paryâya in 1000 sections and the Ratnakûtòa is cited not only by the Sikshâsamuccaya but by Asanga. The Tibetan and Chinese canons contain sections with this name comprising forty- eight or forty- nine items among which are the three important treatises about Amitâbha's paradise and many dialogues called Paripròicchâ, that is, questions put by some personage, human or superhuman, and furnished with appropriate replies. The Chinese Ratnakûtòa is said to have been compiled by Bodhiruchi (693- 713 A.D.) but of course he is responsible only for the selection not for the composition of the works included.

12. The *Gunòa- kâranòdòa- vyûha* and *Kâranòdòa- vyûha* are said to be two recensions of the same work, the first in verse the second in prose. Both are devoted to the praise of Avalokita who is represented as the presiding deity of the universe. He has refused to enter Buddhahood himself until all living creatures attain to true knowledge and is specially occupied in procuring the release of those who suffer in hell. The Gunòa- kâranòdòa- vyûha contains a remarkable account of the origin of the world which is said to be absent from the prose version.

    The primeval Buddha spirit, Âdi- Buddha or Svayambhû, produces Avalokita by meditation, and Avalokita produces the material world and the gods of Hinduism from his body, Siva from his forehead, Nârâyanòa from his heart and so on. As such doctrines are not known to have appeared in Indian Buddhism before the tenth century it seems probable that the versified edition is late. But a work with the title Ratna- kâranòdòaka- vyûha- sûtra was translated into Chinese in 270 and the Kâranòdòa- vyûha is said to have been the first work translated into Tibetan.

13. The *Karunòâa- punòdòarîka* or Lotus of Compassion is mainly occupied with the description of an imaginary continent called Padmadhâtu, its Buddha and its much splendour. It exists in Sanskrit and was translated into Chinese about 400 A.D. (Nanjio, No. 142).

14. The *Mahâvairocanâbhisambhodhi* called in Chinese Ta- jih-ching or Great Sun sutra should perhaps be mentioned as it is the principal scripture of the Chên- yen (Japanese Shingon) school. It is a late work of unknown origin. It was translated into Chinese in 724 A.D. but the Sanskrit text has not been found.

There are a great number of other sutras which are important for the history of literature, although little attention is paid to them by Buddhists at the present day. Such are the Mahayanist version of the Mahâparinirvânòa recounting the death and burial of the Buddha and the Mahâsannipâta- sûtra, which apparently includes the Sûryagarbha and Candragarbha sutras. All these works were translated into Chinese about 420 A.D. and must therefore be of respectable antiquity. Besides the sutras, there are many compositions styled Avadânas or pious legends. These, though recognized by Mahayanists, do not as a rule contain expositions of the Sûnyatâ and Dharma- kâya and are not sharply distinguished from the more imaginative of the Hinayanist scriptures. But they introduce a multiplicity of Buddhas and Bodhisattvas and represent Sâkyamuni as a superhuman worker of miracles.

They correspond in many respects to the Pali Vinaya but teach right conduct not so much by precept as by edifying stories and, like most Mahayanist works they lay less stress upon monastic discipline than on unselfish virtue exercised throughout successive existences. There are a dozen or more collections of Avadânas of which the most important are the Mahâvastu and the Divyâvadâna. The former is an encyclopædic work which contains *inter alia* a life of Sâkyamuni. It describes itself as belonging to the Lokottaravâdins, a section of the Âryamahâ- sanghikas. The Lokottaravâdins were an ancient sect, precursors of the Mahayana rather than a branch of it, and much of the Mahâvastu is parallel to the Pali Canon and may have been composed a century or two before our era. But other parts seem to belong to the Gandharan period and the mention of Chinese and Hunnish writing points to a much later date.

If it was originally a Vinaya treatise, it has been distended out of all recognition by the addition of legends and anecdotes but it still retains a certain amount of matter found also in the Pali and Tibetan Vinayas. There were probably several recensions in which successive additions were made to the original nucleus. One interpolation is the lengthy and important section called Daœabhûmika, describing the career of a Bodhisattva. It is the only part of the Mahâvastu which can be called definitely Mahayanist. The rest of the work marks a transitional stage in doctrine, just as its language is neither Prakrit nor Sanskrit but some ancient vernacular brought into partial conformity with Sanskrit grammar. No Chinese translation is known.

The *Divyâvadâna* is a collection of legends, part of which is known as the Asokâvadâna and gives an edifying life of that pious monarch. This portion was translated into Chinese A.D. 317- 420 and the work probably dates from the third century of our era. It is loosely constructed: considerable portions of it seem to be identical with the Vinaya of the Sarvâstivâdins and others with passages in the works of Aœvaghosha. The Avadânas lie on the borderland between scripture and pious literature which uses human argument and refers to scripture for its authority. Of this literature the Mahayanist church has a goodly collection and the works ascribed to such doctors as Aœvaghosha, Nâgârjuna, Asanga and Vasubandhu hold a high place in general esteem. The Chinese Canon places many of them in the Pitakas (especially in the Abhidharma Pitaka) and not among the works of miscellaneous writers.

The Mahayanist scriptures are still a living force. In Nepal the nine Dharmas receive superstitious homage rather than intelligent study, but in Tibet and the Far East the Prajñâpâramitâ, the Lotus and the sutras about Amitâbha are in daily use for public worship and private reading. I have heard the first- named work as well as the Lêng- yen- ching expounded, that is, read aloud with an extempore paraphrase, to lay congregations in China, and the section of it called the Diamond Cutter is the book which is most commonly in the hands of religious Tibetans. The Lotus is the special scripture of the Nichiren sect in Japan but is universally respected. The twenty-fourth chapter which contains the praises of Avalokita is often printed separately.

The Amitâbha sûtras take the place of the New Testament for the Jôdô and Shin sects and copies of them may also be found in almost every monastery throughout China and Annam. The Suvarnòa- prabhâsa is said to be especially popular among the Mongols and Chinese Buddhists who read the Hua- yen (Avatamòsaka) every day. Modern Japanese writers quote frequently from the Lankâvatâra and Kâœyapa-parivarta but ther is no any instance of these works being in popular use. The obscurity surrounding the history of the Mahayanist Canon in India and it may seem to throw doubt on the authenticity of these scriptures. Unauthentic they certainly are in the sense that European criticism is not likely to accept as historical the discourses which they attribute to the Buddha and others, but there is no reason to doubt that they are treatises composed in India early in our era and representing the doctrines then prevalent.

The religious public of India has never felt any difficulty in accepting works of merit- and often only very moderate merit- as revelations, whether called Upanishads, Puranas, Sutras or what not. Only rarely have such works received any formal approbation, such as recognition by a council. Indeed it is rather in Ceylon, Burma, Tibet and China than in India itself that authoritative lists of scriptures have been compiled. The natural instinct of the Hindus was not to close the Canon but to leave it open for any additions which might be vouchsafed. Two sketches of an elastic Mahayanist Canon of this kind are preserved, one in the Sikshâsamuccaya attributed to Sântideva, who probably flourished in the seventh century, and the other in a little work called the Duration of the Law, reporting a discourse by an otherwise unknown Nandimitra, said to have lived in Ceylon 800 years after the Buddha's death.

The former is a compendium of doctrine illustrated by quotations from what the author regarded as scripture. He cites about a hundred Mahayanist sutras, refers to the Vinaya and Divyâvadâna but not apparently to the Abhidharma. He mentions no Tantras and not many Dhâranòîs. The second work was translated by Hsüan Chuang and was therefore probably written before 600 A.D. Otherwise there is no external evidence for fixing its date. It represents Nandimitra as explaining on his deathbed the steps taken by the Buddha to protect the True Law and in what works that Law is to be found. Like the Chinese Tripitaka it recognizes both Mahayanist and Hinayanist works, but evidently prefers the former and styles them collectively Bodhisattva- Pitòaka. It enumerates about fifty sutras by name, beginning with the Prajñâ- pâramitâ, the Lotus and other well- known texts. Then there is a list of works with titles ending in Samâdhi, followed by others called Paripròicchâ or questions.

A new category seems to be formed by the Buddhâvatamòsaka- sûtra with which the sutras about Amitâbha's Paradise are associated. Then ther is the Mahâsannipâta- sûtra associated with works which may correspond to the Ratnakûtòa division of the Chinese Canon. The writer adds that there are "hundreds of myriads of similar sutras classified in groups and categories." He mentions the Vinaya and Abhidharma without further particulars, whereas in describing the Hinayanist versions of these two Pitakas he gives many details. The importance of this list lies in the fact that it is Indian rather than in its date, for the earliest catalogue of the Chinese Tripitaka compiled about 510 is perhaps older and certainly ampler.

But if the catalogue stood alone, it might be hard to say how far the selection of works in it was due to Chinese taste. But taking the Indian and Chinese evidence together, it is clear that in the sixth century Indian Mahayanists (*a*) tolerated Hinayanist scriptures while preferring their own, (*b*) made little use of the Vinaya or Abhidharma for argument or edification, though the former was very important as a code, (*c*) recognized extremely numerous sutras, grouped in various classes such as Mahâsannipâta and Buddhâvatamòsaka, (*d*) and did not use works called Tantras. Probably much the same is true of the fourth century and even earlier, for Asanga in one work quotes both Maha- and Hinayanist scriptures and among the former cites by name seventeen sutras, including one called Paripròicchâ or questions.

4

The Contents of Early Mahayana Scriptures

The Mahayana scriptures were written probably around the 1st century BCE. Among the earliest major Mahayana scriptures attested to historically are the Perfection of Wisdom (Prajna-Paramita) sutras, the Avatamsaka Sutra, the Lotus Sutra, the Vimalakîrti Sutra, and the Nirvana Sutra. The Mahayana sometimes divides Shakyamuni Buddha's teachings into three general categories, known as "turnings of the wheel of dharma (truth)": the Hinayana, the Prajna Paramita, and the Tathagatagarbha teachings. The Mahayana canon further expanded after Buddhism was transmitted to other countries such as China and Tibet, where the existing texts were translated.

Mahayana as a distinct movement began around the 1st century BCE in the area around the Kushan Empire (now part of Pakistan) before it was transmitted in a highly evolved form to China in the second century CE. According to Akira Hirakawa (A History of Indian Buddhism: From Sakyamuni to Early Mahayana), stupas-which were initially mere monuments to Gautama Buddha-increasingly became the place of devotion and of spreading Buddhism to the masses, the majority of whom were illiterate Hindus.

EPIGRAPHICAL EVIDENCE

One of the first known mentions of the Buddha using the word Bhagavat or Bhagavan ("Supreme Lord") is a dedication on a relic vase inserted in a stupa in Gandhara, written in kharoshthi by an Indo- Greek meridarch (civil governor of a province) named Theodorus in the 1st century BCE:

"Theudorena meridarkhena pratithavida ime sarira sakamunisa bhagavato bahu- jana- stitiye": "The meridarch Theodorus has enshrined relics of Lord Shakyamuni, for the welfare of the mass of the people" (Swât relic vase inscription of the Meridarkh Theodoros)

The earliest stone inscriptions containing recognizably Mahayana formulations and a mention of the Buddha Amitabha were found in the Indian subcontinent in Mathura and dated to around 180 CE. Such inscriptions in Indian proper (Mathura) are rather late and few (the next known one is dated to the end of the 3rd century), in comparison to the multiplicity of Mahayana writings transiting from Central Asia to China at that time, and the involvement of Central Asian Buddhist monks, suggesting the focus of Mahayana development was probably in the northwest.

SCRIPTURES

The first known Mahayana texts are translations made into Chinese by the Kushan monk Lokaksema in the Chinese capital of Luoyang, between 178 and 189 CE. Lokaksema's work includes the translation of the Pratyutpanna Sutra, containing the first known mentions of the Buddha Amitabha and his Pure Land, said to be at the origin of Pure Land practice in China, and the first known translations of the Prajñâpâramitâ Sûtra, a founding text of Mahayana Buddhism.

THE 4TH BUDDHIST COUNCIL

The formal rise of Mahayana Buddhism has been dated to around the middle of the 2nd century CE, when the Kushan emperor Kanishka convened the 4th Buddhist Council in Gandhara, which confirmed the formal scission of Mahayana Buddhism from the traditional Nikaya schools of Buddhism.

EXPANSION (1ST C.CE–10TH C.CE)

From the 1st century CE and within the space of a few centuries, Mahayana was to flourish and spread in from India to South- East Asia and towards the north to Central Asia, China, Korea, and Japan, finally reaching Japan via Korea and Korean Buddhist monks in 538 CE. Mahayana disappeared from India during the 11th century, and consequently lost its influence in South- East Asia where it was replaced by Theravada Buddhism from Sri Lanka.

THE EVOLUTION OF THE ORDER AFTER ASOKA

THE BODHISATTVA

Mahayana practitioners seek to follow the bodhisattva path. Central to a bodhisattva's practice are:

- Development of *bodhicitta*, the 'thought of enlightenment,' which inspires one to become a bodhisattva in order to save others.
- Cultivation of compassion (*karuna*). From bodhicitta and an understanding of emptiness (*shunyata*) arises a profound compassion for the suffering of others and a determination to free others from suffering.
- Cultivation of the *paramitas*, the perfections of generosity, virtue (morality), patience (tolerance, forbearance), energy (diligence, courage, enthusiasm, effort), meditation (absorption, concentration, contemplation), and transcendental wisdom.
- The bodhisattva vow, the intention to save all beings by leading them to nirvana, regardless of how long it takes.

Although it is common today for people to talk about acting "like a bodhisattva," in the Mahayana schema a potential bodhisattva is already well- advanced on the path, with a deep understanding of the teachings such as dependent arising, *Karma*, rebirth and emptiness. Some bodhisattvas are said to have already become Buddhas and then chosen to practice as bodhisattvas. Others are said to have postponed their own enlightenment to be bodhisattvas of compassion. Fundamentally a bodhisattva is a Buddha to be, motivated by altruistic compassion.

BODHISATTVA ARCHETYPES

The Mahayana spawned a plethora of Bodhisattva archetypes, bodhisatvas who had reached the highest stages of compassion. These great bodhisattvas such as Manjushri, Avalokiteshvara, and Maitreya came to be visualized as enormously powerful beings–celestial bodhisattvas. The historical Buddha was not an archetypal bodhisattva but was, rather, a human being, one whose life had a profound impact on human history. The dramatic story of his life as Siddhartha Gautama, prior to his becoming the Buddha, or Awakened One, in a sense establishes the basic archetype for all bodhisattva practice.

SHUNYATA (EMPTINESS)

With the rise of the Mahayana, the teaching of no- self (Anatman) becomes the concept of Shunyata ('Emptiness'). This emptiness is not pure nothingness, of course; nor is it a kind of transcendental something. Rather it is a medicine to remedy the compulsive illusion- making habits of our minds, particularly their tendency to think of persons and things as separate, self- created and self- sustaining. Shunyata indicates, therefore, not the presence of something but rather a resounding lack or void, specifically a lack of inherent existence or 'own nature' (svabhava).

This goes as much for dharmas, those ultimate essences of the world- process, as it does for people and things. In Abhidharma there is a general tendency to think that dharmas are somehow real, though not to the extent of posses, sing atman. In the Mahayana, however, dharmas are decreed unequivocally to be empty, along with everything else. Even Emptiness is ultimately empty.

MAHAYANA SUTRAS

Central to the rise of the Mahayana was the new "technology" of the written word. With the development of the Mahayana in the beginning of the Christian era came a new body of scriptures. Mahayana Buddhists believe that the Mahayana sutras, with the possible exception of those clearly of Chinese origin, are an authentic account of teachings given during the Buddha's lifetime. However, Theravada Buddhists believe them to be later inventions of monks striving to change the original teachings of Buddha, and consider the Mahayana sutras apocryphal.

Generally, scholars conclude that the Mahayana scriptures were composed from the first century CE onwards, with some of them having their roots in other scriptures, composed in the first century BCE. Regardless of their authenticity as the teachings of the Buddha, these sutras came to have great authority because they seemed visionary and inspired. With these new sutras came a new Buddhist cosmology. And with this cosmology, which included planes above the human, came the notion that the Mahayna sutras emanated from the Buddha's wisdom, even if not from his earthly life.

PRAJNAPARAMITA (PERFECTION OF WISDOM)

One of the earliest Mahayana sutras–and one of the most important and enduring–is the Prajnaparamita ("Perfection of Wisdom) sutra, which came to exist in many versions, from 100,00 lines to the short Heart Sutra. At first sight, The Perfection of Wisdom is bewildering, full of paradox and apparent irrationality. Yet once one accepts that trying to unravel these texts without experiencing the intuitions behind them is not satisfactory, it becomes clear that paradox and irrationality are the only means of conveying to the reader those underlying intuitions that would otherwise be impossible to express.

Edward Conze succinctly summarized what The Perfection of Wisdom is about, saying, 'the thousands of lines of the Prajñâparamitâ can be summed up in the following two sentences:

1. One should become a bodhisattva (or, Buddha- to- be), i.e. one who is content with nothing less than all-knowledge attained through the perfection of wisdom for the sake of all beings.
2. There is no such thing as a bodhisattva, or as all-knowledge, or as a 'being', or as the perfection of wisdom, or as an attainment. To accept both of these contradictory facts is to be perfect.'

The central idea of The Perfection of Wisdom is complete release from the world of existence. The Perfection of Wisdom goes beyond earlier Buddhist teaching that focused on the rise and fall of phenomena to state that there is no such rise and fall - because all phenomena are essentially void. The earlier perception had been that reality is composed of a multiplicity of things. The Perfection of Wisdom states that there is no multiplicity: all is one. Even existence (samsara) and nirvana are essentially the same, and both are ultimately void. The view of The Perfection of Wisdom is that words and analysis have a practical application in that they are necessary for us to function in this world but, ultimately, nothing can be predicated about anything.

Within this context of voidness, The Perfection of Wisdom offers a way to enlightenment. It represents the formal introduction to Buddhist thought of a practical ideal-the ideal of a bodhisattva. Unlike an arhat or pratyekabuddha, beings who achieve enlightenment but cannot pass on the means of enlightenment to others, a bodhisattva should and does teach. A bodhisattva must practice the six perfections: giving, morality, patience, vigour, contemplation and wisdom. Wisdom is the most important of these because it dispels the darkness of sensory delusion and allows things to be seen as they really are.

THE MIDDLE WAY SCHOOL

Along with the new sutras came commentaries that laid out the philosophical basis of Mahayana beliefs. Of all the commentators, Nagarjuna is the most celebrated. (In fact, he is often referred to as the second Buddha.) Nagarjuna is said to have systematized the Prajnaoparamita teachings and to have founded the Madhyamaka or "Middle Way" school. He used the traditional concept of the 'middle way' in a sophisticated dialectical manner, and in so doing pushed the implications of certain of the early teachings to their logical conclusion. When discussing the doctrine of origination- in-dependence, the early Theravada scholastic tradition, known as the Abhidhamma ('higher dharma'), had understood this doctrine as referring to the origination and destruction of real elements, which they termed 'dharmas'.

Dharmas were thought of as the building- blocks of which all phenomena were composed. They were conceived of as impermanent, but none the less real. On this basis, objects such as tables and chairs were analysed as compounds of elements rather than as entities having an enduring nature of their own. A chair, for example, might be seen as consisting only of legs, a seat, and a back: there is no 'chair' over and above these parts. Nagarjuna, however, interpreted the doctrine of origination-in- dependence in a more radical way. He taught that dharmas were not just impermanent, but lacked any inherent reality at all. He summed this up by saying that all phenomena-tables, chairs, mountains, people- are simply *empty* of any real being. The Madhyamaka argued strongly, however, that this was not a doctrine of nihilism: the teaching does not claim that things do not exist, merely that they do not exist as independent realities in the way people normally assume.

It claimed that the true status of phenomena is something midway between existence and non- existence, and it was from this interpretation of the 'middle way' that the school derived its name. This line of thought had another important implication, namely that there can be no difference between nirvana and the realm of cyclic rebirth *(samsara)*. If everything is void of real existence, Nagarjuna reasoned, then in a profound sense everything is on the same footing, so on what basis can the distinction between nirvana and *samsara* be made? No difference can be found in things themselves since they are all ultimately 'empty;' the difference, therefore, must lie in our perception of them. The example is given of the person who mistakes a coil of rope for a snake at twilight and becomes terrified.

When he realizes his mistake his fear subsides and his desire to run away disappears. What is needed for liberation, then, Nagarjuna reasoned, is essentially correct vision-to see things as they really are-rather than to embark on a flight from one supposedly imperfect reality (samsara) to a better one (nirvana). Nirvana is thus reinterpreted by the Madhyamaka as a purified vision of what is seen by the ignorant as samsara. It follows that nirvana is here and now if we could but see it. The removal of spiritual ignorance and the realization that things are empty destroys the fear- or craving- we have for them. Nagarjuna and his followers called this complex of ideas "the doctrine of emptiness" *(Sunyavada)* and it has been the inspiration of Mahayana thought down the centuries.

TRANSCENDENTAL BUDDHA

With the rise of Mahayana sutras a new vision of Buddhist history and the essential nature of Buddha came into. The Theravadan idea of the Buddha achieving enlightenment in one human lifetime was replaced with the vision of the Buddha as a being who had been enlightened for endless aeons who compassionately took birth as Siddhartha Gautama in order to assist the humans beings of our era. Being eternal and omnipresent, this transcendental Buddha could apprear in different forms at different times and could reveal different aspects of the Dharma at different times and to different people.

MAHAYANA AND THERAVADA

None of the Buddha's early teachings is rejected by the Mahayana, although they are sometimes reinterpreted in radical ways. The Mahayana saw itself as recovering their true meaning which, it claimed, had been lost sight of by the early tradition. Indeed, much of what is found in the Mahayana is not new. For example, the notion of selfless compassion- which finds expression in the bodhisattva ideal- was already evident in the

Buddha's life of service to others. The doctrine of emptiness can be seen in embryonic form in the teachings on impermanence and no- self. Finally, the meditator's experience of the mind in the higher trances as luminous and pure, could easily foreshadow the conclusion that consciousness itself is the underlying reality.

The areas where the Mahayana was most innovative were in its revamped Buddhology and the devotional cults which sprang up around the various Buddhas and bodhisattvas on balance it is most likely that devotionalism- along with other innovations was an autonomous development which arose naturally at a certain cycle in the evolution of Buddhism as ideas implicit in the early teachings were worked out.

FROM KANISHKA TO VASUBANDHU

Tradition, as mentioned above, connects the rise of the Mahayana with the reign of Kanishka. Materials for forming a picture of Indian life under his rule are not plentiful but it was clearly an age of fusion. His hereditary dominions were ample and he had no need to spend his reign in conquests, but he probably subdued Kashmir as well as Khotan, Yarkand and Kashgar. Hostages from one of these states were sent to reside in India and all accounts agree that they were treated with generosity and that their sojourn improved the relations of Kanishka with the northern tribes. His capital was Purushapura or Peshawar, and the locality, like many other features of his reign, indicates a tendency to amalgamate India with Persia and Central Asia.

It was embellished with masterpieces of Gandharan sculpture and its chief ornament was a great stûpa built by the king for the reception of the relics of the Buddha which he collected. This building is described by several Chinese pilgrims and its proportions, though variously stated, were sufficient to render it celebrated in the entire Buddhist world. It is said to have been several times burnt, and rebuilt, but so solid a structure can hardly have been totally destroyed by fire and the greater part of the monument discovered in 1908 probably dates from the time of Kanishka. The base is a square measuring 285 feet on each side, with massive towers at the corners, and on each of the four faces projections bearing staircases.

The sides were ornamented with stucco figures of the Buddha and according to the Chinese pilgrims the superstructure was crowned with an iron pillar on which were set twenty- five gilded disks. Inside was found a metal casket, still containing the sacred bones, and bearing an inscription which presents two points of great interest. Firstly it mentions "Agiœala the overseer of works at Kanishka's vihâra," that is, probably Agesilaus, a foreigner in the king's service. Secondly it states that the casket was made "for the acceptance of the teachers of the Sarvâstivâdin sect," and the idea that Kanishka was the special patron of the Mahayana must be reconsidered in the light of this statement.Legends ascribe Kanishka's fervour for the Buddhist faith not to education but to conversion.

His coinage, of which abundant specimens have been preserved, confirms this for it presents images of Greek, Persian, Indian and perhaps Babylonian deities showing how varied was the mythology which may have mingled with Gandharan Buddhism. The coins bearing figures of the Buddha are not numerous and, as he undoubtedly left behind him the reputation of a pious Buddhist, it is probable that they were struck late in his reign and represent his last religious phase. Hsüan Chuang repeats some legends which relate that he was originally anti- Buddhist and that after his conversion he summoned a council and built a stupa. The substance of these legends is probable. Kanishka as a barbarian but docile conqueror was likely to adopt Buddhism if he wished to keep abreast of the thought and civilisation of his subjects, for at that time it undoubtedly inspired the intellect and art of north-western India.

Both as a statesman and as an enquirer after truth he would wish to promote harmony and stop sectarian squabbles. His action resembles that of Constantine who after his conversion to Christianity proceeded to summon the Council of Nicaea in order to stop the dissensions of the Church and settle what the tenets of the religion he had embraced, a point about which both he and Kanishka seem to have felt some uncertainty. Our knowledge of Kanishka's Council depends chiefly on the traditions reported by Hsüan Chuang which present many difficulties. He tells us that the king, acting in consultation with Parœva, issued summonses to all the learned doctors of his realm. They came in such crowds that a severe test was imposed and only 499 Arhats were selected.

There was some discussion as to the place of meeting but finally Kashmir was selected and the king built a monastery for the Brethren. When the Council met, there arose a question as to whether Vasumitra (who is not further described) should be admitted seeing that he was not an Arhat but aspired to the career of a Bodhisattva. But owing to the interposition of spirits he was not only admitted but made president. The texts of the Tripitaka were collected and the Council "composed 100,000 stanzas of Upadeœa Sâstras explanatory of the canonical sûtras, 100,000 stanzas of Vinaya- vibhâshâ Sâstras explanatory of the Vinaya and 100,000 of Abhidharma-vibhâshâ Sâstras explanatory of the Abhidharma.

For this exposition of the Tripitaka all learning from remote antiquity was thoroughly examined; the general sense and the terse language (of the Buddhist scriptures) was again and again made clear and distinct, and learning was widely diffused for the safe- guiding of disciples. King Kanishka caused the treatises when finished to be written out on copper plates and enclosed these in stone boxes which he deposited in a tope made for the purpose. He then ordered spirits to keep and guard the texts and not to allow any to be taken out of the country by heretics; those who wished to study them could do so in the country. When leaving to return to his own country, Kanishka renewed Asoka's gift of all Kashmir to the Buddhist Church."

Paramârtha (499- 569 A.D.) in his *Life of Vasubandhu* gives an account of a council generally considered to be the same as that described by Hsüan Chuang, though the differences in the two versions are considerable. He says that about five hundred years after the Buddha's death (*i.e.* between 87 B.C. and 13 A.D. if the Buddha died 487 B.C.) an Indian Arhat called Katyâyanî- putra, who was a monk of the Sarvâstivâdin School, went to Kipin or Kashmir. There with 500 other Arhats and 500 Bodhisattvas he collected the Abhidharma of the Sarvâstivâdins and arranged it in eight books called Ka- lan- ta (Sanskrit *Grantha*) or Kan- tu (Pali *Gantho*). This compilation was also called Jñâna- prasthâna. He then made a proclamation inviting all who had heard the Buddha preach to communicate what they remembered.

Many spirits responded and contributed their reminiscences which were examined by the Council and, when they did not contradict the sûtras and the Vinaya, were accepted, but otherwise were rejected. The selected pieces were grouped according to their subject- matter. Those about wisdom formed the Prajñâ Grantha and those about meditation the Dhyâna Grantha and so on. After finishing the eight books they proceeded to the composition of a commentary or Vibhâshâ and invited the assistance of Acevaghosha. When he came to Kashmir, Katyâyanî- putra expounded the eight books to him and Acevaghosha put them into literary form. At the end of twelve years the composition of the commentary was finished. It consisted of 1,000,000 verses.... Katyâyanî- putra set up a stone inscribed with this proclamation.

"Those who hereafter learn this law must not go out of Kashmir. No sentence of the eight books or of the Vibhâshâ must pass out of the land, lest other schools or the Mahayana should corrupt the true law." This proclamation was reported to the king who approved it. The sages of Kashmir had power over demons and set them to guard the entrance to the country, but we are told that anyone desirous of learning the law could come to Kashmir and was in no way interrupted. There follows a story telling how, despite this prohibition, a native of Ayodhya succeeded in learning the law in Kashmir and subsequently teaching it in his native land.

Paramârtha's account seems exaggerated, whereas the prohibition described by Hsüan Chuang is intelligible. It was forbidden to take the official copies of the law out of Kashmir, lest heretics should tamper with them. Târanâtha gives a singularly confused account of the meeting, which he expressly calls the third council, but makes some important statements about it. He says that it put an end to the dissensions which had been distracting the Buddhist Church *for nearly a century* and that it recognized all the eighteen sects as holding the true doctrine: that it put the Vinaya in writing as well as such parts of the Sûtra- pitòaka and Abhidharma as were still unwritten and corrected those which already existed as written texts: that all kinds of Mahayanist writings appeared at this time but that the Srâvakas raised no opposition.

It is hard to say how much history can be extracted from these vague and discrepant stories. They seem to refer to one assembly regarded (at least in Tibet) as the third council of the Church and held under Kanishka four or five hundred years after the Buddha's death. As to what happened at the council tradition seems to justify the following deductions, though as the tradition is certainly jumbled it may also be incorrect in details.

a. The council is recognized only by the northern Church and is unknown to the Churches of Ceylon, Burma and Siam. It seems to have regarded Kashmir as sacred land outside which the true doctrine was exposed to danger.

b. But it was not a specially Mahayanist meeting but rather a conference of peace and compromise. Târanâtha says this clearly: in Hsüan Chuang's account assemblies of Arhats (which at this time must have meant Hinayanists) elect a president who was not an Arhat and according to Paramârtha the assembly consisted of 500 Arhats and 500 Bodhisattvas who were convened by a leader of the Sarvâstivâdin School and ended by requesting Aœvaghosha to revise their work.

c. The literary result of the council was the composition of commentaries on the three Pitakas. One of these, the

Abhidharma- mahâvibhâshâ- œâstra, translated into Chinese in 437- 9 and still extant, is said to be a work of encyclopædic character, hardly a commentary in the strict sense. Paramârtha perhaps made confusion in saying that the Jñâna- prasthâna itself was composed at the council.

The traditions indicate that the council to some extent sifted and revised the Tripitaka and perhaps it accepted the seven Abhidharma books of the Sarvâstivâdins. But it is not stated or implied that it composed or sanctioned Mahayanist books. Târanâtha merely says that such books appeared at this time and that the Hinayanists raised no active objection. But if the above is the gist of the traditions, the position described is not clear. The council is recognized by Mahayanists yet it appears to have resulted in the composition of a Sarvâstivâdin treatise, and the tradition connecting the Sarvâstivâdins with the council is not likely to be wrong, for they are recognized in the inscription on Kanishka's casket, and Gandhara and Kashmir was their headquarters.

The decisions of councils are often politic rather than logical and it may be that the doctors summoned by Kanishka, while compiling Sarvâstivâdin treatises, admitted the principle that there is more than one vehicle which can take mankind to salvation. Perhaps some compromise based on geography was arranged, such as that Kashmir should be left to the Sarvâstivâdin School which had long flourished there, but that no opposition should be offered to the Mahayanists elsewhere.

The relations of the Sarvâstivâdins to Mahayanism are exceedingly difficult to define and there are hardly sufficient materials for a connected account of this once important sect, but I will state some facts about it which seem certain.

It is ancient, for the Kathâvatthu alludes to its doctrines. It flourished in Gandhara, Kashmir and Central Asia, and Kanishka's casket shows that he patronized it. But it appears to have been hardly known in Ceylon or Southern India. It was the principal northern form of Hinayanism, just as the Theravâda was the southern form. I- Ching however says that it prevailed in the Malay Archipelago. Its doctrines, so far as known, were Hinayanist but it was distinguished from cognate schools by holding that the external world can be said to exist and is not merely a continual process of becoming.

It had its own version of the Abhidharma and of the Vinaya. In the time of Fa- Hsien the latter was still preserved orally and was not written. The adherents of this school were also called Vaibhâshikas, and Vibhâshâ was a name given to their exegetical literature. But the association of the Sarvâstivâdins with Mahayanists is clear from the council of Kanishka onwards. Many eminent Buddhists began by being Sarvâstivâdins and became Mahayanists, their earlier belief being regarded as preliminary rather than erroneous. Hsüan Chuang translated the Sarvâstivâdin scriptures in his old age and I- Ching belonged to the Mûlasarvâstivâdin school; yet both authors write as if they were devout Mahayanists.

The Tibetan Church is generally regarded as an extreme form of Mahayanism but its Vinaya is that of the Sarvâstivâdins. Though the Sarvâstivâdins can hardly have accepted idealist metaphysics, yet the evidence of art and their own version of the Vinaya make it probable that they tolerated a moderate amount of mythology, and the Mahayanists, who like all philosophers were obliged to admit the provisional validity of the external world, may also have admitted their analysis of the same as provisionally valid. The strength of the Hinayanist schools lay in the Vinaya. The Mahayanists showed a tendency to replace it by legends and vague if noble aspirations. But a code of discipline was necessary for large monasteries and the code of the Sarvâstivâdins enjoyed general esteem in Central Asia and China.

Three stages in the history of Indian Buddhism are marked by the names of Aœvaghosha, Nâgârjuna and the two brothers Asanga and Vasubandhu. It would be easier to give a precise description of its development if we were sure which of the works ascribed to these worthies are authentic, but it seems that Aœvaghosha represents an ornate and transitional phase of the older schools leading to Mahayanism, whereas Nâgârjuna is connected with the Prajñâ- pâramitâ and the nihilistic philosophy. Asanga was the founder of the later and more scholastic system called Yogâcâra and is also associated with a series of revelations said to have been made by Maitreya.

As mentioned above, tradition makes Aœvaghosha, one of the most brilliant among Sanskrit writers, live at the court of Kanishka and according to some accounts he was given to the Kushans as part of a war indemnity. The tradition is confirmed by the style and contents of his poems and it has been noted by Foucher that his treatment of legends is in remarkable accord with their artistic presentment in the Gandharan sculptures. Also fragmentary manuscripts of his dramas discovered in Central Asia appear to date from the Kushan epoch. Aœvaghosha's rank as a poet depends chiefly on his Buddhacarita, or life of the Buddha up to the time of his enlightenment.

It is the earliest example of a Kâvya, usually translated as artificial epic, but here literary skill is subservient to the theme and does not, as too often in later works, overwhelm it. The Buddha is its hero, as Râma of the Râmâyana, and it sings the events of his earlier life in a fine flow of elaborate but impassioned language. Another of his poems, discovered only a few years ago, treats of the conversion of Nanda, the Buddha's half- brother. Various other works are ascribed to Aœvaghosha and for the history of Buddhism it is of great interest to decide whether he was really the author of *The Awakening of Faith.*

This skilful exposition of a difficult theme is worthy of the writer of the Buddhacarita but other reasons make his authorship doubtful, for the theology of the work may be described as the full- blown flower of Mahayanism untainted by Tantrism. It includes the doctrines of Bhûta- tathatâ, Âlaya-vijñâna, Tathâgatagarbha and the three bodies of Buddha. It would be dangerous to say that these ideas did not exist in the time of Kanishka, but what is known of the development of doctrine leads us to expect their full expression not then but a century or two later and other circumstances raise suspicions as to Aœvaghosha's authorship. His undoubted works were translated into Chinese about 400 A.D. but *The Awakening of Faith* a century and a half later.

Yet if this concise and authoritative compendium had existed in 400, it is strange that the earlier translators neglected it. It is also stated that an old Chinese catalogue of the Tripitaka does not name Aœvaghosha as the author. The undoubted works of Aœvaghosha treat the Buddha with ornate but grave rhetoric as the hero of an epic. His progress is attended by miracles such as Indian taste demands, but they hardly exceed the marvels recounted in the Pali scriptures and there is no sign that the hero is identified, as in the Ramayana of Tulsi Das or the Gospel according to St. John, with the divine spirit. The poet clearly feels personal devotion to a Saviour. He dwells on the duty of teaching others and not selfishly seeking one's own salvation, but he does not formulate dogmas.

The name most definitely connected with the early promulgation of Mahayanism is Nâgârjuna. A preponderance of Chinese tradition makes him the second patriarch after Aœvaghosha and this agrees with the Kashmir chronicle which implies that he lived soon after Kanishka. He probably flourished in the latter half of the second century. But his biographies extant in Chinese and Tibetan are almost wholly mythical, even crediting him with a life of several centuries, and the most that can be hoped is to extract a few grains of history from them. He is said to have been by birth a Brahman of Vidarbha (Berar) and to have had as teacher a Sudra named Saraha or Râhulabhadra.

When the legend states that he visited the Nâgas in the depths of the sea and obtained books from them, it seems to admit that he preached new doctrines. It is noticeable that he is represented not only as a philosopher but as a great magician, builder, physician, and maker of images. Many works are attributed to him but they have not the same authenticity as the poems of Aœvaghosha. Some schools make him the author of the Prajñâ- pâramitâ but it is more usually regarded as a revelation. The commentary on it known as Mahâ- prajñâ- pâramitâ- œâstra is generally accepted as his work. A consensus of tradition makes him the author of the

Mâdhyamika aphorisms of which some account has been given above. It is the principal authority of its school and is provided with a commentary attributed to the author himself and with a later one by Candrakîrti.

There is also ascribed to him a work called the Suhrillekha or friendly letter, a compendium of Buddhist doctrines, addressed to an Indian king. This work is old for it was translated into Chinese in 434 A.D. and is a homily for laymen. It says nothing of the Mâdhyamika philosophy and most of it deals with the need of good conduct and the terrors of future punishment, quite in the manner of the Hinayana. But it also commends the use of images and incense in worship, it mentions Avalokita and Amitâbha and it holds up the ideal of attaining Buddhahood. Nâgârjuna's authorship is not beyond dispute but these ideas may well represent a type of popular Buddhism slightly posterior to Aœvaghosha.

In most lists of patriarchs Nâgârjuna is followed by Deva, also called Âryadeva, Kânòadeva or Nîlanetra. I- Ching mentions him among the older teachers and a commentary on his principal work, the Sataœâstra, is attributed to Vasubandhu. Little is known of his special teaching but he is regarded as an important doctor and his pupil Dharmatrâta is also important if not as an author at least as a compiler, for Sanskrit collections of verses corresponding to the Pali Dhammapada are ascribed to him. Âryadeva was a native of southern India. The next epoch in the history of Buddhism is marked by the names of Asanga and Vasubandhu. The interval between them and Deva produced no teacher of importance, but Kumâralabdha, the founder of the Sautrântika school and perhaps identical with Kumârata the eighteenth Patriarch of the Chinese lists, may be mentioned.

Hsüan Chuang says that he was carried off in captivity by a king who reigned somewhere in the east of the Pamirs and that he, Aœvaghosha, Nâgârjuna and Deva were styled the four shining suns. Asanga and Vasubandhu were brothers, sons of a Brahman who lived at Peshawar. They were both converted from the Sarvâstivâdin School to Mahayanism, but the third brother Virincivatsa never changed his convictions. Tradition connects their career with Ayodhya as well as with Peshawar and Vasubandhu enjoyed the confidence of the reigning monarch, who was probably Candragupta I. This identification depends on the hypothesis that Vasubandhu lived from about 280 to 360 A.D. which, as already mentioned, seems to me to have been proved by M. Péri.

The earlier Gupta kings though not Buddhists were tolerant, as is shown by the fact that the king of Ceylon was allowed to erect a magnificent monastery at Nâlanda in the reign of Samudragupta (*c.* 330- 375 A.D.). Asanga founded the school known as Yogâcâra and many authorities ascribe to him the introduction of magical practices and Tantrism. But though he is a considerable figure in the history of Buddhism, I doubt if his importance or culpability is so great as this. For if tradition can be trusted, earlier teachers especially Nâgârjuna dealt in spells and invocations and the works of Asanga known to us are characterized by a somewhat scholastic piety and are chiefly occupied in defining and describing the various stages in the spiritual development of a Bodhisattva.

It is true that he admits the use of magical formulæ as an aid in this evolution but they form only a slight part of his system and it does not appear that the Chên- yen or Shingon sect of the Far East (the Sanskrit Mantrayâna) traced its lineage back to him. Our estimate of his position in the history of Buddhism must depend on our opinion as to the authorship of *The Awakening of Faith.* If this treatise was composed by Aœvaghosha then doctrines respecting the three bodies of Buddha, the Tathâgatagarbha and the Âlaya- vijñâna were not only known but scientifically formulated considerably before Asanga. The conclusion cannot be rejected as absurd- for Aœvaghosha might speak differently in poems and in philosophical treatises- but it is surprising, and it is probable that the treatise is not his.

If so, Asanga may have been the first to elaborate systematically (though not to originate) the idea that thought is the one and only reality. Nâgârjuna's nihilism was probably the older theory. It sounds late and elaborate but still it follows easily if the dialectic of Gotama is applied uncompromisingly not only to our mental processes but to the external world. Yet even in India the result was felt to be fantastic and sophistical and it is not surprising if after the lapse of a few generations a new system of idealism became fashionable which, although none too intelligible was abstruse rather than paradoxical. Asanga was alleged to have received revelations from Maitreya and five of his works are attributed to this Bodhisattva who enjoyed considerable honour at this period. It may be that the veneration for the Buddha of the future, the Messiah who would reign over his saints in a pure land, owed something to Persian influence which was strong in India during the decadence of the Kushans.

Both Mithraism and Manichæism classified their adepts in various ranks, and the Yogâcâra doctors who delight in grading the progress of the Bodhisattva may have borrowed something from them. Asanga's doctrine of defilement (kleœa) and purification may also owe something to Mani, as suggested by S. Lévi. In spite of his literary merits Asanga remains a doctor rather than a saint or poet. His speculations have little to do with either Gotama or Amitâbha and he was thus not in living touch with either the old or new schools. His brother Vasubandhu had perhaps a greater position. He is reckoned as the twentieth Patriarch and Tibetan tradition connects him with the worship of Amitâbha.

Paramârtha's life of Vasubandhu represents him as having frequented the court of Vikramâditya (to be identified with Candragupta I), who at first favoured the Sânkhya philosophy but accorded some patronage to Buddhism. During this period Vasubandhu was a Sarvâstivâdin but of liberal views and while in this phase wrote the Abhidharma- koœa, a general exposition of the Abhidharma, mainly according to the views of the Vaibhâshikas but not without criticism. This celebrated work is not well known in Europe but is still a text- book amongst Japanese Buddhist students. It gained the esteem of all schools and we are given to understand that it presupposed the philosophy of the Vibhâshâ and of the Jñâna- prasthâna.

According to Paramârtha the original work consisted of 600 aphorisms in verse which was sent by the author to the monks of Kashmir. They approved of the composition but, as the aphorisms were concise, asked for fuller explanations. Vasubandhu then expanded his verses into a prose commentary, but meanwhile his views had undergone a change and when he disapproved of any Vaibhâshika doctrine, he criticized it. This enlarged edition by no means pleased the brethren of Kashmir and called forth polemics. He also wrote a controversial work against the Sânkhya philosophy. Late in life Vasubandhu, moved by the entreaties of his brother Asanga, became a devout Mahayanist and wrote in his old age Mahayanist treatises and commentaries.

THE CHINESE PILGRIMS VIEW

About the time of Vasubandhu there existed four schools of Indian Buddhism called Vaibhâshika, Sautrântika, Mâdhyamika and Yoga or Yogâcâra. They were specially concerned with philosophy and apparently cut across the older division into eighteen sects, which at this period seem to have differed mainly on points of discipline. Though, not of great practical importance they long continued to play a certain part in controversial works both Buddhist and Brahmanic. The first two which were the older seem to have belonged to the Hinayana and the other two even more definitely to the Mahayana. I- Ching is quite clear as to this. "There are but two kinds of the so- called Mahayana" he says, "first the Mâdhyamika, second the Yoga.... These two systems are perfectly in accordance with the noble doctrine. Can we say which of the two is right? Both equally conform to truth and lead us to Nirvana" and so on. But he does not say that the other two systems are also aspects of the truth.

This is the more remarkable because he himself followed the Mûla- sarvâstivâdins. Apparently Sarvâstivâdin and Vaibhâshika were different names for the same school, the latter being applied to them because they identified themselves with the commentary (Vibhâshâ) already mentioned whereas the former and older designation came to be used chiefly with reference to their disciplinary rules. Also there were two groups of Sarvâstivâdins, those of Gandhara and those of Kashmir. The name of Vaibhâshika was applied chiefly to the latter that, if we may find a kernel of truth in legends which are certainly exaggerated, endeavoured to make Kashmir a holy land with a monopoly of the pure doctrine. Vasubandhu and Asanga appear to have broken up this isolation for they first preached the Vaibhâshika doctrines in a liberal and eclectic form outside Kashmir and then by a natural transition and development went over to the Mahayana.

But the Vaibhâshikas did not disappear and were in existence even in the fourteenth century. Their chief tenet was the real existence of external objects. In matters of doctrine they regarded their own Abhidharma as the highest authority. They also held that Gotama had an ordinary human body and passed first into a preliminary form of Nirvana when he attained Buddhahood and secondly into complete Nirvana at his death. He was superhuman only in the sense that he had intuitive knowledge and no need to learn. Their contempt for sutras may have been due to the fact that many of them discountenance the Vaibhâshika views and also to knowledge that new ones were continually being composed. I- Ching, who ends his work by asserting that all his statements are according to the Ârya-mûla- sarvâstivâda- nikâya and no other, gives an interesting summary of doctrine.

"Again I say: the most important are only one or two out of eighty thousand doctrines of the Buddha: one should conform to the worldly path but inwardly strive to secure true wisdom. Now what is the worldly path? It is obeying prohibitive laws and avoiding any crime. What is the true wisdom? It is to obliterate the distinction between subject and object, to follow the excellent truth and to free oneself from worldly attachments: to do away with the trammels of the chain of causality: further to obtain merit by accumulating good works and finally to realize the excellent meaning of perfect reality."

Such a statement enables us to understand the remark which he makes elsewhere that the same school may belong to the Hinayana and Mahayana in different places, for, whatever may be meant by wisdom which aims at obliterating the difference between subject and object, it is clearly not out of sympathy with Yogâcâra doctrines. In another place where he describes the curriculum followed by monks he says that they learn the Yogâcârya- œâstra first and then eight compositions of Asanga and Vasubandhu. Among the works prescribed for logic is the Nyâyadvâra- œâstra attributed to Nâgârjuna. The monk should learn not only the Abhidharma of the Sarvâstivâdins but also the Âgamas, equivalent to the Sûtra-pitòaka. So the study of the sûtras and the works of Asanga and Vasubandhu is approved by a Sarvâstivâdin.

The Sautrântikas, though accounted Hinayanists, mark a step in the direction of the Mahayana. The founder of the school was Kumarâlabdha, mentioned above. In their estimation of scripture they reversed the views of the Vaibhâshikas, for they rejected the Abhidharma and accepted only the sûtras, arguing that the Abhidharma was practically an extract from them. As literary criticism this is correct, if it means that the more ancient sûtras are older than the oldest Abhidharma books. But the indiscriminate acceptance of sûtras led to a creed in which the supernatural played a larger part. The Sautrântikas not only ascribed superhuman powers to the Buddha, but believed in the doctrine of three bodies. In philosophy, though they were realists, they held that external objects are not perceived directly but that their existence is inferred.

Something has already been said of the two other schools, both of which denied the reality of the external world. The differences between them were concerned with metaphysics rather than theology and led to no popular controversies. Up to this point the history of Indian Buddhism has proved singularly nebulous. The most important dates are a matter of argument, the chief personages half mythical. But when the records of the Chinese pilgrims commence we are in touch with something more solid. They record dates and facts, though we must regret that they only repeat what they heard and make no attempt to criticize Indian traditions or even to weave them into a connected chronicle. Fa- Hsien, the first of these interesting men, left China in 399 and resided in India from 405 to 411, spending three years at Pataliputra and two at Tamralipti.

He visited the Panjab, Hindustan and Bengal and his narrative leaves the impression that all these were in the main Buddhist countries: of the Deccan which he did not visit he heard that its inhabitants were barbarous and not Buddhists, though it contained some Buddhist shrines. Of the Middle Kingdom (which according to his reckoning begins with Muttra) he says that the people are free and happy and neither kills any living creature nor drink intoxicating liquor. He does not hint at persecution though he once or twice mentions that the Brahmans were jealous of the Buddhists. Neither does he indicate that any strong animosity prevailed between Maha and Hinayanists. But the two parties were distinct and he notes which prevailed in each locality.

He left China by land and found the Hinayana prevalent at Shen- shen and Wu- i (apparently localities not far from Lob-Nor) but the Mahayana at Khotan. Nearer India, in countries apparently corresponding to parts of Kashmir and Gilgit, the monks were numerous and all Hinayanist. The same was the case in Udyana, and in Gandhara the Hinayanists were still in the majority. In the Panjab both schools were prevalent but the Hinayana evidently strong. In the district of Muttra the Law was still more flourishing, monasteries and topes were numerous and ample alms were given to the monks. He states that the professors of the Abhidharma and Vinaya made offerings to those works, and the Mahayanists to the book Prajñâ- pâramitâ, as well as to Mañjuœrî and Kwan- shih- yin. He found the country in which are the sacred sites of Srâvasti, Kapilavastu and Kusinârâ sparsely inhabited and desolate, but this seems to have been due to general causes, not especially to the decay of religion.

He mentions that ninety- six varieties of erroneous views are found among the Buddhists, which points to the existence of numerous but not acutely hostile sects and says that there still existed, apparently in Koœala, followers of Devadatta who recognized three previous Buddhas but not Sâkyamuni. He visited the birth- places of these three Buddhas which contained topes erected in their honour. He found Magadha prosperous and pious. Of its capital, Patna, he says "by the side of the topes of Asoka has been made a Mahayana monastery very grand and beautiful, there is also a Hinayana one, the two together containing 600 or 700 monks." It is probable that this was typical of the religious condition of Magadha and Bengal. Both schools existed but the Mahayana was the more flourishing.

Many of the old sites, such as Râjagròiha and Gaya, were deserted but there were new towns near them and Bodh Gaya was a place of pilgrimage with three monasteries. In the district of Tamralipti (Tamluk) on the coast of Bengal were 22 monasteries. As his principal object was to obtain copies of the Vinaya, he stayed three years in Patna seeking and copying manuscripts. In this he found some difficulty, for the various schools of the Vinaya, which he says were divided by trivial differences only, handed down their respective versions orally. He found in the Mahayanist monastery one manuscript of the Mahâsânghika rules and considered it the most complete, but also took down the Sarvâstivâdin rules. After the death of Vasubandhu few names of even moderate magnitude stand out in the history of Indian Buddhism.

The changes which occurred were great but gradual and due not to the initiative of innovators but to the assimilative power of Hinduism and to the attractions of magical and emotional rites. But this tendency, though it doubtless existed, did not become conspicuous until about 700 A.D. The accounts of the Chinese pilgrims and the literature which has been preserved suggest that in the intervening centuries the monks were chiefly occupied with scholastic and exegetical work. The most distinguished successors of Asanga were logicians, among whom Dinnâga was pre- eminent. Sthiramati and Gunòamati appear to have belonged to the same school and perhaps Bhavaviveka too. The statements as to his date are inconsistent but the interesting fact is recorded that he utilized the terminology of the Sânkhya for the purposes of the Mahayana.

Throughout the middle ages the study of logic was pursued but Buddhists and Jains rather than by Brahmans. Vasubandhu composed some treatises dealing exclusively with logic but it was his disciple Dinnâga who separated it definitely from philosophy and theology. As in idealist philosophy, so in pure logic there was a parallel movement in the Buddhist and Brahmanic schools, but if we may trust the statements of Vâcaspatimiœra (about 1100 A.D.) Dinnâga interpreted the aphorisms of the Nyâya philosophy in a heterodox or Buddhist sense. This traces the beginnings of Indian logic to a Brahmanic source but subsequently it flourished greatly in the hands of Buddhists, especially Dinnâga and Dharmakîrti.

The former appears to have been a native of Conjevaram and a contemporary of Kâlidâsa. Both the logician and the poet were probably alive in the reign of Kumâragupta (413- 455). Dinnâga spent much time in Nâlanda, and though the Sanskrit originals of his works are lost the Tibetan translations are preserved. The Buddhist schools of logic continued for many centuries. One flourished in Kashmir and another, founded by Candragomin, in Bengal. Both lasted almost until the Mohammedan conquest of the two countries. From about 470 to 530 A.D. northern India groaned under the tyranny of the Huns. Their King Mihiragula is represented as a determined enemy of Buddhism and a systematic destroyer of monasteries. He is said to have been a worshipper of Siva but his fury was probably inspired less by religious animosity than by love of pillage and slaughter.

About 530 A.D. he was defeated by a coalition of Indian princes and died ten years later amid storms and portents which were believed to signify the descent of his wicked soul into hell. It must have been about this time that Bodhidharma left India for he arrived in Canton about 520. According to the Chinese he was the son of a king of a country called Hsiang-Chih in southern India and the twenty- eighth patriarch and he became an important figure in the religion and art of the Far East. But no allusion to him or to any of the Patriarchs after Vasubandhu has been found in Indian literature nor in the works of Hsüan Chuang and I- Ching. The inference is that he was of no importance in India and that his reputation in China was not great before the eighth century: also that the Chinese lists of patriarchs do not represent the traditions of northern India.

Religious feeling often ran high in southern India. Buddhists, Jains and Hindus engaged in violent disputes, and persecution was more frequent than in the north. It is easy to suppose that Bodhidharma being the head of some heretical sect had to fly and followed the example of many monks in going to China. But if so, no record of his school is forthcoming from his native land, though the possibility that he was more than an individual thinker and represented some movement unknown to us cannot be denied. We might suppose too that since Nâgârjuna and Âryadeva were southerners, their peculiar doctrines were coloured by Dravidian ideas. But our available documents indicate that the Buddhism of southern India was almost entirely Hinayanist, analogous to that of Ceylon and not very sympathetic to the Tamils.

The pilgrims Sung- Yün and Hui- Shêng visited Udyana and Gandhara during the time of the Hun domination (518-521). They found the king of the former a pious Buddhist but the latter was governed by an Ephthalite chieftain, perhaps Mihiragula himself, who was a worshipper of demons. Of the Yetha or Ephthalites they make the general observation that "their rules of politeness are very defective." But they also say that the population of Gandhara had a great respect for Buddhism and as they took back to China 170 volumes, "all standard works belonging to the Great Vehicle," the Ephthalite persecution cannot have destroyed the faith in north- western India. But the evil days of decay were beginning. Henceforward we have no more pictures of untroubled piety and prosperity. At best Buddhism receives royal patronage in company with other religions; sectarian conflicts increase and sometimes we hear of persecution. About 600 A.D. a king of Central Bengal named Saœânka who worshipped Siva attempted to extirpate Buddhism in his dominions and destroyed the Bo tree at Bodh Gaya.

On the other hand we hear of the pious Pûrnòavarman, king of Magadha, who made amends for these sacrileges, and of Sîlâditya, king of the country called Mo- lo- po by the Chinese, who was so careful of animal life, that he even strained the water drunk by his horses and elephants, lest they should consume minute insects. We know more of Indian Buddhism in the seventh century than in the periods which precede or follow it. The epoch was marked by the reign of the great king, or rather emperor, Harsha- Vardhana (606- 648 A.D.), and the works written by Bânòa, Bhartrihari and others who frequented his court have come down to us. Also we are fortunate in possessing the copious narrative of Hsüan Chuang, the greatest of the Chinese pilgrims, who spent sixteen years (629- 645) in India as well as the work known as the "Record of the Buddhist religion as practised in India and the Malay Archipelago," composed by I- Ching who travelled in those countries from 671 to 695. I- Ching also wrote the lives of sixty Chinese pilgrims who visited India during the seventh century and probably there were many others of whom we have no record.

The reign of Harsha is thus illustrated by a number of contemporary dateable works unusual in India. The king himself wrote some Buddhist hymns, and three dramas are ascribed to him but were probably composed by some of the literary men whom he patronized. For all that, the religious ideas which they contain must have had his approval. The Ratnâvalî and Priyadarœikâ are secular pieces and so far as they have any religious atmosphere it is Brahmanic, but the Nàgânanda is a Buddhist religious drama which opens with an invocation of the Buddha and has a Jâtaka story for its plot. Bânòa was himself a devout Brahman but his historical romance Harshacarita and his novel called Kâdambarî both describe a mixture of religions founded on observation of contemporary life. In an interesting passage he recounts the king's visit to a Buddhist ascetic.

The influence of the holy man causes the more intelligent animals in his neighbourhood, such as parrots, to devote themselves to Buddhist lore, but he is surrounded by devotees of the most diverse sects, Jains, Bhâgavatas, Pâncarâtras, Lokâyatikas with followers of Kapila, Kanòâda and many other teachers. Mayûra, another literary protégé of Harsha's, was like Bâna a Brahman, and Subandhu, who flourished a little before them, ignores Buddhism in his romance called Vâsavadattâ. But Bhartrihari, the still popular gnomic poet, was a Buddhist. It is true that he oscillated between the court and the cloister no less than seven times, but this vacillation seems to have been due to the weakness of the flesh, not to any change of convictions. For our purpose the gist of this literature is that Hinduism in many forms, some of them very unorthodox, was becoming the normal religion of India but that there were still many eminent Buddhists and that Buddhism had sufficient prestige to attract Harsha and sufficient life to respond to his patronage.

About 600 A.D. India was exhausted by her struggle with the Huns. After it there remained only a multitude of small states and obscure dynasties, but there was evidently a readiness to accept any form of unifying and tranquillizing rule and for nearly half a century this was provided by Harsha. He conquered northern India from the Panjab to Bengal but failed to subdue the Deccan. Though a great part of his reign was spent in war, learning and education flourished. Hsüan Chuang, who was his honoured guest, gives a good account of his administration but also makes it plain that brigandage prevailed and that travelling was dangerous. After 643 Harsha, who was growing elderly, devoted much attention to religion and may be said to have become a Buddhist, while allowing himself a certain eclectic freedom. Several creeds were represented among his immediate relatives.

Devotion to Siva was traditional in the family: his father had been a zealous worshipper of the Sun and his brother and sister were Buddhists of the Sammitîya sect. Harsha by no means disowned Brahmanic worship, but in his latter years his proclivity to Buddhism became more marked and he endeavoured to emulate the piety of Asoka. He founded rest houses and hospitals, as well as monasteries and thousands of stupas. He prohibited the taking of life and the use of animal food and of the three periods into which his day was divided two was devoted to religion and one to business. He also exercised surveillance over the whole Buddhist order and advanced meritorious members. Hsüan Chuang has left an interesting account of the religious fêtes and spectacles organized by Harsha.

At Kanauj he attended a great assembly during which a solemn procession took place every day. A golden image of Buddha was borne on an elephant and Harsha, dressed as Indra, held a canopy over it, while his ally Raja Kumara, dressed as Brahmâ, waved a fly- whisk. It was subsequently washed by the king's own hands and in the evening his Majesty, who like Akbar had a taste for religious discussion, listened to the arguments of his Chinese guest. But the royal instructions that no one was to speak against the Master of the Law were so peremptory that even his biographer admits there was no real discussion. These edifying pageants were interrupted by disagreeable incidents which show that Harsha's tolerance had not produced complete harmony.

A temporary monastery erected for the fêtes caught fire and a fanatic attempted to stab the king. He confessed under examination that he had been instigated to the crime by Brahmans who were jealous of the favours which the Buddhists received. It was also established that the incendiaries were Brahmans and, after the ringleaders had been punished, five hundred were exiled. Harsha then proceeded to Allahabad to superintend a quinquennial distribution of alms. It was his custom to let treasure accumulate for five years and then to divide it among holy men and the poor. The proceedings lasted seventy- five days and the concourse which collected to gaze and receive must have resembled the fair still held on the same spot.

Buddhists, Brahmans and Jains all partook of the royal bounty and the images of Buddha, Sûrya and Siva were worshipped on successive days, though greater honour was shown to the Buddha. The king gave away everything that he had, even his robes and jewels, and finally, arrayed in clothes borrowed from his sister, rejoiced saying "all I have has entered into incorruptible and imperishable treasuries." After this, adds Hsüan Chuang, the king's vassals offered him jewels and robes so that the treasury was replenished. This was the sixth quinquennial distribution which Harsha had held and the last, for he died in 648. He at first favoured the Hinayana but subsequently went over to the Mahayana, being moved in part by the exhortations of Hsüan Chuang.

Yet the substance of Hsüan Chuang's account is that though Buddhism was prospering in the Far East it was decaying in India. Against this can be set instances of royal piety like those described, the fame enjoyed by the shrines and schools of Magadha and the conversion of the king of Tibet in 638 A.D. This event was due to Chinese as well as Indian influence, but would hardly have occurred unless in north-eastern India Buddhism had been esteemed the religion of civilization. Still Hsüan Chuang's long catalogue of deserted monasteries has an unmistakable significance. The decay was most pronounced in the north- west and south. In Gandhara there were only a few Buddhists: more than a thousand monasteries stood untenanted and the Buddha's sacred bowl had vanished. In Takshaœîla the monasteries were numerous but desolate: in Kashmir the people followed a mixed faith.

Only in Udyâna was Buddhism held in high esteem. In Sind the monks were numerous but indolent. No doubt this desolation was largely due to the depredations of Mihiragula. In the Deccan and the extreme south there was also a special cause, namely the prevalence of Jainism, which somewhat later became the state religion in several kingdoms. In Kalinga, Andhra and the kingdom of the Colas the pilgrim reports that Jains were very numerous but counts Buddhist monasteries only by tens and twenties. In Dravida there were also 10,000 monks of the Sthavira School but in Malakuta among many ruined monasteries only a few were still inhabited and here again Jains were numerous.

For all Central India and Bengal the pilgrim's statistics tell the same tale, namely that though Buddhism was represented both by monasteries and monks, the Deva-temples and unbelievers were also numerous. The most favourable accounts are those given of Kanauj, Ayodhya and Magadha where the sacred sites naturally caused the devout to congregate. The statistics which he gives as to sects are interesting. The total number of monks amounted to about 183,000. Of these only 32,000 belonged definitely to the Mahayana: more than 96,000 to the Hinayana and 54,500 studied both systems or at any rate resided in monasteries which tolerated either course of study. Some writers speak as if after our era Mahayanism was predominant in India and the Hinayana banished to its extreme confines such as Ceylon and Kashmir. Yet about A.D. 640 this zealous Mahayanist states that half the monks of India were definitely Hinayanist while less than a fifth had equally definite Mahayanist convictions.

The Mahayana laid less stress on monasticism than the Hinayana and therefore its strength may have lain among the laity, but even so the admitted strength of the Hinayana is remarkable. Three Hinayanist schools are frequently mentioned, the Sthaviras, Sarvâstivâdins and Sammitîyas. The first are the well- known Sinhalese sect and were found chiefly in the south (Conjeevaram) and in East Bengal, besides the monks of the Sinhalese monastery at Gaya. The Sarvâstivâdins were found, as their history would lead us to expect, chiefly in the north and beyond the frontiers of India proper. But both were outnumbered by the Sammitîyas, who amounted to nearly 44,000 monks. The chief doctrine of this sect is said to have been that individuals (puggalo) exist as such in the truest sense.

This doctrine was supported by reference to the sutra known as the Burden and the Burden bearer. It does not assert that there is a permanent and unchangeable soul (attâ) but it emphasizes the reality and importance of that personality which all accept as true for practical purposes. It is probable that in practice this belief differed little from the ordinary Brahmanic doctrine of metempsychosis and this may be one reason for the prevalence of the sect. I- Ching, though he does not furnish statistics, gives a clear conspectus of Buddhist sects as they existed in his time. He starts from the ancient eighteen sects but divides them into four groups or Nikayas.

- The Ârya- Mahâsanghika- nikâya. This comprised seven subdivisions but was apparently the least influential school as it was not predominant anywhere, though it coexisted with other schools in most parts. The Lokottaravâdins mentioned by Hsüan Chuang as existing at Bamiyan belonged to it. They held that the Buddha was not subject to the laws of nature.
- Ârya- Sthavira- nikâya. This is the school to which our Pali Canon belongs. It was predominant in southern India and Ceylon and was also found in eastern Bengal.
- The Ârya- Mûla- sarvâstivâda- nikâya with four subdivisions. Almost all belonged to this school in northern India and it was nourishing in Magadha.
- The Ârya- Sammitîya- nikâya with four subdivisions flourished in Lâtòa and Sindhu. Thus the last three schools were preponderant in southern, northern and western India respectively.

All were followed in Magadha, no doubt because the holy places and the University of Nâlandâ attracted all shades of opinion, and Bengal seems to have been similarly catholic. This is substantially the same as Hsüan Chuang's statement except that I- Ching takes a more favourable view of the position of the Sarvâstivâda, either because it was his own school or because its position had really improved.

It would seem that in the estimation of both pilgrims the Maha- and Hinayana are not schools but modes in which any school can be studied. The Nikâya or school appears to have been chiefly, though not exclusively, concerned with the rule of discipline which naturally had more importance for Buddhist monks than it has for European scholars. The observances of each Nikâya were laid down in its own recension of the scriptures which was sometimes oral and sometimes in writing. Probably all the eighteen schools had separate Vinayas, and to some extent they had different editions of the other Pitakas, for the Sarvâstivâdins had an Abhidharma of their own.

But there was no objection to combining the study of Sarvâstivâdin literature with the reading of treatises by Asanga and Vasubandhu or sutras such as the Lotus, which I- Ching's master read once a day for sixty years. I- Ching himself seems to regard the two Vehicles as alternative forms of religion, both excellent in their way, much as a Catholic theologian might impartially explain the respective advantages of the active and contemplative lives. "With resolutions rightly formed" he says "we should look forward to meeting the coming Buddha Maitreya. If we wish to gain the lesser fruition (of the Hinayana) we may pursue it through the eight grades of sanctification. But if we learn to follow the course of the greater fruition (of the Mahayana) we must try to accomplish our work through long ages."

I- Ching observes that both Vehicles agree in prescribing the same discipline, in prohibiting the same offences and enjoining the practice of the noble truths. His views, which are substantially those of Hsüan Chuang, must be those current in the seventh century when the Hinayana was allowing the Mahayana to overgrow it without resistance, but the relations of the two creeds are sometimes stated differently. For instance the Angulimâliya sutra, known only in a Tibetan translation, states that whereas for the Hinayana such formulæ as the four truths and the eightfold path are of cardinal importance, the Mahayana does not recognize them, and it is undoubtedly true that the Vaipulya sutras frequently ignore the familiar doctrines of early Buddhism and hint that they belong to a rudimentary stage of instruction.

I- Ching makes no mention of persecution but he deplores the decay of the faith. "The teaching of the Buddha is becoming less prevalent in the world from day to day" he says. "When I compare what I have witnessed in my younger days and what I see today in my old age, the state is altogether different and we are bearing witness to this and it is hoped we shall be more attentive in future." Though he speaks regretfully of lax or incorrect discipline, he does not complain of the corruption of the faith by Tantrism and magical practices. He does however deprecate in an exceedingly curious passage the prevalence of religious suicide.

Except for progressive decay, the condition of Indian Buddhism as described by the two pilgrims is much the same. Meals were supplied to monks in the monasteries and it was no longer usual to beg for food in the streets, since the practice is mentioned by I- Ching as exceptional. On Upavasatha days it was the custom for the pious laity to entertain the monks and the meal was sometimes preceded by a religious service performed before an image and accompanied by music. I- Ching describes the musical services with devout enthusiasm. "The priests perform the ordinary service late in the afternoon or in the evening twilight. They come out of the monastery and walk three times round a stupa, offering incense and flowers.

Then they all kneel down and one of them who sing well begins to chant hymns describing the virtues of the great Teacher and continues to sing ten or twenty œlokas. They then return to the place in the monastery where they usually assemble and, when all have sat down, a reciter mounting the lion- seat (which is near the head priest) reads a short sutra. Among the scriptures for such an occasion the 'Service in three parts' is often used. This is a selection of Aœvaghosha. The first part contains ten œlokas of a hymn. The second part is a selection from some scripture consisting of the Buddha's words. Then there is an additional hymn as the third part of the service, of more than ten œlokas, being prayers that express the wish to bring one's merits to maturity. After the singing the assembled Bhikshus exclaim Subhâshita or Sâdhu that is well- said or bravo. The reader descends and the Bhikshus in order salute the lion- seat, the seats of Bodhisattvas and Arhats, and the superior of the monastery."

I- Ching also tell us of the ceremonial bathing of images and preface his description by the remark that "the meaning of the Truths is so profound that it is a matter beyond the comprehension of vulgar minds while the ablution of the holy images is practicable for all. Though the Great Teacher has entered Nirvana yet his image exists and we should worship it with zeal as though in his presence. Those who constantly offer incense and flowers to it are enabled to purify their thoughts and those who perpetually bathe his image are enabled to overcome the sins that involve them in darkness."

He appears to contemplate chiefly the veneration of images of Sâkyamuni but figures of Bodhisattvas were also conspicuous features in temples, as we know not only from archæology but from the biography of Hsüan Chuang, where it is said that worshippers used to throw flowers and silk scarves at the image of Avalokita and draw auguries from the way they fell. Monasteries were liberally decorated with statues, carvings and pictures. They often comprised several courts and temples. Hsüan Chuang says that a monastery in Magadha which he calls Ti- lo- shi- ka had "four courts with three storeyed halls, lofty terraces and a succession of open passages.... At the head of the road through the middle gate were three temples with disks on the roof and hung with small bells; the bases were surrounded by balustrades, and doors, windows, beams, walls, and stairs were ornamented with gilt work in relief."

In the three temples were large images representing the Buddha, Târâ and Avalokita? The great centres of Buddhist learning and monastic life, mentioned by both pilgrims, were Valabhî or Balabhi in Gujarat and Nalanda. The former was a district rather than a single locality and contained 100 monasteries with 6000 monks of the Sammitîya School. Nalanda was in Magadha not far from Gaya. The date of its foundation is unknown but a great temple (though apparently not the first) was built about 485 A.D. Fa- Hsien mentions a village called Nala but without indicating that it was a seat of learning. Hence it is probable that the University was not then in existence or at least not celebrated.

Hsüan Chuang describes it as containing six monasteries built by various kings and surrounded by an enclosing wall in which there was only one gate. I- Ching writing later says that the establishment owned 200 villages and contained eight halls with more than 3000 monks. In the neighbourhood of the monastery were a hundred sacred spots, several marked by temples and topes. It was a resort for Buddhists from all countries and an educational as well as a religious centre. I-Ching says that students spent two or three years there in learning and disputing after which they went to the king's court in search of a government appointment. Successful merit was rewarded not only by rank but by grants of land.

Both pilgrims mention the names of several celebrities connected with Nalanda. But the worthies of the seventh century did not attain to more than scholastic eminence. The most important literary figure of the age is Sântideva of whose life nothing is known. His writings however prove that the Buddhism of this period was not a corrupt superstition, but could inspire and nourish some of the most beautiful thoughts which the creed has produced.

5

Mahayana Texts Composed during the Kusana Dynasty

Buddhist texts can be categorized in a number of ways. The Western terms "scripture" and "canonical" are applied to Buddhism in inconsistent ways by Western scholars: for example, one authority refers to "scriptures and other canonical texts", while another says that scriptures can be categorized into canonical, commentarial and pseudo-canonical. A rather more definite division is that between Buddhavacana (the Word of the Buddha) and other texts. The former, including the Sutras (Sanskrit) or Suttas (Pali) are held to be the literal words of the historical Buddha or close approximations thereof. The latter are the various commentaries on canonical texts and other treatises on the Dharma, as well as collections of quotations, histories, grammars, and other texts. Sometimes texts that are considered commentaries by some are regarded by others as Buddhavacana.

Within Buddhavacana, there is a chronological difference between the early Buddhist texts (e.g. the Pali Canon and the Agamas), and the Mahayana sutras. Whereas some scholars believe that some portions of the Pali Canon and Agamas could contain the actual substance of the historical teachings (and possibly even the words) of the Buddha, this is not the case for the Mahayana sutras, for which only adherence to the spirit of the Buddha would be claimed by non- fundamentalist

Mahayanists. Some of these distinctions are arbitrary, and some texts fall between categories or can be associated with more than one. Many later Chinese scriptures were explicitly not of Indian origin, but have been widely accepted as valid sutras on their own merits by Chinese and East Asian Buddhists of the Mahayana tradition.

Recently an important archaeological discovery was made, consisting of the earliest known Buddhist manuscripts, recovered from the ancient civilization of Gandhara in north central Pakistan (near Taxila just south west of the capital Islamabad). These fragments, written on birch bark, are dated to the 1st century and have been compared to the Dead Sea scrolls in importance. Donated to the British Library in 1994, they are now being studied in a joint project at the University of Washington.

BUDDHAVACANA

These are, in some way or other, texts associated with one of the Buddhas. Different schools, however, are not always in agreement about which texts are Buddhavacana, and the various collections of Buddhist literature contain widely varying numbers and types of texts. According to most early schools of Buddhism, the texts come in three types:

- Sutras (i.e. discourses)
- Vinaya (relating to the rules of monastic discipline)
- Abhidharma (analytical texts)

Together these three make up what is known in Sanskrit as the Tripitaka and in Pali as the Tipitaka. Both the sutras and the vinaya of every Buddhist school contain a huge variety of documents including discourses on the Dharma, commentaries on other teachings, cosmological and cosmogonical texts, stories of the Buddha's previous lives, and various lists. Traditionally, the Theravada and other Nikaya schools believe, more or less literally, that most of these texts contain the actual words of the Buddha. The Theravada canon, also known as the Pali Canon after the language it was written in, contains some four million words.

Later texts, such as the Mahayana Sutras, are also traditionally considered by Mahayanists to be the word of the Buddha, but transmitted either in secret, via lineages of supernatural beings (such as the nagas), or revealed directly from other Buddhas or bodhisattvas. Some 600 Mahayana Sutras have survived in Sanskrit, or in Chinese and/or Tibetan translation. The earliest Mahayana texts were composed in a 'Middle Indo- Âryan' language which was Sanskritised during the Gupta era when Sanskrit became the official language of the Indian court. Most of the Mahayana sutra texts are composed in what is called Buddhist Hybrid Sanskrit, a Middle Indo- Âryan Prakrit with ornaments and flourishes designed to imitate Sanskrit.

The Tibetan Kangyur, which belongs to the various schools of Tibetan Vajrayana Buddhism, in addition to containing sutras and vinaya, also contains tantras. The division of texts into the traditional three yanas may obscure the process of development that went on, and there is some overlap in the traditional classifications. For instance, there are so- called *proto- Mahayana* texts, such as the Ajitasena Sutra, which are missing key features that are associated with Mahayana texts. Some Pali texts also contain ideas that later became synonymous with the Mahayana. The Garbhâvakrânti Sûtra is included in both the Vinaya Pitaka of the Mulasarvastivada, one of the early schools, and the Ratnakuta, a standard collection of Mahayana sutras.

Some Mahayana texts are also thought to display a distinctly tantric character, particularly some of the shorter Perfection of Wisdom Sutras. An early tantra, the Mahavairocana Abhisambodhi Tantra, is also known as the Mahavairocana Sutra. At least some editions of the Kangyur include the Heart Sutra in the tantra division. Such overlap is not confined to "neighbouring" yanas: at least nine "Sravakayana" ("Hinayana") texts can be found in the tantra divisions of some editions of the Kangyur. One of them, the Atanatiya Sutra, is also included in the Mikkyo (esoteric) division of the standard modern collected edition of Sino-Japanese Buddhist literature. (A variant of it is also found in the Digha Nikaya of the Pali Canon.) Some Buddhist texts evolved to become a virtual canon in them, and are referred to as *vaipulya* or extensive sutras. Scholars think, for instance, that the Golden Light Sutra constellated around the celebrated third chapter.

The Avatamsaka Sutra is another example of a single Sutra made up of many other sutras, many of which, particularly the Gandavyuha Sutra still circulate as separate texts. The Avatamsaka Sutra and the White Lotus Sutra are associated with the idea of the Ekayana or One Vehicle. The texts claim to unify all the teachings that have come before into a greater whole. Shingon Buddhism developed a system which assigned authorship of the early sutras to Gautama Buddha in his physical manifestation, of the *Ekayana* sutras to the Buddhas as Sambhoghakaya, and the Vajrayana texts to the Buddha as Dharmakaya.

OTHER TEXTS

Other texts have been important from very early in Buddhism. Extensive commentaries exist in Pali for the Pali Canon and in Tibetan, Chinese and other East Asian languages. Important examples of non- canonical texts are the Visuddhimagga, or *Path of Purification*, by Buddhaghosa, which is a compendium of Theravada teachings that include quotes from the Pali Canon. The Milinda Pañha or *Questions of Milinda*, sometimes included in the Pali Canon and perhaps regarded by some as Buddhavacana, is a popular condensation of the Dharma in the form of a dialogue between the Buddhist sage Nâgasena and the Indo- Greek King Menander.

The treatise *Awakening of Faith in the Mahayana* (attributed by the faithful to Aœvagho°a) strongly influenced East Asian Mahayana doctrine and inspired numerous commentaries authored by early Chinese and Korean Buddhist teachers. Shantideva's *Bodhicaryavatara* has been influential in both Mahayana and Vajrayana, and his Shikshasamucaya contains references to texts which are no longer extant in any other form. The Platform Sutra attributed to Huineng is on the borders of Buddhavacana; it is one of a very few texts not thought to be spoken by the Buddha that has the label "sutra." One should note, however, that this distinction may be an artifact of translation; in the original Chinese, the Platform Sutra is a *jîng*, a term that may be translated as "sutra", but is also applied to a variety of other classic texts, such as the Daodejing and the Shi Jing.

In the Platform Sutra, Hui Neng gives an autobiographical account of his succession as Zen Patriarch, as well as teachings about Zen theory and practice. The Zen and Ch'an school in particular rely on non- canonical accounts of Zen masters lives and teachings, for example the *Blue Cliff Record*. Tibetan Buddhism has a unique and special class of texts called terma (Tibetan gTer- ma). These are texts (or ritual objects, etc.) which are held to have been either composed or hidden by tantric masters and/or elementally secreted or encoded in the elements and retrieved, accessed or rediscovered by other tantric masters when appropriate. Termas are discovered by a tertön (Tibetan gTer- stons), whose special function is to discover these texts.

Some termas are hidden in caves or similar places, but a few are said to be 'mind termas' which are 'discovered' in the mind of the tertön. The Nyingma school (and Bön tradition) has a large terma literature. Many of the terma texts are said to have been written by Padmasambhava, who is particularly important to the Nyingmas. Probably the best known terma text is the so- called "Tibetan book of the dead", the Bardo thodol. Other types of texts which have been important are the histories of Buddhism in Sri Lanka, the *Dipavamsa* and *Mahavamsa*.

TEXTS OF THE EARLY SCHOOLS

Although many versions of the texts of the early Buddhist schools exist, the most complete canon to survive is the Pali Canon of the Theravadin School, which preserved the texts in the Pali language. Also large parts of the Sarvastivada and Dharmaguptaka texts are extant. The Pali literature has been divided by one scholar into roughly three periods. The early, or classical, period begins with the Pali Canon itself and ends with the Milindha- pañha about the turn of the Christian era. After a period of being in comparative disuse or decline, Pali underwent a renaissance in the 4th or 5th century with the help of Buddhaghosa, and this period lasted until the 12th Century.

The third period coincides with major political changes in Burma and lasted for some time in Sri Lanka, and much longer in Burma. The other (parts of) extant versions of the Tipitakas of early schools include the agamas, which includes texts of the Sarvastivada and the Dharmaguptaka. Parts of what is likely to be the canon of the Dharmaguptaka can be found amongst the Gandharan Buddhist Texts. Several early Vinaya Pitakas (from various schools) are also kept in the Chinese (Mahayana) Canon.

VINAYA

The vinaya literature is primarily concerned with aspects of the monastic discipline. However, vinaya as a term is also contrasted with Dharma, where the pair (Dhamma- Vinaya) means something like 'doctrine and discipline'. The vinaya literature in fact contains a considerable range of texts. There are, of course, those which discuss the monastic rules, how they came about, how they developed, and how they were applied. But the vinaya also contains some doctrinal expositions, ritual and liturgical texts, biographical stories, and some elements of the "Jatakas", or birth stories.

Paradoxically, the text most closely associated with the vinaya, and the most frequently used portion of it, the *Pratimoksha*, is in itself not a canonical text in Theravada, even though almost all of it can be found in the canon.

Six complete vinayas survive:

- Theravada, written in Pali.
- Mula- Sarvâstivâda, written in Sanskrit, but surviving complete only in Tibetan translation.
- Mahâsânghika, Sarvâstivâda, Mahîshâsika, and Dharmagupta, originally in Indian languages, but only surviving in Chinese translation.

In addition, portions survive of a number of vinayas in various languages. The *Mahâvastu* compiled by the Lokottaravadin sub- school of the Mahâsânghika was perhaps originally the preamble to their vinaya that became detached; hence, rather than dealing with the rules themselves, it takes the form of an extended biography of the Buddha, which it describes in terms of his progression through ten bhumis, or stages. This doctrine was later taken up by the Mahayana in a modified form as Vasubandhu's Ten Stages Sutra.

SUTRA

The Sutras (Sanskrit; Pali *Sutta*) are mostly discourses attributed to the Buddha or one of his close disciples. They are all, even those not actually spoken by him, considered to be 'Buddhavacana' or the word of the Buddha, just as in the case of all canonical literature. The Buddha's discourses were perhaps originally organised according to the style in which they were delivered; there were originally nine, but later twelve, of these. The Sanskrit forms are:

- Sûtra: prose discourses, especially short declarative discourses.
- Geya: mixed prose and verse discourse. Identified with the Sagâthâvagga of the SaAyutta Nikâya.
- Vyâkarana: explanation, analysis. Discourses in question and answer format.
- Gâthâ: verse.
- Udâna: inspired speech.
- Ityukta: beginning with 'thus has the Bhagavan said'.
- Jâtaka: story of previous life.
- Abhutadharma: concerning wonders and miraculous events.
- Vaipulya either 'extended discourses' or 'those giving joy' (cf Mahayana Texts).
- Nidâna: in which the teachings are set within their circumstances of origin.
- Avadâna: tales of exploits.
- Upadesha: defined and considered instructions.

The first nine are listed in all surviving agamas, with the other three added in some later sources. In Theravada, at least, they are regarded as a classification of the whole of the scriptures, not just suttas. The scheme is also found in Mahayana texts. However, some time later a new scheme of organisation was imposed on the canon, and it is this scheme which most people are familiar with. The scheme organises the suttas into:

Long discourses

These range in length up to 95 pages. The Pali Digha Nikaya contains 34 texts, including the Mahâparinibbâna Sutta and the Brahmajâla Sutta. The Dîrghâgama of the Dharmagupta also survives, in Chinese translation, and contains 30 sutras.

Medium- length discourses

These are the rest of the sutras of any length, and the Pali Majjhima Nikaya has 152 suttas. The Madhyamâgama of the Sarvâstivada containing 222 sutras survives in Chinese translation.

Connected discourses

This grouping consists of many short texts connected by theme, setting, or interlocutor. The Pali Samyutta Nikaya contains more than 2,800 suttas. The Samyuktâgama of the Sarvâstivada containing only 1,300 sutras survives in Chinese translation.

Numbered discourses

Sutras have the same number of doctrinal items comprising over 2,300 suttas in the Pali Anguttara Nikaya. The Chinese canon contains an Ekottarâgama which is thought by some scholars to belong to the Mahâsanghika School.

Miscellaneous texts

Not all schools had this category, but the Pali Khuddaka Nikaya has several well- known and loved texts, including:

- The *Dhammapada*: a collection of sayings and aphorisms.
- The *Udana*: a collection of inspired sayings in verse usually with a prose introduction that sets a context of sorts for the saying.
- The *Sutta Nipata*: parts of the Sutta Nipata, such as the Ammhakavagga and the Pârâyanavagga, are thought by some scholars to represent the earliest strata of the written canon. Many of the features of later texts, such as numbered lists of teachings, or complex doctrinal categories, are not present.
- *Theragâthâ* and *Therîgâthâ* two collections of biographical verse related to the disciples of the Buddha (male and female respectively.)
- *Jataka*: poems related to the so- called 'birth stories' which recount former lives of the Buddha. These remain popular in many forms of Buddhism.

Many of these texts are available in translation as well as in the original language. The Dhammapada, for instance, has a Pali version, three Chinese versions, a Tibetan version, and a Khotanese version.

Abhidharma

Abhidharma (in Pali, *Abhidhamma*) means 'further Dharma' and is concerned with the analysis of phenomena. It grew initially out of various lists of teachings such as the 37 Bodhipaksika- dharmas or the 37 Factors leading to Awakening. The Abhidharma literature is chiefly concerned with the analysis of phenomena and the relationships between them. The Theravâda Abhidhamma survives in the Pali Canon. Outside of the Theravada monasteries the Pali Abhidharma texts are not well- known.

A Sarvastivada Abhidharma, composed in Sanskrit, survives in Chinese and Tibetan traditions. Though the Theravâdin Abhidhamma is well preserved and best known, it should be noted that a number of the early Eighteen Schools each had their own distinct Abhidharma collection with not very much common textual material, though sharing methodology. Not all schools accepted the Abhidharma as canonical. The Sautrântika, for instance, held that the canon stopped with the vinaya and sutras. The rejection by some schools that dharmas (i.e. phenomena) are ultimately real, which the Theravada Abhidhamma, for instance, insists, is thought to be an important factor in the origin of the Mahayana.

Other texts

One early text not usually regarded as Buddhavacana is probably the *Milinda pañha* (literally *The Questions of Milinda*). This text is in the form of a dialogue between Nagasena, and the Indo- Greek King Menander (Pali: Milinda). It is a compendium of doctrine, and covers a range of subjects. It is included in some editions of the Pali Canon. The Pali texts have an extensive commentarial literature much of which is still untranslated. These are largely attributed to Buddhaghosa. There are also sub- commentaries or commentaries on the commentaries. Buddhaghosa was also the author of the *Visuddhimagga*, or *Path of Purification*, which is a manual of doctrine and practice according to the Theravada school.

MAHAYANA TEXTS

PERFECTION OF WISDOM TEXTS

These deal with prajñâ (wisdom or insight). Wisdom in this context means the ability to see reality as it truly is. They do not contain an elaborate philosophical argument, but simply try to point to the true nature of reality, especially through the use of paradox. The basic premise is a radical non-dualism, in which every dichotomist way of seeing things is denied: so phenomena are existent, or non- existent, but are marked by sunyata, emptiness, and an absence of any essential unchanging nature. The Perfection of Wisdom in One Letter illustrates this approach by choosing to represent the perfection of prajñâ with the Sanskrit/Pali short *a* vowel- which, as a prefix, negates a word's meaning (e.g., changing *svabhava* to *asvabhava*, "with essence" to "without essence"; cf.

mu); which is the first letter of Indic alphabets; and which, as a sound on its own, can be seen as the most neutral/basic of speech sounds (cf Aum and bija).

Many sutras are known by the number of lines, or slokas, that they contained. Edward Conze, who translated nearly all of the Perfection of Wisdom sutras into English, identified four periods of development in this literature:

1. 100BCE- 100CE: Ratnagunasamcayagatha and the Astasaharika (8,000 lines).
2. 100- 300CE: a period of elaboration in which versions in 18,000, 25,000, and 100,000 lines are produced. Possibly also the Diamond Sutra.
3. 300- 500CE : a period of condensation, producing the well known Heart Sutra, and the Perfection of Wisdom in one letter.
4. 500- 1000CE : texts from this period begin to show a tantric influence.

The Perfection of Wisdom texts have influenced every Mahayana school of Buddhism.

SADDHARMA- PUNDARIKA

Also called the Lotus Sutra, White Lotus Sutra, Sutra of the White Lotus, or Sutra on the White Lotus of the Sublime Dharma. Probably composed in its earliest form in the period 100 BCE–100 CE, the White Lotus proposes that the three yanas (Shravakayana, Pratyekabuddhayana, and Bodhisattvayana) are not in fact three different paths leading to three goals, but one path, with one goal.

The earlier teachings are said to be of 'skillful means' in order to help beings of limited capacities. Notable for the (re)appearance of the Buddha Prabhutaratna, who had died several aeons earlier, because it suggests that a Buddha is not inaccessible after his parinirvana, and also that his life- span is said to be inconceivably long because of the accumulation of merit in past lives. This idea, though not necessarily from this source, forms the basis of the later Trikaya doctrine later associated particularly with the Tien Tai in China (Tendai in Japan) school and the Nichiren schools in Japan.

PURE LAND SUTRAS

There are three major sutras that fall into this category: the Infinite Life Sutra, also known as the Larger Pure Land Sutra; the Amitabha Sutra, also known as the Smaller Pure Land Sutra; and the Contemplation Sutra, or Visualization, Sutra. These texts describe the origins and nature of the Western Pure Land in which the Buddha Amitabha resides. They list the forty- eight vows made by Amitabha as a bodhisattva by which he undertook to build a Pure Land where beings are able to practise the Dharma without difficulty or distraction. The sutras state that beings can be reborn there by pure conduct and by practices such as thinking continuously of Amitabha, praising him, recounting his virtues, and chanting his name. These Pure Land sutras and the practices they recommend became the foundations of Pure Land Buddhism, which focus on the salvific power of faith in the vows of Amitabha.

THE VIMALAKIRTI NIRDESHA SUTRA

It composed in its earliest form some time before 150CE. The Bodhisattva Vimalakirti appears in the guise of a layman in order to teach the Dharma seen by some as a strong assertion of the value of lay practice. Doctrinally similar to the Perfection of Wisdom texts, another major theme is the Buddhafield (Buddha- kshetra), which was influential on Pure Land schools. Very popular in China and Japan where it was seen as being compatible with Confucian values.

SAMADHI SUTRAS

Amongst the very earliest Mahayana texts, the Samadhi Sutras are a collection of sutras which focus on the attainment of profound states of consciousness reached in meditation, perhaps suggesting that meditation played an important role in early Mahayana and includes the Pratyutpanna Sutra and the Shurangama- samadhi Sutra.

CONFESSION SUTRAS

The Triskandha Sutra, and the Suvarnaprabhasa Sutra (or Golden Light Sutra) focuses on the practice of confession of faults. The Golden Light Sutra became especially influential in Japan, where one of its chapters (on the Universal Sovereign) was used by the Japanese emperors to legitimise their rule, and it provided a model for a well- run state.

THE AVATAMSAKA SUTRA

A large composite text consists of several parts most notably of the Dasabhumika Sutra and the Gandavyuha Sutra. It exists in three successive versions, two in Chinese and one in Tibetan. New sutras were added to the collection in both the intervals between these. The Gandavyuha sutra is thought to be the source of a sect that was dedicated specifically to Vairocana and that later gave rise to the Mahavairocana- abhisambodhi tantra, which became one of two central texts in Shingon Buddhism, and is included in the Tibetan canon as a carya class tantra. The Avatamsaka Sutra became the central text for the Hua- yen (Jp. Kegon) school of Buddhism, the most important doctrine of which is the interpenetration of all phenomena.

THIRD TURNING SUTRAS

Sutras which primarily teach the doctrine of *vijnapti- matra* or 'representation- only', associated with the Yogacara School. The *Sandhinirmocana Sutra* (c 2nd Century CE) is the earliest surviving sutra in this class (and according to some Gelugpa authorities the only one). This sutra divides the teachings of the Buddha into three classes, which it calls the "Three Turnings of the Wheel of the Dharma." To the first turning, it ascribes the *Agamas* of the Shravakas, to the second turning the lower Mahayana sutras including the *Prajna- paramita Sutras,* and finally sutras like it are deemed to comprise the third turning. Moreover, the first two turnings are considered, in this system of classification, to be provisional while the third group is said to present the final truth without a need for further explication (*nitartha*).

TATHAGATAGARBHA CLASS SUTRAS

Especially the Tathagatagarbha Sutra, the Shrîmâlâdevi-simhanâda Sûtra (Srimala Sutra), the Angulimaliya Sutra, the

Anunatva- Apurnatva- Nirdesa Sutra, and the Mahayana Mahaparinirvana Sutra (which is very different in character from the Pali Mahaparinibbana Sutta). These texts teach that every being has a Tathagatagarbha: variously translated as Buddha nature, Buddha seed, and Buddha matrix. It is this Buddha nature, Buddha Essence or Buddha Principle, this aspect of every being which is enlightened, that enables beings to be liberated and one of the most important responses of Buddhism to the problem of immanence and transcendence.

The Tathagatagarbha doctrine was very influential in East Asian Buddhism, and the idea in one form or another can be found in most of its schools. The well- known *Lankavatara Sutra*, composed sometime around the 4th century CE, is sometimes included in the *vijnapti- matra* group associated with the Yogacara teachings; however D.T. Suzuki sees the Lankavatara as clearly pre- dating and distinguished from Yogacara. The Lankavatara teaches *cittamatra* (mind only) not that of *vijnaptimatra* of the Yogacara.

Also, central to the Lankavatara is the identity of the *alayavjnana* with the *tathagata- garbha* and the Lankavatara's central message that the *tathagata- garbha* is what makes possible the turning inward (*paravritti* or *paravrtti*) of awareness to realize the Buddha's psychological transformation in practical life, while the "tathagata- garbha" system was unknown or ignored by the progenitors of the Yogacara system. The Lankavatara Sutra was influential in the Chan or Zen schools.

Collected Sutras

Two very large sutras are again actually collections of other sutras. The Mahâratnakûta Sûtra contains 49 individual works, and the Mahâsamnipâta Sûtra is a collection of 17 shorter works. Both seem to have been finalised by about the 5th century, although some parts of them are considerably older.

Transmigration Sutras

A number of sutras which focus on the actions that lead to existence in the various spheres of existence, or which expound the doctrine of the twelve links of pratitya-samutpada or dependent- origination.

Discipline Sutras

Sutras which focus on the principles and guides the behaviour of Bodhisattvas including the Kâshyapa- parivarta, the Bodhisattva- prâtimoksa Sûtra, and the Brahmajâla Sûtra.

Sutras devoted to individual figures

A large number of sutras which describe the nature and virtues of a particular Buddha or Bodhisattva and/or their Pure Land, including Mañjusri, Ksitigarbha, the Buddha Akshobhya, and Bhaishajyaguru also known as the Medicine Buddha.

PROTO- MAHAYANA SUTRAS

Early in the 20th Century, a cache of texts was found in a mound near Gilgit, Afghanistan. Amongst them was the Ajitasena Sutra. The Ajitasena Sutra appears to be a mixture of Mahayana and pre- Mahayana ideas. It occurs in a world where monasticism is the norm, which is typical of the Pali Suttas; there is none of the usual antagonism towards the Shravakas (also called the Hinayana) or the notion of Arahantship, which is typical of Mahayana Sutras such as the White Lotus, or Vimalakirti Nirdesha. However, the sutra also has an Arahant seeing all the Buddha fields, it is said that reciting the name of the sutra will save beings from suffering and the hell realms, and a meditative practice is described which allows the practitioner to see with the eyes of a Buddha, and to receive teachings from them that are very much typical of Mahayana Sutras.

Ruling line descended from the Yuezhi, a people that ruled over most of the northern Indian subcontinent, Afghanistan, and parts of Central Asia during the first three centuries of the Common Era. The Yuezhi conquered Bactria in the 2nd century BCE and divided the country into five chiefdoms, one of which was that of the Kushans (Guishuang). A hundred years later the Kushan chief Kujula Kadphises (Qiu

Jiuque) secured the political unification of the Yuezhi kingdom under himself. Under Kaniska I (flourished 1st century CE) and his successors, the Kushan kingdom reached its height. It was acknowledged as one of the four great Eurasian powers of its time (the others being China, Rome, and Parthia).

The Kushans were instrumental in spreading Buddhism in Central Asia and China and in developing Mahayana Buddhism and the Gandhara and Mathura schools of art. The Kushans became affluent through trade, particularly with Rome, as their large issues of gold coins show. These coins, which exhibit the figures of Greek, Roman, Iranian, Hindu, and Buddhist deities and bear inscriptions in adapted Greek letters, are witness to the toleration and to the syncretism in religion and art that prevailed in the Kushan Empire. After the rise of the Sâsânian dynasty in Iran and of local powers in northern India, Kushan rule declined.

The Kushan Empire (c. 1st–3rd century) of Ancient India originally formed in Bactria, on either side of the middle course of the Oxus River or Syr Darya in what is now northern Afghanistan, southern Tajikistan and Uzbekistan. At its cultural zenith, circa 105–250 CE, it extended from what is now Afghanistan to Pakistan and down into the Ganges river valley in northern India. The empire was created by the Kushan branch of the Yuezhi confederation, believed to have been an Indo- European people from the eastern Tarim Basin, China, possibly related to the Tocharians. They had diplomatic contacts with Rome, Persia and China, and for several centuries were at the center of exchange between the East and the West.

Chinese sources describe the *Guishuang, i.e.* the "Kushans", as one of the five aristocratic tribes of the Yuezhi, also spelled Yueh- chi,, a loose confederation of supposedly Indo-European peoples. The Yuezhi are also generally considered as the easternmost speakers of Indo- European languages, who had been living in the arid grasslands of eastern Central Asia, in modern- day Xinjiang and Gansu, possibly speaking versions of the Tocharian language, until they were driven west by the Xiongnu in 176–160 BCE. The five tribes constituting the Yuezhi are known in Chinese history as Xiûmì, Guishuang, Shuangmi, Xidun, and Dûmì.

Historian John Keay contextualizes the movements of the Kushan within a larger setting of mass migrations taking place in the region:

Chinese sources tell of the construction of the Great Wall in the third century BC and the repulse of various marauding tribes. Forced to head west and eventually south, these tribes displaced others in an ethnic knock- on effect which lasted many decades and spread right across Central Asia. The Parthians from Iran and the Bactrian Greeks from Bactria had both been dislodged by the Shàkas coming down from somewhere near the Aral Sea. But the Shakas had in turn been dislodged by the Yueh- chi that had themselves been driven west to Xinjiang by the Hiung- nu. The last, otherwise the Huns, would happily not reach India for a long time. But the Yueh- chi continued to press on the Shakas, and having forced them out of Bactria, it was sections or clans of these Yueh- chi who next began to move down into India in the second half of the first century AD."

The Yuezhi reached the Hellenic kingdom of Greco-Bactria, in the Bactrian territory (northernmost Afghanistan and Uzbekistan) around 135 BCE. The displaced Greek dynasties resettled to the southeast in areas of the Hindu Kush and the Indus basin (in present day Pakistan), occupying the western part of the Indo- Greek Kingdom.

EARLY KUSHANS

Some traces remain of the presence of the Kushan in the area of Bactria and Sogdiana. Archaeological structures are known in Takht- I- Sangin, Surkh Kotal (a monumental temple), and in the palace of Khalchayan. Various sculptures and friezes are known, representing horse- riding archers, and significantly men with artificially deformed skulls, such as the Kushan prince of Khalchayan (a practice well attested in nomadic Central Asia). On the ruins of ancient Hellenistic cities such as Ai- Khanoum, the Kushans are known to have built fortresses.

The earliest documented ruler and the first one to proclaim himself as a Kushan ruler was Heraios. He calls himself a "Tyrant" on his coins, and also exhibits skull deformation. He may have been an ally of the Greeks, and he shared the same style of coinage. Heraios may have been the father of the first Kushan emperor Kujula Kadphises.

A MULTI- CULTURAL EMPIRE

In the following century, the *Guishuang* gained prominence over the other Yuezhi tribes, and welded them into a tight confederation under *yabgu* (Commander) Kujula Kadphises. The name *Guishuang* was adopted in the West and modified into *Kushan* to designate the confederation, although the Chinese continued to call them *Yuezhi*. Gradually wresting control of the area from the Scythian tribes, the Kushans expanded south into the region traditionally known as Gandhara (An area lying primarily in Pakistan's Pothowar, and Northwest Frontier Provinces region but going in an arc to include Kabul valley and part of Qandahar in Afghanistan) and established twin capitals near present- day Kabul and Peshawar then known as Kapisa and Pushklavati respectively.

The Kushans adopted elements of the Hellenistic culture of Bactria. They adapted the Greek alphabet (often corrupted) to suit their own language (with the additional development of the letter Þ "sh", as in "Kushan") and soon began minting coinage on the Greek model. On their coins they used Greek language legends combined with Pali legends (in the Kharoshthi script), until the first few years of the reign of Kanishka. After that date, they used Kushan language legends (in an adapted Greek script), combined with legends in Greek (Greek script) and legends in Pali (Kharoshthi script).

The Kushans are believed to have been predominantly Zoroastrian and later Buddhist as well. However, from the time of Wima Takto, many Kushans started adopting aspects of Indian culture. Like the Egyptians they absorbed the strong remnants of the Greek Culture of the Hellenistic Kingdoms, becoming at least partly Hellenised. The first great Kushan emperor Wima Kadphises may have embraced Saivism, as surmised by coins minted during the period. The following Kushan emperors represented both Zoroastrianism and Buddhism.

The rule of the Kushans linked the seagoing trade of the Indian Ocean with the commerce of the Silk Road through the long- civilized Indus Valley. At the height of the dynasty, the Kushans loosely oversaw a territory that extended to the Aral Sea through present- day Uzbekistan, Afghanistan, and Pakistan into northern India. The loose unity and comparative peace of such a vast expanse encouraged long- distance trade, brought Chinese silks to Rome, and created strings of flourishing urban centers.

TERRITORIAL EXPANSION

Direct archaeological evidence of a Kushan rule of long duration is basically available in an area stretching from Surkh Kotal, Begram, the summer capital of the Kushans, Peshawar the capital under Kanishka I, Taxila and Mathura, the winter capital of the Kushans. Other areas of probable rule include Khwarezm (Russian archaeological findings) Kausambi (excavations of the Allahabad University), Sanchi and Sarnath (inscriptions with names and dates of Kushan kings), Malwa and Maharashtra, Orissa (imitation of Kushan coins, and large Kushan hoards). The recently discovered Rabatak inscription tends to confirm large Kushan dominions in the heartland of India. The lines 4 to 7 of the inscription describe the cities which were under the rule of Kanishka, among which six names are identifiable: Ujjain, Kundina, Saketa, Kausambi, Pataliputra, and Champa (although the text is not clear whether Champa was a possession of Kanishka or just beyond it).

Northward, in the 2nd century CE, the Kushans under Kanishka made various forays into the Tarim Basin, seemingly the original ground of their ancestors the Yuezhi, where they had various contacts with the Chinese. Both archaeological findings and literary evidence suggest Kushan rule, in Kashgar, Yarkand and Khotan. As late as the 3rd century CE, decorated coins of Huvishka were dedicated at Bodh Gaya together with other gold offerings under the "Enlightenment Throne" of the Buddha, suggesting direct Kushan influence in the area during that period.

MAIN KUSHAN RULERS

KUJULA KADPHISES (30-80)

According to the *Hou Hanshu*: "the prince (xihou) of Guishuang (Badakhshan and the adjoining territories north of the Oxus), named Kujula Kadphises attacked and exterminated the four other princes (xihou). He set himself up as king of a kingdom called Guishuang." He invaded Anxi (Parthia) and took the Gaofu (Kabul) region. He also defeated the whole of the kingdoms of Puda, and Jibin (Kapisha-Gandhara). Qiujiuque (Kujula Kadphises) was more than eighty years old when he died."

These conquests probably took place sometime between 45 and 60, and laid the basis for the Kushan Empire which was rapidly expanded by his descendants. Kujula issued an extensive series of coins and fathered at least two sons, SadackaGa (who is known from only two inscriptions, especially the Rabatak inscription, and apparently never have ruled), and seemingly Vima Taktu. Kujula Kadphises was the great grandfather of Kanishka.

VIMA TAKTU (80-105)

Vima Takt[u] is not mentioned in the Rabatak inscription. He was the predecessor of Vima Kadphises, and Kanishka I. He expanded the Kushan Empire into the northwest of the Indian subcontinent. The *Hou Hanshu* says:

"His [Kujula Kadphises'] son, Yangaozhen (Vima Taktu), became king in his place. He conquered Tianzhu (Northwestern India) and installed a General to supervise and lead it. The Yuezhi then became extremely rich. All the kingdoms call [their king] the Guishuang (Kushan) king, but the Han call them by their original name, Da Yuezhi."

VIMA KADPHISES (105-127)

Vima Kadphises was a Kushan emperor from around 90-100 CE, the son of Sadashkana and the grandson of Kujula Kadphises, and the father of Kanishka I, as detailed by the Rabatak inscription. Vima Kadphises added to the Kushan territory by his conquests in Afghanistan and north- west India. He issued an extensive series of coins and inscriptions. He was the first to introduce gold coinage in India, in addition to the existing copper and silver coinage.

Kanishka, the fifth Kushan king who flourished for at least 28 years from c. 127, upon his accession, Kanishka ruled a huge territory (virtually all of northern India), south to Ujjain and Kundina and east beyond Pataliputra, according to the Rabatak inscription:

His territory was administered from two capitals: Purushapura (now Peshawar in northern Pakistan) and Mathura, in northern India. He is also credited (along with Raja Dab) for building the massive, ancient Fort at Bathinda (Qila Mubarak), in the modern city of Bathinda, Indian Punjab.

The Kushans also had a summer capital in Bagram (then known as Kapisa), where the "Begram Treasure", comprising works of art from Greece to China, has been found. According to the Rabatak inscription, Kanishka was the son of Vima Kadphises, the grandson of Sadashkana, and the great- grandson of Kujula Kadphises. Kanishka's era is now generally accepted to have begun in 127 on the basis of Harry Falk's ground-breaking research. Kanishka's era was used as a calendar reference by the Kushans for about a century, until the decline of the Kushan realm.

VÂSISHKA

Vâsishka was a Kushan emperor, who seems to have a short reign following Kanishka. His rule is recorded as far south as Sanchi (near Vidisa), where several inscriptions in his name have been found, dated to the year 22 (The Sanchi inscription of "Vaksushana" - i. e. Vasishka Kushana) and year

28 (The Sanchi inscription of Vasaska – i. e. Vasishka) of the Kanishka era. Huvishka (Kushan: Ïïçêé, "Ooishki") was a Kushan emperor from the death of Kanishka (assumed on the best evidence available to be in 140 CE) until the succession of Vasudeva I about forty years later. His rule was a period of retrenchment and consolidation for the Empire. In particular he devoted time and effort early in his reign to the exertion of greater control over the city of Mathura.

Named inscriptions dating from year 64 to 98 of Kanishka's era suggest his reign extended from at least 191 to 225 CE. He was the last great Kushan emperor, and the end of his rule coincides with the invasion of the Sassanids as far as northwestern India, and the establishment of the Indo- Sassanids or Kushanshahs from around 240 CE. The Kushan religious pantheon is extremely varied, as revealed by their coins and their seals, on which more than 30 different gods appear, belonging to the Hellenistic, the Iranian, and to a lesser extent the Indian world. Greek deities, with Greek names are represented on early coins. During Kanishka's reign, the language of the coinage changes to Bactrian (though it remained in Greek script for all kings). After Huvishka, only two divinities appear on the coins: *Ardoxsho* and *Oesho*.

THE KUSHANS AND BUDDHISM

Cultural exchanges also flourished, encouraging the development of Greco- Buddhism, a fusion of Hellenistic and Buddhist cultural elements to expand into central and northern Asia as Mahayana Buddhism. Kanishka is renowned in Buddhist tradition for having convened a great Buddhist council in Kashmir. Kanishka also had the original Gandhari vernacular, or Prakrit, Buddhist texts translated into the language of Sanskrit. Along with the Indian emperors Ashoka and Harsha Vardhana and the Indo- Greek king Menander I (Milinda), Kanishka is considered by Buddhism as one of its greatest benefactors.

KUSHAN ART

The art and culture of Gandhara, at the crossroads of the Kushan hegemony, are the best known expressions of Kushan influences to Westerners. Several direct depictions of Kushans are known from Gandhara, where they are represented with a tunic, belt and trousers and play the role of devotees to the Buddha, as well as the Bodhisattva and future Buddha Maitreya. In the iconography, they are never associated however with the very Hellenistic "Standing Buddha" statues, which might therefore correspond to an earlier historical period. The style of these friezes incorporating Kushan devotees is already strongly Indianized, quite remote from earlier Hellenistic depictions of the Buddha:

Contacts with Rome

Several Roman sources describe the visit of ambassadors from the Kings of Bactria and India during the 2nd century, probably referring to the Kushans.

Historia Augusta, speaking of Emperor Hadrian (117-138) tells:

"Reges Bactrianorum legatos ad eum, amicitiae petendae causa, supplices miserunt"

"The kings of the Bactrians sent supplicant ambassadors to him, to seek his friendship."

Also in 138, according to Aurelius Victor (*Epitome*, XV, 4), and Appian (*Praef.* 7), Antoninus Pius, successor to Hadrian, received some Indian, Bactrian (Kushan) and Hyrcanian ambassadors. The Chinese Historical Chronicle of the Hou Hanshu also describes the exchange of goods between northwestern India and the Roman Empire at that time: "To the west (Tiazhu, northwestern India) communicates with Da Qin (the Roman Empire). Precious things from Da Qin can be found there, as well as fine cotton cloths, excellent wool carpets, perfumes of all sorts, sugar loaves, pepper, ginger, and black salt." The summer capital of the Kushan in Begram has yielded a considerable amount of goods imported from the Roman Empire, in particular various types of glassware.

CONTACTS WITH CHINA

During the 1st and 2nd century, the Kushan Empire

expanded militarily to the north and occupied parts of the Tarim Basin, their original grounds, putting them at the center of the profitable Central Asian commerce with the Roman Empire. They are related to have collaborated militarily with the Chinese against nomadic incursion, particularly when they collaborated with the Chinese general Ban Chao against the Sogdians in 84, when the latter were trying to support a revolt by the king of Kashgar. Around 85, they also assisted the Chinese general in an attack on Turfan, east of the Tarim Basin.

In recognition for their support to the Chinese, the Kushans requested, but were denied, a Han princess, even after they had sent presents to the Chinese court. In retaliation, they marched on Ban Chao in 86 with a force of 70,000, but, exhausted by the expedition, were finally defeated by the smaller Chinese force. The Yuezhi retreated and paid tribute to the Chinese Empire during the reign of the Chinese emperor Han He (89–106). Later, around 116, the Kushans under Kanishka established a kingdom centered on Kashgar, also taking control of Khotan and Yarkand, which were Chinese dependencies in the Tarim Basin, modern Xinjiang. They introduced the Brahmi script, the Indian Prakrit language for administration, and expanded the influence of Greco- Buddhist art which developed into Serindian art.

The Kushans are again recorded to have sent presents to the Chinese court in 158–159 during the reign of the Chinese emperor Han Huan. Following these interactions, cultural exhanges further increased, and Kushan Buddhist missionaries, such as Lokaksema, became active in the Chinese capital cities of Loyang and sometimes Nanjing, where they particularly distinguished themselves by their translation work. They were the first recorded promoters of Hinayana and Mahayana scriptures in China, greatly contributing to the Silk Road transmission of Buddhism.

DECLINE

After the death of Vasudeva I in 225, the Kushan Empire split into western and eastern halves. The Western Kushans (in Afghanistan) were soon subjugated by the Persian Sassanid

Empire and lost Bactria and other territories. In 248 they were defeated again by the Persians, who deposed the Western dynasty and replaced them with Persian vassals known as the Kushanshas (or Indo- Sassanids). The Eastern Kushan kingdom was based in the Punjab. Around 270 their territories on the Gangetic plain became independent under local dynasties such as the Yaudheyas. Then in the mid 4th century they were subjugated by the Gupta Empire under Samudragupta.

In 360 a Kushan vassal named Kidara overthrew the old Kushan dynasty and established the Kidarite Kingdom. The Kushan style of Kidarite coins indicates they considered themselves as Kushans. The Kidarite seem to have been rather prosperous, although on a smaller scale than their Kushan predecessors. These remnants of the Kushan Empire were ultimately wiped out in the 5th century by the invasions of the White Huns, and later the expansion of Islam.

IN FICTION

The Kushan Empire was used to represent a dystopian demonic empire within the hugely popular *Berserk* manga. Its culture is based on that of ancient and medieval India, which was the cultural centre of the real Kushan Empire, including Indian weapons such as chakrams, katars and urumis, and martial arts similar to Kalarippayattu, but adapted for the nihilistic setting. In this fictional setting it is ruled by the Emperor Ganishka, a name based upon the real Kushan Emperor Kanishka.

6

Theory and Practise in Early Mahayana Buddhism

In the late nineteenth and early twentieth centuries, European and Indian scholars were puzzled by the absence of anthropomorphic representations of the historical Buddha Sakyamuni in the earliest surviving Buddhist art. Early Buddhist art, it was assumed, either avoided Buddha images entirely, or favored the use of symbols to refer to the Buddha or important events in the Buddha's life. For example, the depiction of a specific tree in early stone reliefs was interpreted to signify the Buddha's enlightenment beneath the bodhi tree at Bodh Gaya. Similarly, portrayals of the wheel representing Buddhist law were often thought to be symbolic representations of the Buddha's first sermon at Sarnath.

This supposed practice of either avoiding images of the Buddha or using symbols as substitutes for Buddha images became known as "aniconism." For nearly a hundred years, the theory of aniconism has been universally accepted in the interpretation of early Buddhist art. The early twentieth-century writer Alfred Foucher was the first to articulate the theory. He based his ideas on the assumption that the earliest Buddha images were those produced in the Gandhara region of ancient India during the early centuries of the Christian era-more than half a millennium after the Buddha lived. In Gandhara, he surmised, Indian artists were introduced to what he considered a superior sculptural heritage- that of the Greek and classical world- which stimulated the creation of anthropomorphic images of the Buddha.

Indian sentiment was naturally offended at the suggestion that Western influence was required to motivate the production of the Buddha image. Ananda Coomaraswamy took the case to the Art Bulletin, where he contended in a frequently cited article that the impetus for creating the Buddha image was rooted in indigenous beliefs and sculptural traditions. At the same time, Coomaraswamy, like Foucher, accepted the theory of aniconism to explain the art in which portrayals of the Buddha in human form did not occur.

Considering some of the underlying principles of Buddhism, it has not been difficult for scholars to suggest explanations for the absence of anthropomorphic images of the Buddha in early Buddhist art. One author notes that "the Buddha was not shown at all, to symbolize the fact that he was nibbuta (`extinguished')," thus relating the notion of aniconism with the very essence of Buddhism- the cessation of existence in physical form.

Another scholar cites a verse from the Suttanipata, which states, "He who is passionless regarding all desires, Resorts to nothingness," to suggest that the Buddha's transcendence of personal, egoistic existence may be linked with the artistic phenomenon. This author further suggests that "As flame blown by the force of wind goes out and is no longer reckoned. Even so the sage, released from name and form, goes out and is no longer reckoned," and concludes that the absence of Buddha figures in human form in the early art reflects the Buddha's "true Nirvana essence [which is] inconceivable in visual form and human shape." While such concepts are central to Buddhist thinking, they may not be pertinent to the issue of aniconism.

Although such references recur throughout Buddhist literature, they do not directly address the issue of whether a Buddha should be represented in human form. So deeply embedded within a matrix of long- standing views of Buddhist doctrinal, institutional, and sectarian history is the aniconic interpretation of early Buddhist art that any erosion of the theory threatens to crumble the foundations upon which decades of scholarship have been built. Acceptance of a so-called period of aniconism preceding an image- making phase has been so strong that a number of cases may be cited where secure archaeological, inscriptional, and literary evidence to the contrary has been dismissed to accommodate the theory.

Nonetheless, a fresh analysis based on archaeological, literary, and inscriptional evidence casts doubt on the practice of deliberate avoidance of Buddha images. For instance, one of the cornerstones of the aniconic theory has been that the early art reflected "Himayana" forms of Buddhism and that "Himayana" Buddhists had doctrinal proscriptions against the creation of works of art showing Buddhas in their human forms. Proponents of the theory have contended that the practice of creating anthropomorphic representations of the Buddha was initiated only when Mahayana Buddhism began to flourish around the early centuries of the Christian era. However, one respected Buddhologist has recently suggested on the basis of textual evidence that "Hinayanists" were probably as receptive to the making of the image as Mahayanists.

Another distinguished Buddhologist has concluded that the association of the Buddha image solely with Mahayana is incorrect and that "almost all the Hinayana schools were actively interested in and concerned with images and the cult of images." Indeed, in the entire corpus of Buddhist literature, scholars have been able to find only a single, indirect reference to a proscription against the creation of Buddha images, and that is limited to the context of a single Buddhist sect. Archaeological evidence also challenges one of the mainstays of the aniconic theory, namely, the long- held conviction that the Buddha image was first created during the Kusana period around the first or second century A. D.

Recently a number of sculpted Buddha images belonging to the pre- Kusana period have been identified. The existence of these pre- Kusana sculpted Buddhas undermines the theory that Kusana patronage was responsible for the introduction of anthropomorphic Buddha images. The early date of these images confirms that representations of Buddhas were being produced at the same time as the so- called aniconic reliefs, thus suggesting that the absence of Buddha images in the reliefs cannot be attributed to widespread prohibitions against the creation of Buddha images. The widening gap between recent historical, art- historical and textual evidence and the traditional aniconic theory raises many questions. Can it still be assumed that the pre- Kusana reliefs that do not depict the Buddha in human form reflect a deliberate avoidance of his portrayal?

Might there be other explanations for the apparent absence of Buddha figures in the early reliefs? Can the recently identified Buddha images from pre- Kusana times be reconciled with the other artistic remains of those periods? And, most importantly if the subjects of the hundreds of pre-Kusana reliefs do not contained veiled references to a being that is never shown, what might they have been intended to communicate? At present, I am engaged in a detailed study that explores the early art of Buddhist India with these questions in mind and offers new interpretations of the content of these carvings. The corpus of so called aniconic reliefs displays a variety of subjects, including abstract animal, and foliate motifs, nature spirits, and narrative scenes.

Among these, the narrative scenes are of the greatest importance to the study of the problem of aniconism, for the vast majority are generally identified either as events in the life of the historical Buddha Sakyamuni (ca. 560- 480 B.C.) or as depictions of jataka stories relating his previous lives. The type of relief that is among those that are usually said to illustrate scenes from the life of the Buddha, with the Buddha, however, not depicted. It is possible that most, if not all, of these compositions do not represent events in the life of the Buddha at all, but rather portray worship and adoration at sacred Buddhist sites.

Although some of these reliefs may depict devotions made at sacred sites even while the Buddha was still alive, most of them probably show the sites as they were worshiped after the lifetime of the Buddha. Further, the so- called aniconic symbols, such as empty thrones, trees, wheels, and stupas (hemispherical structures containing relics), were not intended by the makers of the reliefs to serve as surrogates for Buddha images, but were the sacred nuclei of worship at these sites.

The reliefs, then, are essentially "portraits" of the sites and show the practices of pilgrimage and devotion associated with them. A comparison between an iconic image of the Buddha's first sermon and an image that has been identified as an aniconic version of the same scene demonstrates the visual and thematic differences between the two types. In the so- called aniconic type, seen in a first- century A.D. relief at Sanchi, a large wheel is the central object in the composition.

The wheel-the Buddhist wheel of law (righteousness) - is invariably associated with the Buddha's first sermon, during which he is said to have set the wheel of law in motion. Therefore, compositions like this are generally identified as depictions of the Buddha's first sermon with the Buddha not shown in anthropomorphic form. The other image, a second- or third- century A.D. relief from the Gandhara region of Pakistan, is of the "iconic" type and bears a figure of a Buddha seated upon a throne. Like most images showing a Buddha, this carving is later in date than most of the "aniconic" images. In the Gandharan relief, the Buddha is portrayed along with five ascetics and a pair of deer flanking a wheel below.

These elements typify illustrations of the Buddha's first sermon, which he delivered to an audience of five heretics at the Deer Park and at Benares. Three additional figures, distinguished by their costumes, are also in attendance, although their presence is not requisite in the scene. Two observations may be made about reliefs that actually portray Buddha's life events:

1. The place being shown is the place where the event occurred, and
2. The time of the activity depicted in the composition is the time of the event itself.

These two conditions generally are not present or even implicit in reliefs of the "aniconic" type, such as the scene showing the wheel. Earlier scholars have assumed that compositions like this record events during the lifetime of the Buddha, in spite of both the absence of the Buddha and the presence of other elements in the composition that indicate that another activity is occurring. Without accounting for the counterevidence, they have concluded that such compositions represent Buddha life scenes with the Buddha absent. Place and time, which are explicitly indicated in iconic images of Buddha's life events, are key issues in the interpretation of the aniconic reliefs, as may be clarified by examining a recently discovered image from Amaravati.

This second- century A.D. carving depicts neither a nonfigurative subject nor a Buddha. Instead, it shows what a Buddha image placed upon a throne is clearly. The focus of the relief is a rectangular throne, behind which is an asvattha tree, as identified by the shape of its leaves. Upon the throne rests a rounder bearing a figure of a seated Buddha displaying the gesture of reassurance with his right hand. A pair of footprints appears below. To the far right and rear of the pictorial space, a portion of a roofed building or pavilion is visible. Flanking the central throne and tree is a pair of figures (that on the viewer's left being badly damaged).

These figures are seated with one leg pendant on platforms that flank the central altar, and the figure at the right holds a fly whisk over his right shoulder. There is no doubt that this relief represents a certain place. The setting of the relief is strikingly suggested by the building at the right rear, which apparently is included as part of the portrayal of the site. It seems clear that the scene is not an event in the life of Buddha, since the Buddha is not present and he (or another Buddha) is specifically depicted in an image. Because the scene does not represent a life event of the Buddha, one cannot even be certain that the place being depicted is one where an event in the Buddha's Life occurred.

The presence of the asvattha tree might imply that the site was Bodh Gaya, but, as is well known, specimens of the asvattha tree, the enlightenment or bodhi tree of Sakyamuni Buddha, are sacred and are enshrined throughout the Buddhist world. The Buddha in the rounder is not in the earth touching gesture that characterizes representations of his imminent enlightenment at Bodh Gaya, thus providing further evidence that the site is not Bodh Gaya. One can only say that the scene represents a Buddhist sacred spot, or pitha. Regarding the time of the event, the presence of the image suggests that the scene probably occurred after the lifetime of the Buddha.

Scholars have assumed that all the early reliefs of the type under discussion-both the "iconic" and "aniconic" examples-were meant to indicate an event during the lifetime of the Buddha, but it is clear that another alternative exists: I contend that at least some of the so- called aniconic scenes depict sacred locations of Buddhism being visited by laypersons, most likely some time after the Buddha had lived. A number of features in the "aniconic" carvings of this type, such as the devout worshipers in the Sanchi scene, clearly indicate this type of practice.

The strongest and perhaps most unequivocal evidence that the scene showing the veneration of the wheel of law and numerous other so- called aniconic reliefs are depictions of sacred places, with lay practitioners worshiping at them (and not events in the life of the Buddha), is the body of inscriptions associated with some of the "aniconic" reliefs from Bharhut dating from the first century B.C. One critic of my theory has accused me of being "blissfully unaware of the plethora of inscriptions at Bharhut that specifically identify these representations as events in the Buddha's life."

On the contrary, a closer examination of the inscriptions reveals that they argue strongly for my case, because many of the epigraphs clearly indicate places, not events. Indeed, it is precisely the confusion of location and event that is at the root of what I believe to be the misperception about many of the early reliefs. Several examples from Bharhut clarify the issues relating to this confusion. One of the most incontrovertible illustrations is a cat first- century B.C. rounder showing a tree with an altar in front of it being venerated by a male and female couple and a pair of children.

The inscription accompanying this relief says bhagavato Vesabhuna bodhi salo, that is, "The Bodhi tree of the holy Vesabhu (Visvabhu), a Sala tree." The inscription clearly identifies the scene as a representation of the tree of enlightenment (bodhi tree) of the Buddha Visvabhu, one of the mortal Buddhas who preceded Sakyumuni in time. In other words, the relief depicts the tree under which the enlightenment took place, but not the event of Buddha Visvabhu's enlightenment itself. The inscription implies the location-the place where the tree was rooted-while the human figures and other elements in the rounder indicate the activity that is taking place.

The rounder features the tree, an altar for offerings, and the human devotees who are worshiping the tree by draping it with garlands, making offerings, and kneeling in respect. It is clear that the relief illustrates activities that are taking place at the holy site some time after Visvabhu's enlightenment. Further, the scene is clearly an exaltation of Buddhist devotion, specifically lay devotion, since the figures are lay worshipers, as indicated by their secular garb. Several other reliefs from the Bharhut railing show the trees of other mortal Buddhas and are accompanied by inscriptions indicating that the scenes represent the sacred trees at their sacred sites, rather than enlightenment events.

The most detailed of these compositions shows an elaborate temple enshrining an asvattha tree, the bodhi tree of Sakyamuni. This first century B.C. panel is commonly said to represent the enlightenment of the Buddha, with the Buddha absent due to aniconic interdictions. However, the inscription that accompanies this carving says bhagavato Sakamunino bodho, that is, the bodhi (tree) of holy Sakyamuni, and thus parallels the inscription identifying the tree of Buddha Visvabhu.

The composition includes a depiction of a platform with the tree, a building, and worshipers. There is no evidence from surviving literary or archaeological sources that any kind of temple existed at the site when the Buddha meditated under his sacred tree. Indeed, Emperor Asoka (r. cat 272- 231 B.C.) is credited with having built the first important temple at Bodh

Gaya, and therefore the presence of the temple suggests that the depiction shows the site in the Asokan period or later. Furthermore, an examination of the activity in the relief reveals that it is a representation of human devotees, specifically lay devotees, worshiping the sacred spot.

Therefore, though it is certain that the relief portrays the tree under which the Buddha became enlightened at Bodh Gaya, and there is the evidence that the event portrayed is not the enlightenment itself. A comprehensive study of the other inscriptions at Bharhut confirms that many of the compositions commonly identified as Buddha life events with the Buddha lacking are instead depictions of sacred sites, including devotional activities at these sites. The major scholars who have studied the inscriptions during the past century have read the pertinent epigraphs in the manner I describe here.

Nonetheless, those discussing the art have invariably misconstrued the contents of the inscriptions- if they have consulted them at all-to refer to Buddha life events. Thus, their identifications of the activities and subjects shown in the reliefs have conformed to the assumption that the subjects are life scenes with the Buddha absent. Even Heinrich Luders, who so carefully reread and analyzed the inscriptions, entitled one of his chapters "Inscriptions Attached to Scenes of Buddha's Life," in spite of the fact that his own translations of the inscriptions did not support the identification of the scenes as events in the life of the Buddha.

Another example of a so- called aniconic composition that invites a new interpretation is an uninscribed carving from Bharhut traditionally identified as the Buddha's descent from Trayastrimsa heaven at the site of Sankasya. The usual interpretation of this cat first- century B.C. relief is that the ladder by which the Buddha made the descent is shown in the center of the composition, but due to the presumed aniconic proscriptions, the Buddha was not shown. However, the theory that I am proposing- that reliefs like this portray a place but not an event of the Buddha's life- allows another interpretation that perhaps better accounts for the elements depicted in the relief.

The figures appear to move as if in a clockwise procession

around the ladders in the nearly ubiquitous circumambulation ritual used inewitness accounts of Buddhist pilgrims to Sankasya and archaeological evidence at the site indicate that as early as the third century B.C. Sankasya had become a major pilgrimage center and that an actual set of stairs-perhaps the very ones depicted in this relief- were the focal point of worship. Regarding the ladders, the seventh- century Chinese pilgrim Xuanzang (Hsuan- tsang) observed: Some centuries ago, the ladders still existed in their original position, but now they have sunk into the earth and disappeared. The neighbouring princes, grieved at not having seen them, built up of bricks and chased stones ornamented with jewels, on the ancient foundations (three ladders) resembling the old ones.

They are about 70 feet high. Above them they built a vihara in which is a stone image of Buddha, and on either side of this is a ladder with the figures of Brahma and Sakra, just as they appeared when first rising to accompany Buddha in his descent. Thus, at one time the focus of devotion at Sankasya had apparently been a set of stairs erected by the early royalty of India. Therefore, instead of representing the Buddha life event itself, with the main actors missing, the Bharhut carving seems to show a later worship scene at the holy site of Sankasya, where the descent took place.

Another panel from Bharhut, dating from about the first century B.C., shows a subject common in the early Buddhist relief art of India, a depiction of a stupa. Because the Buddha's relics were divided and enshrined in eight stupas shortly after his demise, depictions of stupas in the early art are often said to depict the Buddha's great decease (parinirvana). Yet, as in other reliefs already discussed, the presence of lay worshipers in the composition suggests that the main subject of the carving is the practice of making pilgrimage to the sacred sites where relics of the Buddha were housed.

The pillar crowned with addorsed lions at the left suggests that the stupa site is shown as it appeared after around the third century B.C., when Emperor Asoka erected numerous similar pillars at the sacred sites of Buddhism. Many other reliefs at Bharhut and other sites show a wheel, a tree, a stupa, a pillar, or other type of monument, and I believe these also should be interpreted as depictions of places, not events with the main actors missing. At least by Asoka's time in the third century B.C., numerous places associated with the Buddha had become famous pithas (holy "seats," i.e., holy places), and shrines, pillars, or other monuments had been erected at them.

The almost invariable presence of devotees and worshipers in such compositions suggests that it is not a historical event in the life of the Buddha that is being represented, but rather the activities of darsana-of "seeing" a sacred place, person, or object-and the associated devotional practices. Inasmuch as specific sacred sites were the focus of many of the early reliefs, the significance attached to pilgrimage to these locations forms an important background for understanding early Buddhist art. The Buddha himself, upon his deathbed, instructed his followers to make pilgrimage to the sites of the four main events of his life: his birth, enlightenment, first sermon, and death (parinirvana).

The practice of making such pilgrimages was popularized in the third century B.C. by Emperor Asoka, Buddhism's paradigmatic lay devotee, whose pious journey was immortalized in the Asokovadana. The same text also records Asoka's well- known embellishment of the sacred sites of Buddhism with architectural and artistic creations, some of which may be depicted in the "aniconic" compositions.

The presence of lay worshipers in virtually all of the reliefs in question supports the theory that they record a practice of lay devotion. A number of reliefs specifically show devotees performing the Buddhist rite of circumambulation, which may be ascertained by the depiction of the figures as if turning in space as they walk around a sacred object of devotion.

The reinterpretation of the reliefs as depictions of places rather than events bears directly upon the issue of whether the various objects that appear in the reliefs, like wheels, sacred trees, stupas, or pillars, are "symbolic" representations of the Buddha. If we consider that these reliefs may represent sacred places, then it would follow that the artists would depict the focal point of worship at each of them. In representations of the site of Bodh Gaya, the temple and/or the tree might be shown; in representations of Sarnath, a wheel or temple with an enclosed wheel could be depicted.

The place where the Buddha's death took place, or the sites where his relics were enshrined, might be shown by a rendering of a stupa. Similarly, depictions of other sites might be portrayed by illustrations of their identifying or most characteristic features. That objects installed at Buddhist sacred sites can be worthy of devotion in their own right and not merely substitute for a forbidden anthropomorphic rendering of a Buddha is attested by a phenomenon seen in Sri Lankan Buddhism. The phenomenon is likely to have had an Indian source, perhaps in the early Buddhism of the period of concern to the aniconic question (ca. second century B.C. through the first century A.D.).

Based on the belief that the Buddha visited their island three times, Sri Lankan Buddhist reveres the places he visited or rested, and sites housing some of his relics. These, along with several other sacred sites, have been codified into a cult of the Sixteen Great Places, which are the focus of Sri Lankan pilgrimage and constitute a central theme in the art and literature of the country. Most Buddhist temples in Sri Lanka bear painted or sculpted depictions of the sixteen sites, and the motif appears commonly on other types of objects, such as Buddhist books covers. At first glance, such depictions could be interpreted as symbolic representations of the Buddha, for they show sacred trees, stupas, or footprints.

However, in Sri Lanka there is no doubt that these are portraits of sacred places. The importance of a cult of pilgrimage to the sacred sites of Buddhism is also verified from Buddhist texts that describe the three types of relics (cetiya) that the Buddha is said to have left after his death:

1. Sariraka (pieces of the body),
2. Paribhogaka (things he used), and
3. Uddesaka (reminders, i.e., representations, or images).

The meaning of sariraka is eminently clear-here, Buddhists refer not only to the cremated ashes of the Buddha, but also to any other bodily relic, such as a hair, a tooth, a fragment of bone, or nails. Small caskets containing such sacred relics became an important focal point of Buddhist worship, and monuments and shrines said to contain such relics are found throughout the Buddhist world. The second category of relic, paribhogaka, includes objects like his robe, begging bowl, turban, and any chair or seat upon which he sat, among others.

The most important of the paribhogaka objects is the bodhi tree at Bodh Gaya. But any place the Buddha visited, rested, or traversed would also be considered paribhogaka. The third of the three types of relics are the uddesaka, specifically, images (pratima) of the Buddha. The aniconic theory encodes the expectation that the image of the Buddha must be of primary importance and that other depictions, such as a bodhi tree, were secondary substitutes for a figurative form. However, in the Buddhist context it is primarily the sariraka and paribhogaka that have provided the main impetus for pilgrimage and reverence at Buddhist sites. In the Mahavamsa, the Buddha is cited as having pronounced: "In remembrance that I have used these, do homage to them."

Further in the "Mahaparinibbanasuttanta," the Buddha explains that such places should be seen and admired, and that whoever dies with a contented mind while on a pilgrimage will be reborn in heaven. In a Sri Lankan monastery, the most important element is the relic, which is enshrined in the mahastupa, the focal point of the monastic plan. Second in importance is the bodhi tree (mahabodhi), and indeed every monastery in Sri Lanka has at least one major bodhi tree. Third in importance is the image house (pratimaghara). Therefore, the image and image hall are far less important than the stupa and the bodhi tree at Sri Lankan monasteries.

While the Sri Lankan evidence does not prove the existence in India of such a ranking, I believe that the importance of sariraka and paribhogaka relics has been greatly underestimated by Western scholars, who have given the idea of the image a primacy that it did not have in the early Buddhist context. I propose that the sacred trees, stupas, and other features that mark special places associated with the

Buddha had inestimable importance in their own right and that the cult of image worship was secondary.

This concept is expressed in the Commentary on the Vibhanga, wherein it states that one obtains Buddhalambanapti (joy or ecstasy derived by looking at or thinking about the Buddha) by looking at a stupa housing a relic of the Buddha or a bodhi tree, but no mention is made of the merit gained by looking at an image of the Buddha.

To view sacred trees, stupas, and other such forms as substitutes or symbols for something else is to misunderstand their intrinsic importance in the Buddhist scheme. Essentially, I suggest that the early Buddhist art of India was not primarily concerned with the biography of gakyamuni Buddha, as has been assumed for so many decades. Instead, an important emphasis was placed on the practice of lay devotion at the sacred sites of Buddhism.

That merit is derived from viewing the sacred traces of the Buddha is clear from the literary sources and, I believe, the surviving artistic remains. That such sanctified places (specifically "seats," or "pithas") are believed to contain great power is also well known throughout the Buddhist world. The many early Buddhist relief sculptures surviving today were not isolated images, but were part of the adornment of major architectural structures. Rather than serving as the focus of these monuments the reliefs played a subsidiary role in the overall schemes. For the most part, the carved reliefs were located on railings and gateways, or, in some cases, as part of the facing of the exterior of stupas.

In their secondary but essential role, the images helped to communicate and reinforce the central meaning of the monuments they adorned. Considering the function of these monuments as repositories or adornments for important Buddhist relics, it is not surprising that depictions of worshipers visiting similar places constitute one of their major artistic themes. Further, since devotion to the relics of the Buddha was an activity specifically associated with the laity rather than with the clergy, the inclusion of lay worshipers as a prominent motif in the carvings is fitting indeed.

If the reinterpretation offered here is valid, one must ask how these artistic remains have been so misunderstood by so many for so long. How did the aniconic idea originate and what arguments were put forth to validate the idea of the avoidance of Buddha images? How did the theory continue to be reinforced and why was it never doubted? The history of the theory provides some of the answers. Although nineteenth- century writers had observed the absence of Buddhas in the early art of India, Foucher was the first scholar to propound the theory of what has come to be known as aniconism in early Buddhist art.

Writing in the early twentieth century, Foucher stated: "When we find the ancient stone- carvers of India in full activity, we observe that they are very industriously engaged in carrying out the strange undertaking of representing the life of Buddha without Buddha." Foucher further asserted: "Such is the abnormal, but indisputable fact of which every history of Buddhist art will have at the outset to render account." Characterizing this phenomenon as a "monstrous abstention," he read into the reliefs what a modern European scholar unacquainted with the practices of early Buddhism might have expected to be there.

His premise that the lack of a Buddha image reflected an abnormality became the foundation stone for the view that the art created by these early Buddhists was a substitute for something else that had been deliberately avoided. Ultimately, Foucher's measuring rod of expectations led him and his followers to overlook the intrinsic message of the art. The problem-the misunderstanding of the thematic content of the art-is inextricably related to and has been perpetuated by the terminology that has been used to describe this artistic phenomenon.

Using a term aniconism that defined a phenomenon according to what it is not, scholars have been overly concerned with what they believe should be in the art rather than with what is actually there. Believing that the scenes shown on the monuments were meant to illustrate episodes in the life of the Buddha, Foucher of course found the absence of the Buddha figure perplexing. Inferring that the objects in the reliefs such as trees, stupas, and thrones were intended as symbols for something that was not shown, namely, an anthropomorphic representation of the Buddha, Foucher and his followers were led astray from the intrinsic meaning of the art.

While virtually all other authors espousing the aniconic theory have assumed that there were religious interdictions against the creation of the Buddha image, Foucher himself expressly stated that he knew of no textual proscriptions against such a practice. Foucher toyed with a number of suggestions to explain the aniconic phenomenon and finally concluded that the explanation is "in appearance simpleminded enough, but one which, in India, is still sufficient for all: 'If they did not do it, it was because it was not the custom to do it.'"

The insubstantiality of his explanation makes it difficult to comprehend how the theory he propounded ever took root and has been embraced so tenaciously by generations of scholars. Indeed, the development and passionate advocacy of the aniconic theory constitutes an intriguing chapter in intellectual history and involves an array of political, social, and cultural factors.

For instance, it is doubtful that the theory of aniconism would have achieved its sanctified place in art- historical writings if the related issue of where the first Buddha image was made had not been so hotly debated. Foucher and his Western followers believed that the Buddha image was first created in the GrecoRoman- influenced region of Gandhara, thus claiming an essentially Western origin for the idea of the image.

Ananda Coomaraswamy and his Indian nationalist sympathizers, perhaps attempting to cast off the yoke of Western imperialism, asserted a strictly Indian origin at Mathura. In retrospect, the arguments can be viewed in light of twentieth- century political issues that polarized European and Indian scholars. Yet so intent was each cultural camp on claiming the primacy of its contribution to Buddhist art, that other, potentially more important issues were overlooked. Indeed, throughout the debate, what I believe to be a more fundamental question was never posed: Was there really an aniconic period?

Because the idea of an aniconic period was never doubted, the preconceptions associated with the theory of aniconism have saturated art- historical thinking for nearly a century. The idea of aniconism has been so thoroughly embedded in scholarly thought that it has led scholars to misread inscriptions, dismiss literary documentation attesting to an early image tradition, and express skepticism about scientific archaeological data confirming the early existence of Buddha images. Perhaps the most serious and far- reaching consequence has been in the area of interpretation, in which scholars have misunderstood the subject matter of the images and misread the overall message of the monuments the sculpted images adorned.

Assuming that the points I make in my full- length study are valid, the conclusions will require a reexamination and probably a revision of virtually all of these areas of study. I have suggested that the subjects in a specific type of composition are not substitutes or symbols for something else, but are important emblems of Buddhist devotion in their own right. While these early reliefs do not contain Buddha figures, this absence is not to be explained by an aniconic proscription or by the belief that these common motifs reflect a substitution for a figure of a Buddha.

Expressing concepts central to the practice of Buddhism during this period, particularly relating to the exaltation of lay worship, such carvings are completely compatible with the recently proven existence of Buddha images even from early periods of Indian history. The emphasis on sacred pithas and pilgrimage to them in Buddhism has never waned, although the "aniconic" period was brought to a close many centuries ago. A record left by the thirteenth- century monk Dharmasvamin of his visit to Bodh Gaya is especially interesting in light of the problem of aniconism. Like earlier pilgrims to the sacred site, Dharmasvamin did not find the living Buddha at Bodh Gaya.

Instead, what he described is not unlike what we see in some of the so- called aniconic reliefs, for he said that "inside the courtyard stood the empty throne of Sakyamuni . . . which was worshipped, and an eternal offering lamp was kept in front of it." Today, the sacred spot is also vacant, as it has been for two and a half millennia. We, like the countless pilgrims who have visited Bodha Gaya since the time the great sage sat there in deepest meditation, cannot expect to see him there in the flesh.

Yet we should not be disappointed at the sight of an empty seat, for the power of the sacred Pitha still resonates and can be felt by anyone who stands in the presence of the spot where the Buddha- to- sat and was sheltered by the sacred tree on the day of his awakening. Introduction doubts have often been expressed about the relationship between Buddhism and human rights. It is true that Buddhist scriptures do not allude directly in either content or form to the modern idea of protecting human rights.

The same could be said however for the Christian Bible and other texts. Why then are Christianity and Buddhism judged differently in terms of their contribution to human rights theory? The answer lies in their respective development of a sense of purpose in terms of grappling with the various problems of modern society while remaining grounded in sacred texts written in ancient times, and how much effort has been made to interpret those texts.

INTERPRETING BUDDHIST SCRIPTURES

As stated at the beginning, previous failure to identify ideas shared by Buddhism and human rights theory may be attributed to a lack of awareness of how to interpret Buddhist scriptures. Let us therefore contemplate a method of interpreting these scriptures, from three different perspectives. First, we need to recognize the breadth of Buddhist concepts. Christianity has altered over the centuries from its inception to the present day, and now take many forms, for example the Catholic, Protestant and the Eastern Orthodox churches.

Buddhism has undergone changes in the same way, and is now broadly speaking divided into two streams: Theravada Buddhism in the south, and Mahayana Buddhism in the north of Asia. Among Western scholars however there is a tendency to concentrate on the historical origins of Buddhism and solely on Theravada, in what therefore becomes a limited understanding of Buddhist ideology. In extreme cases this has even meant actively downplaying the significance of Mahayana Buddhism, based on a theory that Mahayana Buddhism was not even the teaching of Shakyamuni, the historical Buddha.

However like Christianity, we need to view Buddhism more broadly not simply in terms of its origins, but including its historical development and current position. It is important to consider the words of professor emeritus Masato Nagao on this issue. According to Professor Nagao, the writings of Buddhism have three meanings. One, the teachings preached by the Buddha (Shakyamuni); two, teachings related to Buddha (laws and truths), and three, teachings designed to enable people living now to achieve Buddha status. Here I would like to pay particular attention to the third variety of teaching.

In Buddhology, the scriptures written in Balinese are believed to express most directly the words of Shakyamuni, and Theravada Buddhism to be based on these scriptures. However, if we take a broader view of the concepts of Buddhism and include teachings for the purpose of attaining Buddhahood, the scriptures of Mahayana Buddhism are also of obvious importance. Buddhism has developed historically as a teaching to enable people to achieve Buddhahood. A "living Buddhism" perspective is therefore also essential. Christianity has theology, which is more than Biblical interpretation and commentary.

Christian theology has always endeavored to address the various issues faced by Christians and Christian societies. Particularly in the West Christianity has historically been "living Christianity" developing with the times. Buddhism too should not be restricted by the preference for tranquility observed in its past history- it is only natural that Buddhist ideology continues to develop amid the turbulence of modern society.

Secondly, there is the problem of how to interpret the Buddhist scriptures. Attempting to describe Buddhism by extracting single phrases holds little meaning. Obviously scriptures written in ancient times will not have direct links to modern ideas of human rights. Even if one were to find a phrase of the scriptures linked to a specific human right found in modern constitutions, e.g. freedom of speech, such a link would be superficial, and logically not really supportable. More important is to find out what these scriptures are attempting to convey through their words and expressions, in other words, identifying in them principles and ideas.

Finding principles and ideas in texts in this way is the act of interpretation. And this interpreting of Buddhist scriptures must be concerned with more than syntax and logic: it must also take into account the historical background of the time. Even more important however is to realize that interpreting scriptures is not a oneway process in which we receive messages from the past. For the very reason that Buddhism is alive here and now, anyone endeavoring to interpret its writings needs to be aware of issues facing the world today as they look for answers in the past.

In other words this interpreting needs to be a two- way process. Previous discourse on the relationship between Buddhism and human rights has been defective because researchers focused on individual phrases in their interpretation of Buddhist scriptures, to the detriment of seeking out principles and ideas, and because their awareness of social issues was insufficient. This was not a problem with the scriptures themselves, but meant a need to question the method used to interpret them. Moreover an awareness of social issues means more than being deeply conscious of problems in society. It is a matter of whether one can feel "pain" when approaching such problems.

This pain felt for others could be described as sensitivity to human rights. This sensitivity to human rights demands that pain be alleviated, in other words the construction of a theory of human rights for the purpose of salvation. Awareness of social issues requires this sensitivity to human rights plus a legal logical structure for the practical protection of human rights. Thirdly, we must search for Buddhist ideas that fit with discourse on human dignity in law. Of course Buddhism does not discuss human dignity as such, but there are individual concepts within it that equate to that of human dignity, because Buddhism presents us with an image of the way human beings should live, and this image can be linked to legal discourse on human dignity.

By Buddhist ideas, my focus here is particularly on Mahayana Buddhism, the reason being that as the name Mahayana implies, it has developed as a Buddhist movement with an emphasis on *bosatsu- gyo* (bodhisattva practice) among ordinary people. As a movement of the people Mahayana Buddhism offers a guide for life that is intimately linked to everyday life. It is difficult to derive any concrete discussion of what defines a human being, of human dignity, from a Buddhism in which the primary emphasis is on holy places and rituals removed from everyday living. Discourse on human existence in Mahayana Buddhism has both epistemological and prescriptive aspects, which are not clearly distinguished.

Plus it encompasses many ideas, not arranged in any particular order or formed into any kind of system. My discussion here is purely one of the significance of these ideas in terms of legal discourse on the issue of human dignity. Of course, this assumes one is interpreting scriptures by reading them from a fixed perspective. From here I shall continue my examination of Buddhist ideology by focusing on the concepts of Buddha- nature, dependent origination and *Karma*.

7

Human Dignity in Mahayana Buddhism

THE DOCTRINE OF BUDDHA- NATURE

The doctrine of Buddha- nature or inherent Buddhahood is unique to Mahayana Buddhism. The Nirvana Sutra states that "all sentient creatures possess Buddha- nature." From the doctrine of Buddha- nature we can derive much related to the concept of human dignity. First it is important to make people aware that they themselves possess Buddhanature (the dignity of human beings). As society demands greater economic efficiency, as we are controlled in so many ways, transformed into "things" and relegated to a state of passivity, the doctrine of Buddha- nature can give us pride as human beings. This does not mean simply recognizing the Buddha- nature in ourselves.

The "all" of "all sentient creatures" also means having consideration for the Buddha- nature of all people. In Japanese we use the word *jinken* (human rights) and occasionally *kenri* (right) for human rights, however the character (*ri*- benefit or gain) used here is not really suitable for use in a translation of "right." In the early Meiji years the characters are said to have been used for kenri and this is the *dori*- reason, justice. Human rights should therefore not be a tool for personal gain, but based on a sense of reason and justice that respects human dignity, both that of the self and of others.

Furthermore, because the doctrine of Buddha- nature maintains that all people possess an inherent Buddhahood, it may be described as a doctrine of true equality. It is well known that the historical Buddha or Shakyamuni criticized the social discrimination and caste system of his age. The scriptures state that "People are not born base. Nor are they born Brahmins. By their actions they become base, and by their actions they become Brahmins." (Suttanipata) In this sense the doctrine of Buddha- nature has much in common with the natural rights concept of people being born free and equal. However it pays to remember that while Buddha- nature is a doctrine of equality, it is not a mechanical (formal) doctrine of equality. Buddhanature is said to consist of wisdom and mercy, however this wisdom is wisdom used to enable us to live better lives, in other words, that which works to enable us to maximize our innate potential.

That is, the doctrine of Buddha- nature shows that (all) individuals have equal potential for self- realization, however the way in which this self- realization is manifested will not necessarily be identical. A mechanical doctrine of equality furthermore would in fact lack the perspective of salvation for people actually living in disadvantaged circumstances. The question of a precise definition of equality is one of the main topics in human rights today, however while everyone may approve of outlawing irrational discrimination, there are no clear ideological guidelines for more active ways of making equality reality.

If however we interpret equality as the potential for self-realization as found in the doctrine of Buddha- nature, we may deduce from this a consideration for others from a sympathetic point of view, for example for a socially disadvantaged person who has used their wisdom to overcome their circumstances. Up to now I have said that Buddha- nature is wisdom, however whatever its precise meaning may be it is certainly not a particularly idealized version of a specific state of being or reality. The Buddha- nature doctrine of Mahayana Buddhism does not equal a fixed ideal state.

The doctrine of Buddha- nature is composed of "Buddha" and "nature," and does not mean departing from human form to become a Buddha, but demonstrating the nature and abilities of a Buddha while remaining a human being. It was T'ien- t'ai the "Great Teacher" of China who formulated a very clear theory on this point in his doctrine of Ten Worlds. T'ien-t'ai constructed a doctrine of 10 worlds or realms of human life ranging from hell to Buddhahood, and using the Lotus Sutra to prove his theory of "mutual possession of the Ten Worlds," described the relationship between Buddhahood and the other nine worlds as "the nine worlds are Buddhahood" and "earthly desires are enlightenment," by which he meant that a person can attain Buddhahood while still a human being.

"Earthly desires are enlightenment" refers to working toward self- realization while carrying on an everyday existence. In other words, the fundamental position of Mahayana Buddhism is not one of fleeing from pain and conflict to arrive at some pure destination, nor of ignoring the physical and spiritual desires we possess as human beings. Compared to Christian ideology therefore there are some obvious differences. The God of Christianity transcends human beings. Human dignity is said to have its basis in the fact that human beings "are created in the image of God."

In addition Kant, also a major influence on human rights doctrine in the West, maintained that people capable of rational self- determination have dignity. In any case, both share an emphasis on rationality and spirituality in their definition of human dignity, and assume transcendence from the practical state of everyday living. In contrast, in the doctrine of Ten Worlds, Buddhahood does not transcend the other nine worlds, but is manifested alongside the physical desires and social attachments of the worlds of hell, hungry spirits, Animals and asuras.

In other words, the doctrine of Buddha- nature as seen in that of the Ten Worlds is not slanted exclusively toward lofty spirituality, but amid the conflicts of body and mind and of society, seeks not to destroy these things, but to use our wisdom to make the most of them. I have on a previous occasion dubbed this feature of the doctrine of Buddha- nature "concrete corporeality," however I believe it deserves closer examination here. The reason is that in "concrete corporeality" we may deduce a way of thinking intimately connected with the roots of democracy, not only the concerns of individuals.

In Christianity it could be said that a vertical relationship exists between God and human beings, in that an absolute entity transcending humanity, known as God, saves people from conflict and woe. If we replace this God with temporal law, then law becomes the absolute entity. For example, it is frequently said that "equality in the eyes of God" has developed into "equality in the eyes of the law." However the doctrine of Buddha- nature maintains that each of us has an inherent Buddhahood, leading easily to the logical conclusion that we may seek counsel with others to attain a result. Mahayana Buddhism attaches importance to the horizontal relationships between people, and in this we may find an affinity with democracy, i.e. "control by the people."

Dependent Origination

Buddhism preaches a doctrine of dependent origination as represented by the twelve linked chain of dependent origination or causation. The doctrine of the twelve- linked chain of dependent origination shows a logical progression from the ignorance of the individual to their enlightenment, however the doctrine of dependent origination preached in Mahayana Buddhism today has a broader logic structure than this. For example, the Miscellaneous Agama Sutra states most directly, "When there is this, that is. With the arising of this, that arises. When this is not, neither is that. With the cessation of this, that ceases." The problem however is how to interpret this.

Here we may find a mode of thought that does not perceive various beings including human beings as separate or fixed, but which understands things always in terms of their relation to others. To look at this understanding of relationships another way, it means that relationships with others are always open. We can imagine two different viewpoints arising from this doctrine of dependent origination. In one, we see this connection as meaning not viewing things as fixed, but constantly changing. The other viewpoint emphasizes this connection as coexistence with others, a symbiotic relationship.

The first viewpoint echoes that of Nagarjuna of India, who described dependent origination as "non substantiality." If we believe things to always be changing, we may draw conclusions such as the following: human beings sometimes believe the situations in which they find themselves to be absolute, become attached to them, and are vulnerable to disappointment. However the doctrine of dependent origination teaches us that by viewing situations as temporary, as a phase in a continual process of change, we may perceive the first step in escape from these situations. Potential for change is by no means confined to the realm of the individual.

According to the doctrine of dependent origination, social systems are not rigid either. Changes to social systems tend to be viewed as undesirable by those in possession of political power at the time (i.e. those with a vested interest in the status quo). For examples we need only think of the caste system of India, or the Edo Period Japan structure of warrior, farmer, artisan and merchant classes. Advocate the doctrine of dependent origination in such situations, and naturally it becomes a criticism of the status quo. However whether it be an individual or an entire social system, this concept of change is not a passive one in which people simply accepts change as it occurs.

The doctrine of dependent origination in Mahayana Buddhism includes not only the knowledge of change, but maintains that change should occur to achieve an ideal. On an individual level this means enlightenment and the manifestation of Buddhahood, and in social systems too demands reforms to make these developments possible. To recap what I have discussed so far: understanding our lives as one phase in a process of continual change means at the individual level always having hope and not falling into the trap of disappointment and attachment to the status quo, and behaving in a benevolent manner toward others regardless of our present relationship with them (social status, gender etc.).

If this is what constitutes an open person, then on the social level this person will demand an open society always accepting of all kinds of people, and with the potential for change. Next let us turn to the second viewpoint we may derive from the doctrine of dependent origination- that of symbiosis. From this viewpoint, the connection described earlier may be seen as the relationship of mutual dependency between human beings. This means overcoming egotism or self- interest. In the modern world, urbanization has weakened ties among family members and within local communities, and rather than caring for others, there is a growing tendency to use them for our own ends.

This type of behavior could be described as a closed relationship with other people. So how does the doctrine of dependent origination address this situation? The catch- cry of the French Revolution, which was grounded in the concept of natural rights, was "Liberty, fraternity, equality." This fraternity referred to solidarity with others, however as we have already seen, today this spirit of fraternity is disappearing. In reaction to this we may identify two streams of modern legal thought: that of the "libertarians" who value greater freedom for the individual, and of the "communitarians" who desire greater communality.

Buddhism is generally believed to place more emphasis on communality, and this has been described a feature of Buddhism contrasting with the individualism of the West. What we need to be careful of here however is over- simplifying this dichotomy of the individual- community: because if more emphasis is placed on the community or communality this categorization could serve to equate Buddhism with complete annihilation of the individual, and quite frankly to stress the opposing natures of Buddhist communality and Western individualism so much that Buddhist communality becomes annihilation of the individual would be a serious mistake.

In the doctrine of dependent origination found in Mahayana Buddhism, by understanding people in terms of their interdependence, we first of all open up human relationships that had been closed by selfinterest, and begin to have consideration for others. This does not mean however a fusion of the self and others in a relationship in which the self is annihilated. If we add the Buddha- nature to this equation, what is does mean is being aware of the Buddha- nature within ourselves, and respecting the Buddha- nature in others, and that this is part of the relationship of interdependence between us all?

In a communality that involves annihilation of the self, a doctrine of dependent origination showing the connection between the self and others could not exist. Let us explain this in terms of the *bosatsu- gyo* (bodhisattva practice) of Mahayana Buddhism. *Bosatsu- gyo* has been described as putting mercy into practice, feeling the pain of others, and extending to them the hand of salvation. This must be an action taken toward another person in accordance with our autonomous will and practice, and our wishes as individuals. Furthermore it is not a one- way action performed on another person: by taking that action toward the person it simultaneously becomes a "two- way street" in which we reveal our own Buddhanature.

In conclusion, the symbiotic viewpoint that may be derived from the doctrine of dependent origination is the overcoming of our closed- off egotism, and does not mean annihilation of the individual. It is an attempt to create communality from the autonomy of individuals. So far incidentally I have discussed the doctrine of dependent origination, as it relates both to individuals and to society, in terms of the connections between people. However, the doctrine of dependent origination may also be thought to include the relationship between human beings and the natural world.

In Buddhist tradition this may be seen in Japan in the idea of "trees, plants, the land, all can attain Buddhahood"- the perception that Buddha- nature may be found not only in human beings but also in the vegetation around us. In view of this, we need to consider the Buddhahood not only of humans but also of nature. Moreover Mio- lo of China preached the oneness of life and its environment, demonstrating a mutually dependent relationship between human beings and the environment with human beings as the focus. Our own experience tells us that people create environments and alter them, and are also influenced by their environment. The richness of nature enriches human beings spiritually; however destruction of the environment does more than inflict damage on that spirituality: in the worst scenario it may place us in real physical jeopardy.

To understand the danger of this, we can do no better than to recall the book *Silent*. It is too late to realize the importance of nature when its destruction is already a physical threat to human beings. Such destruction is the ultimate manifestation of many years of abuse, and treating only its symptoms is by this stage no longer adequate. It is instead an issue we need to think about every day, at the very basic level of what form the relationship between human beings and the natural world should take.

The view that "trees, plants, the land, all can attain Buddhahood" lies at the very heart of this idea, and is the departure point from which it develops. The need to establish rights for the environment so frequently stressed these days is also an issue that ought to be considered not in terms of policy responses to problems such as environmental destruction and pollution, but in terms of one origin of the concept of human dignity. *Karma* So far I have discussed the doctrine of dependent origination mainly as it relates to the connections between people and between people and nature, i.e. spatial relationships and the horizontal aspect of dependent origination.

The doctrine of dependent origination however also has a vertical dimension of temporal connection, known as the doctrine of *Karma*. *Karma* or *go* in Japanese literally means "action." In Buddhism there are three types of action- physical, verbal and mental, that is to say a temporal connection between actions in a broad sense. Physical action is that which involves the body, verbal our use of words as means of expression, and mental what lies in our hearts, and collectively these may be thought to represent action in the wider sense of the word. What then is the temporal relationship between these three types of action? Most simply, it may be expressed in the oft- heard saying, "As ye sow, so shall ye reap."

In other words, perform good deeds and you will reap good results, while the reverse also applies. Just as the connectivity and possibility of change of the horizontal doctrine of dependent origination are not confined to a simple awareness but are prescriptive in nature, so the doctrine of *Karma*, having as it does the "As ye sow, so shall ye reap" causative relationship, is prescriptive in terms of telling us we should have the correct causes, take the correct action. If this is the meaning of the doctrine of *Karma*, then in it we may identify a number of different viewpoints. One is that because results are influenced by the actions of individuals, the self-determination of the individual is important. And, if we respect the right to self- determination of the individual, we may also say that they have responsibility for themselves.

Determination and responsibility are two sides of the same coin. Earlier I stated that Buddhism did not mean the annihilation of individuality, and the doctrine of *Karma*, while preaching the causality of our actions, indeed precisely because it does so, also asks penetrating questions about the self-determination and responsibility of individuals. A second viewpoint is that this prescriptiveness possesses a broader morality than the legal prescriptions of the state. In an ordinary society, unless one violates a law of the nation, malicious or discriminatory statements, or actions taken purely out of self-interest may well be permitted. However, the doctrine of *Karma* is stricter than this, as may be observed in the concept of "mental action," i.e. if a person is bad within themselves, they will be called to account for the results.

It must be said however that this strict morality is not morality in the sense of a penalty imposed objectively by the state, but always a morality in which the individual themselves makes a subjective judgement. The third viewpoint, in connection with this, lies in the separation of the doctrine of *Karma* from that of environmental determinism. In the doctrine of *Karma*, respect for self- determination viewed from another angle means that the environment can be altered by the actions of the self.

This does not mean that we are totally free of the influence of the environment, but that we can take autonomous action in various environmental conditions to change our environment. I would like to contemplate this point further, while touching on the past misuse of the doctrine of *Karma* in Japanese Buddhism. Japanese Buddhism frequently preaches a doctrine of *Karma* known as *shukugo* in which the pain of this world is deemed to be the result of misdeeds in the past. In this doctrine the past determines the present, and it is a doctrine of environmental determinism for the individual living now.

This is not an issue of fundamental Buddhist ideology, but was merely an attempt by those in political power at the time to shift the responsibility for social problems onto the victims of discrimination, in which the priesthood colluded with the authorities to justify this discrimination in the name of Buddhism. The substance of the Buddhist doctrine of *Karma* lies in the positive idea that a person living now can overcome their past and not be bound by it, to look to the future and lead a creative life. In the earlier discussion on dependent origination the focus was on overcoming a rigid set of circumstances and being closed to others.

This being the case, naturally the doctrine of *Karma* should also refute the idea of being bound by the past found in the doctrine of *shukugo*. Fourthly, the doctrine of *Karma* is said to include the *Karma* of individuals (*fugugo*) and of society (*gugo* or "common *Karma*"), which transcends the individual. In this case the theory of common or collective *Karma* means that if a large number of people behave badly, this bad behavior will combine to form a bad social consciousness. This social consciousness will eventually be transformed into a social system.

This way of thinking also contends that social consciousness and social systems will be passed down through the generations and in turn provide norms for the consciousness and behavior of individuals. According to the Buddhist scriptures preaching the doctrine of common *Karma*, the caste system of India was formed when the avarice, envy and pride of the people created discrimination within society, which then became a social system. The doctrine of common *Karma* contends that there are social problems that cannot be attributed to the *Karma* of individuals.

In saying this however, what the doctrine of common *Karma* really means is that even though we may refer to something known as "the social system," ultimately this system is created by the *Karma* of people, and precisely because of this, in accordance with the right to self- determination and responsibility of each individual we should face the future and take the proper actions to bring about a revolution in social consciousness and social systems. The Buddhist scriptures do not refer directly to specific modern human rights; however in them we may identify a concept that forms the foundation of human rights.

To borrow the terminology of modern human rights we may call this the concept of human dignity. In order however to discover this type of concept and see it begin to take form in the scriptures, we must engage in the act of interpretation. To do so it is important to understand Buddhism as "living Buddhism," and to reinterpret the Buddhist sutras in light of our awareness of problems in modern society. This ideological task requires the practical study of various Buddhist doctrines carried out to date by religious groups, and in addition to Buddhology, which involves philological and corroborative research on Buddhism, a new Buddhist theology.

In one of its rulings, the US Supreme Court, quoting a section from the report of the Second Vatican Council, commented that "People are looking to religion for answers to the riddles posed by human existence. In other words, religion is what we look to answer the questions of what is a human being, and what is the meaning and purpose of our lives." It would be correct to view the purpose of the Supreme Court in quoting this extract as an expectation of answers from various religions to the question of the meaning of human existence, which lies at the root of human rights. This chapter is one answer from Mahayana Buddhism.

THE VERBAL COMMUNICATION IN EARLY BUDDHISM

Buddhism is one of the great religions of the world that has had a profound impact on humankind. It has influenced religious, philosophical, moral, ethical, philosophical, cultural, and ethical thinking in very significant ways. For a religion to have that kind of impact, it must possess very interesting approaches to the issue of human communication. The Buddha was a communicator par excellence; he was a supremely influential teacher, and that influence is largely attributable to his success as a communicator. The Buddha preached to the people in a language that was readily understandable. He paid great care and attention to the psychological background and disposition of his potential audiences. He structured his messages in a way that would appeal to the lay persons readily.

From a communications viewpoint, the rhetorical strategies adopted by the Buddha in his teachings are multi-faceted and most fascinating, and merit close study. The way he used parables, allegories, tropes, wit, humour, innovative narrative strategies, and parallelisms deserve a separate study. Just to cite a few examples, let us first consider his use of parables. Once a woman who was deeply distraught by the death of her son came to the Buddha and implored him to restore his son to life. Realizing that she could be taught the truth of existence, the Buddha asked her to go back to the city, make the rounds of the total city, and to locate a house in which no one had ever died, and fetch tiny grains of mustard from that house.

The mother, with great expectations, went from house to house, but could not locate a house in which someone had not died. Before long, she realized the lesson that the Buddha intended to teach her. Saying that death occurs to everyone, she buried him. Buddhist literature is replete with such illustrative parables that vividly convey religious messages. Another distinguishing features of the Buddha as a communicator as his efficacious use of diverse rhetorical strategies. For example, in the following passage taken from the discourse on the snake (*uraga sutta*), the careful use of a trope for communicative purposes is powerfully exemplified.

He who gives up anger which has arisen, as the snake poison diffused in the body is removed by antidotes, that monk gives up the cycle of existence as the snake sheds its old, decayed skin. He who has completely destroyed lust as one cuts off a lotus flower in a lake, that monk gives up the cycle of existence as the snake sheds its old, decayed skin. He who has completely destroyed craving like drying up a once swiftly- flowing river, that monk gives up the cycle of existence as the snake sheds its old, decayed skin. He who has completely destroyed pride like a weak bridge of reeds swept away by a mighty flood, that monk gives up the cycle of existence as the snake sheds its old, decayed skin.

He who does not see any substantiality in forms of becoming as one does not find flowers on a fig tree, that monk gives up the cycle of existence as the snake sheds its old, decayed skin. He who has no ill- temper within him and who has overcome all forms of becoming, that monk gives up the cycle of existence as the snake sheds its old, decayed skin. What is interesting to observe about these statements is the functional way in which a dominant trope organizes and orchestrates the flow of thought. The trope of the snake shedding its old, decayed skin provides a useful epistemological vantage point while extending the moral discursive boundaries.

The way epistemology and troping combine these statements is fascinating. As a supremely persuasive communicator, the Buddha often deployed various narrative strategies to convey his intended message. In the following example, what we see is the vivid use of dramatic parallelism for communicative purposes. This is a dialogue that takes place between the Buddha and Dhaniya, the herdsman. The dialogue deals with the clash between worldly security and spiritual emancipation. Dhaniya was a herdsman who lived at the time when the Buddha was staying at Savatthi. It was the monsoon season, just before the onset of rain.

He had built strong shelters for himself, his family, and the cattle on the bank of the river Mahi. The Buddha, however, realized that this family was in danger of being overwhelmed by the flood and appeared in the cattle- keeper's shelter just when he was rejoicing in his comfort and security.

Dhaniya: I have cooked my rice and milked the cows. I dwell with my people near the bank of the Mahi. My house is thatched, the fire is kindled. Therefore, rain, or cloud, if you like!

The Buddha: I am free from anger, from passion; I abide for the night near the bank of the river Mahi. My house (body) is uncovered; the fire of passion is extinguished. Therefore, rain, or cloud, if you like!

Dhaniya: Gadflies and mosquitoes are not fund. My meadows are abounding with grass on the marshy land. The cattle can endure the rain when it comes. Therefore, rain, or cloud, if you like!

The Buddha: By me is made a well- constructed raft (path). I have passed over the floods to Nibbana. There is no further use of the raft. Therefore, rain, or cloud if you like!

Dhaniya: Gopi, my wife, is not wanton and is obedient to me. For a long time she has lived with me pleasantly. Of her, I do not hear any evil whatever.

The Buddha: My mind is obedient and free from passion. For a long time it has been trained and well subdued. So evil is not to be found in me. What we find in this interesting exchange that centers on material security and spiritual emancipation, illusion and reality is the vivid deployment of the rhetorical strategies of dramatic parallelisms and verbal puns.

It is primarily through these communication devices that the intended effects are secured. Buddhist literature is replete with examples of this nature that display the mastery of communication strategies characteristic of the Buddha. This is indeed a topic that merits close and sustained study, and I shall leave it for a later occasion. In this chapter, my objective is to discuss the idea of verbal communication as inscribed in early Buddhism. This objective, to be sure, is closely related to the issue of rhetorical and communicational strategies that I have been discussing so far.

THE BUDDHIST ATTITUDE TO LANGUAGE

The attitude to language reflected in early Buddhism is inseparably linked to the central tenets of Buddhism, namely, the ideas of insubstantiality, impermanence, and causality. Indeed, it is these concepts that lend depth and definition to the Buddhist attitude to language and verbal communication. In order to understand the distinctiveness of the Buddhist approach to language and verbal communication, we need to place it alongside some of the dominant views that were current at the time in India. One such view was that language was sacred, that it was a divine creation, and that it was an instrument of divine will.

Buddhism repudiated that view. Closely allied to this notion was that language incarnated essences and carried metaphysical meanings. Buddhism rejected this view as well. What is interesting about the Buddhist approach to language and verbal communication is that it marks the middle path, the avoidance of extremes that has always characterized Buddhist thought. The Buddhist approach to language avoided the essentialism that was dominant in many other views current at the time; it also repudiated a totally materialistic approach to language that advanced the view that it was totally arbitrary. As I shall explain presently, the Buddhist approach to language places emphasis on a different set of interests in keeping with its epistemology and moral imperatives.

The idea that verbal communication is based on convention and social practices, is central to Buddhist thinking, which has no truck with the divine origins of language. This is vividly illustrated in the famous discourse on the origins (*agganna sutta*). In his explication, the Buddha tells the two

Brahmins, Vasettha and Bharadvaja, that human society came to be what is through a process of evolution. Social institutions, then, were created not by some divine power or creator but by the dynamics of social growth. Hinduism stresses the fact that the world was produced by the Brahma as well as the caste system.

Buddhism maintains that they were the outcome of social evolution, and that language is one such result. Hence, Buddhism discards the view of language as a divine creation. According to Buddhism, language has to be understood as a social practice inflected by convention and agreed upon by the people who use it. What this means is that language is not divinely- ordained or ironclad, and that it evolves in conformity to the movement of convention. In the Buddhist literature there are copious references to agreement among the users (*sammuti*) or the practice of users (*vohara*).

Hence, language as a product of social interaction is central to the Buddhist perspective on verbal communication. When we examine the early discourses on Buddhism, we can identify five central concepts that are deployed in discussions of language. They are etymology (*nirutti*), generality (*samanna*), usage (*vohara*), consensus (*sammuti*) and conceptuality (*pannatti*). Among these the ideas of etymology and generality were current at the time. However, the Buddha was not obsessed with these in the way that some others had been; he did not reify them in the way that others did. He was much more interested in the ideas of usage, convention, and conceptuality because they enabled him to focus on the idea of language as a social institution and social practice that responds to changing social and cultural forces.

LANGUAGE AS A SOCIAL PRACTICE

The Buddhist perspective on language and verbal communication that stresses the ideas of language as a social practice as a phenomenon that is consensus- driven, along with the central tenet of Buddhism regarding causality- the dependent co- origination and its concomitant multi- causality focuses on a very important dimension of communication. In

Western communication theory, until recent times, the process of communication was conceptualized in terms of solitary addressers and addresses or senders and receivers, and the focus was how messages were conveyed from one solitary mind to the other.

This is indeed a Cartesian legacy. What this leaves out of consideration is the all too important fact that verbal communication takes place within specific contexts of operation. What the Buddhist attitude to language does is to focus on the commonly shared world that senders and receivers share and how it constitutes a very important facet of the communicated meaning and the communicative event. Contexts and conventions that Buddhism focuses on are sets of practices and concerns that deepen the communicative act that is being performed. Hence, the Buddhist way of reconceptualizing verbal communication opens up very productive pathways of inquiry.

Verbal communication, according to the Buddhist view of things, is a social practice that underlines commonalities of usage, consensus, and mutuality. At the same time, verbal communication is understood within a moral space that imparts a sense of gravitas to the communicative event. Let me quote from the Buddhist text the discourse on wholesome speech (*subhasita sutta*) in addressing a group of monks. The Buddha said, "Speech which has four characteristics is speech well spoken, blameless, and not censured by the wise; namely, the speech of a monk who speaks only what is wholesome and not what is unwholesome, who speaks only what is worthy and not hat is unworthy, who speaks only what is pleasant and not what is unpleasant, who speaks only what is truthful and not what is untruthful. Speech characterized by these four factors is well spoken, and not ill spoken, blameless, and not censured by the wise.

This is what the master said." Having said this, he went on, as a teacher, to say this: Wholesome speech, the saints say, is the foremost. One should speak what is worthy and not what is unworthy, and this is the second. One should speak what is pleasant and not unpleasant, and this is the third. One should speak what is truthful and not what is false, and this is the fourth. These passages clearly establish the fact tat the Buddhist conception of verbal communication takes place in a moral space where normative imperatives play a significant rule. The fact that one should be truthful in speech is a desideratum that is constantly encircled in Buddhist popular discourse. For example, in the popular compilation *The Dhammapada*, it is stated that there is no sin that cannot be committed by a person who states falsehoods and violates virtuous speech.

Hence, what we find in the early Buddhist attitude to speech and verbal communication is the idea that a speech event is more than an exchange of information; there should be some direction, edifying impulse, to the entire communication event. In other words, Buddhists would maintain that speech acts, communicative interactions, and verbal interchanges are not value- free. There should be a discernible point to the direction in which such an event or interchange develops. The ideal speech situation proposed by the well- known social philosopher and communication theorist, Jurgen Habermas (1984) would share this viewpoint.

THE BUDDHA'S PHILOSOPHY OF LANGUAGE

The Buddha was a supremely effective communicator who interacted with various types of people, educated and uneducated, pious and impious. So far, I have been discussing the Buddhist attitude to communication in general and the Buddha's communications with ordinary people. At times, he had to engage theoreticians, logicians, and scholars of various persuasions.

In those instances, his strategy was different, arising largely out of the subject- matter and the context. For example, the Buddha stressed the conscious and responsible utilization of language. He said at one point, "these two conditions, monks, contribute to the confusion and disappearance of the genuine doctrine. Which two? An ill- placed terminology (*dunnikkhatan ca padavyanjanam*) and a meaning ill- conveyed (*attho ca dunnito*)? When the terminology is ill- placed, the meaning is also not approvingly conveyed."

This is indeed a comment that carries great implications for verbal communication. The way the Buddha responded to questions of metaphysics, to unanswerable questions, and to profitless queries reflects his deep- seated ideas about verbal communication and rationality. With regard to questions and challenges about the nature of reality and truth, the Buddha adopted a four- fold method of approach. First, he saw certain questions as meriting categorical or direct explication. Second, there were those questions that demanded to be explained analytically. Third, there were questions that invited explication only after a counter- question was posed.

Fourth, there were those questions that should be laid aside. The last mentioned questions were those that could not be meaningfully answered in terms of experience or those that had little relevance to the problematic issues countenanced by human beings. What this mode of responding to questions reflects is another facet of the Buddha's views on language, truth and reality, and its implications for communication. As has been remarked by Kalupahana (1999), the Buddha adopted a number of important measures to safeguard the validity of linguistic communication. First, he paid great attention to the interconnections between experience and articulation in language.

This led him into the investigations into the growth of language. Second, there is always the danger of language slipping into metaphysical modalities of thinking and expression. This meant the constant guarding against the perils of substantialism and absolutism. In order to avoid this, the Buddha often deployed passive forms, the aorists, and past participles instead of active forms. Third, he sought to scrutinize concepts while paying close attention to the ways in which they changed in their usage over time. What this meant was that he focused on the mutability and changeability of concepts.

Fourth, he was sensitive to the inherent limitations of experience and language, and paid sustained attention to the complex ways in which they wee intertwined and intersected. Fifth, lowing from this, he sought to maintain a balance between experience and explication and focus on the blind spots of rationalities. Sixth, he sought to construct a philosophy of language that was in keeping with his privileged epistemology and moral imagination. These considerations of the Buddha gave the Buddhist perspective on language and verbal communication its distinctive outlook. As students of communication, it is of the utmost importance that we pay focused attention on each of these considerations.

IMPLICATIONS FOR COMMUNICATION THEORY

Against this background of discussion, I wish to draw out a number of important themes embedded in the Buddhist approach to language that we as students of communication should find to be extremely productive and relevant to our pursuits. These themes should prove to be of great heuristic value in our efforts to re- think communication theory and its implications. First, according to early Buddhist thinking, as I stated earlier in this chapter, language comes into being as a social practice based on usage and convention and is not a divinely- ordained product. This focuses on the non-essentialist and non- absolutist approach to language advocated by Buddhism.

It was seen as an instrument, but a purposive one that best operated within a normative space. The idea of convention and consensus as guiding linguistic communication has to be considered very carefully. As has been pointed out by Tilakaratne (1993), while recognizing and explicating the non-absolutist nature of language, the Buddha unambiguously underlined the need to adhere to linguistic conventions if the wider society has opted to abide by them. This is borne out in the following passage.

There are these three linguistic conventions or usages of words or terms, which have been distinct in the past, are distinct in the present, and will be distinct in the future, and which are not ignored by the wise Brahmans and recluses. Whatever material form (*rupa*) that has been, which has ceased to be, which is past and has changed, is called, reckoned, and termed "has been" (*ahosi*) and is not reckoned as "it exists" (*atthi*) or as "it will be" (*bhavissati*), this is repeated for the other four aggregates: feelings, perceptions, disposition, and consciousness.

Whatever material form has not arisen nor come to be is called, reckoned as "it exists" (*atthi*) or as "it has been" (*ahosi*). Whatever material form has arisen, and has manifested itself, is called, reckoned, or termed "it exists" (*atthi*), and is not reckoned or termed "it has been" (*ahosi*) nor as "it will be" (*bhavissati*). It is clear from this passage that the Buddha admonishes his followers not to transgress the conventions of time cited above.

Conventions, to be sure, transform themselves over time, and what Buddhism points out is that in adhering to convention, one must be prudent and exercise discriminatory judgment. This attitude to linguistic convention carries with it important implications for verbal communication. The second important theme from a communications viewpoint that is significant in early Buddhist writings is the idea of linguistic embeddedness that characterizes a communicative event.

A communicative event does not signify the sending of a message by a solitary sender to a solitary receiver; it takes place within a linguistic context in which both are embedded, and this linguistic context forms a vital part of the meaning of the communication act. It is important to bear in mind the fact that consciousness is forged in the linguistic signs produced by the participants in the communicative act. The individual consciousness is nurtured on signs, and it mirrors their logic and imperatives. Indeed, the logic of consciousness is the logic of semiotic interactions of a given communicative event. Indeed, if we deprive consciousness of its semiotic content, there would be nothing left in it.

Let us explore this notion a little more deeply. Language consists of signs; they arise only on the basis of inter-individual interaction or intersubjectivity. Signs are organized socially and are fuelled by intersubjective interactions. It is only under these conditions that signs come into life in verbal communication. Hence, when we discuss the nature and significance of verbal communication, it is always important to bear in mind the importance of the social context which invests the communicative event with meaning.

The early Buddhist attitude to language that we have discussed leads us productively in this direction. In verbal communication, a transaction takes place between the addresser and the addressee through the medium of language. The linguistic and social environment in which this transaction occurs determines its nature and meaning. The orientation of the word towards the addressees carries with it an extremely high significance. In point of fact, the word constitutes a two-sided act. It is determined equally by the person whose word it is as much as for whom it is intended.

The word, then, is the product of the reciprocal relationship between the speaker and the listener, the sender and the receiver. In a communication act, each and every word expresses the one in relation to the other. I give my words verbal shape keeping in mind the image of the intended receiver. In an act of communication, the word can be regarded as a bridge thrown between myself and the potential interlocutor. If one end of the bridge is dependent on me, the other is dependent in my addressee.

According to the Buddhist approach to language and communication, a word is a territory shared by both the addresser and the addressee, by the sender and the receiver. Consequently, in an act of communication, we can identify three important constituent elements. First, there is the physical act of speaking, the production and emittance of sound. Second, there is the act of creating verbal signs, drawing upon the social stock of signs available to the speaker. Third, there is the manipulation and orchestration of the verbal sign so as to set in motion a communication process, and this is totally determined by the social relations that exist between the participants in the communicative event.

Therefore, we see clearly the importance of the social context as a generator of communication. As we examine Buddhist expository writings on this theme, what we come to realize is that Buddhism placed great emphasis on language as a sign system within which individual words as well as clusters of words acquire the force of meaning. What this means is that both senders and receivers, owing to their shared backgrounds and contexts, respond to words as both articulatory patterns as well as hermeneutic patterns, based on prior experiences.

This embeddedness in a common sign system, and its implications, are clearly established in Buddhist writings. This is a line of approach underlined by the Buddhist perspective on language and communication. A third theme which emerges from early Buddhist expository writings is the self-reflectivity and introspection that characterizes human communication. For Buddhists, to use the terminology of communication scholars, in communication, intrapersonal communication is as important as interpersonal communication.

According to Buddhism, ultimately, language and communication should lead to spiritual liberation. Hence, introspection, self- reflectivity, intrapersonal communication is of paramount importance. For Buddhists, this self- reflexivity is built into the very process of linguistic communication. In communication, Buddhists stress, one is not involved in merely stringing together a cluster of words but also reflecting on them. Communication presupposes this reflective act. This self-reflexivity is vitally connected to our attitude to the world in which we live as well as to the people in society with whom we interact.

Hence, according to Buddhism, to communicate, to use language to interact with others, is to adopt a moral posture. From this flows the inescapable fact that language deals not only with information and knowledge but also with feelings, at times directly and at times obliquely. Therefore, to communicate in language, according to Buddhism, is to be aware of how one is constituted as a human being. This is a very important facet of communication that has been relatively ignored by contemporary communication scholars both in the West and the East. Earlier, I discussed the importance of the context in verbal communication from a Buddhist perspective.

This gives rise to another theme; the fourth in my list that I wish to broach, namely, the importance of the public space in verbal communication. Meaningful verbal communication arises from, and leads to, an identifiable public space. By public space, I refer to the arena in which we discuss, argue over, explore, matters of common interest as human beings. As I pointed out earlier, for Buddhists verbal communication implies a social activity with a purpose and certain gravitas. This is because language is seen as a precious resource that should ultimately pave the way for human welfare.

There are different ways in which the relationship between language and the public space has been glossed. Some would argue that while language shapes the public space, the public space in turn shapes language. Those who subscribe to a Wittgensteinian (1958) approach to things would argue that there must exist a consensus in judgments as a pre- condition of language being a mode of communication, and that is what the public space does. As there needs to be public agree criteria for meaningful verbal communication to take place, the public space becomes important. A linguistic concept, if it is not shared or shareable, does no lend itself communication and hence the importance of Wittgenstein's arguments against private language.

Those who favor a more symbolically- oriented approach, like some modern anthropologists, would maintain that a community comes into being as a symbolically constructed system of values, norms, codes, and conventions of behavior and judgment, and that the public face of language enables this to happen. Buddhist theorists of communication, while not disagreeing with these propositions, would go a step further and assert that thinking and language are inextricably linked, and that thinking is language. Thinking takes place in public. Even when one is thinking in solitude, one is interacting with others. Hence thinking and the public space are vitally connected.

A Buddhist approach to communication would stress this dimension of verbal interaction. Fifth, the idea of meaning is pivotal to the early Buddhist understanding of verbal communication. In Buddhist writings, communication is perceived as a quest for meaning, where the sender and receiver act as co-investigators of meaning. Even in the case of intrapersonal communication, the quest for meaning is a joint one, because an imaginary interlocutor or set of interlocutors is posited. Buddhists maintain that human beings inhabit a world of meaning, and hence any meaningful communicative event must be involved in the exploration of meaning. The sender and the receiver are embedded in a linguistic and social context, that is to say, in a context of meaning.

They are co- discoverers of meaning. Consequently, the common pursuit of meaning becomes an important consideration in the eyes of Buddhist thinkers. According to the Buddhist way of thinking, a human being is a linguistic animal as well as a self- interpreting animal; human beings are sharers of meaning. Hence, questions of meaning are not only of paramount importance to him or her but also inescapably and irreducibly present in human interaction. As in the case of Jurgen Habermas' (1984) ideal speech situation, in the Buddhist thinking also, there is a strong ethical component to linguistic communication.

MANIPULATIVE AND TRANSACTIONAL MODELS

In keeping with this tenor of thinking, the early conceptualizations of communication adhered to a transportational and manipulative view of communication. According to Osgood (1957) in the most general sense, we have communication whenever one system, a source, influences another, the destination, by manipulation of alternative signals which can be transmitted over the channels connecting them. Shannon and Weaver (1949) conceptualized communication as the procedures by which one mind affects another.

Since then, communication scholars have abandoned this manipulative notion and gradually moved towards a transitional notion. For example, George Gerbner (1956) saw communication as the interaction through messages. Kincaid (1979) defined communication as a process of convergence in which information is shared by participants in order to arrive at a mutual understanding. Pearce and Cronen (1980) explicated communication as the co- creation and co-management of reality. Since the 1980s, communication scholars have moving along this path and focusing on the interactional aspects of communication and reciprocities of meaning- making.

It is evident, therefore, that the idea of communication has undergone significant transformations during the past two and a half decades. Broadly speaking, then, there are two generic models of communication: the manipulative and the transactional. The models of communication advanced by scholars such as Lasswell (1948), Shannon and Weaver (1949), Osgood (1957), Westley and MacLean (1957) and Berlo (1960) can be termed manipulative. On the other hand, the models associated with Barnlund (1970) Schramm (1973), Kincaid (1970), and Pearce and Cronen (1980) paved the way for transactional models.

This is, of course, not to suggest that there are no variations and differences of emphases in the models included in each generic category. However, one can justifiably categorize them into two broad groupings. The differences between these two generic models can be represented schematically as follows:

1. Linear and one- way Non- linear and two- way.
2. Emphasis on sender Emphasis on relationship between two.
3. Focus on persuasion Focus on understanding.
4. Attention on psychology Attention on psychology and social effects.
5. Mechanistic Organic.
6. De- contextualized Contextualized.

We see, therefore, that the transactional models have made significant progress over the manipulative models in conceptualizing communication. This applies to verbal communication as well. Despite their manifest differences, both types of models agree on fundamental consideration, namely, the adoption of an instrumentalist view of language. In both types of models, language is seen as an instrument of manipulation or as an instrument which facilitates a two- way transaction. Language is never perceived or explained in a more fundamental way as constitutive of meaning.

Speaking of verbal communication, we can identify two approaches. The first recognizes language as an instrument of meaning. The second privileges language as constitutive of meaning. It is only in very recent times that such an approach to verbal communication has made its appearance. The second approach to verbal communication has two dimensions.

1. The idea that language is not a mere instrument or tool of communication but is constitutive of the meaning of verbal communication.
2. The idea that language arises out of the social matrix in which the users live.

Outside of this social interaction there is no verbal communication; no such entity can come into being. The Buddhist approach to language and verbal communication, as we have discussed so far, clearly belongs to the second constitutive approach. However, it needs to be noted that there are some important differences that mark the Buddhist approach off from the generality of approaches that belong to this category. First, there is a much greater emphasis placed on the idea of consciousness in the Buddhist perspective. Consciousness is crucial to language formation and use.

Second, the idea of intrapersonal communication is as important as interpersonal communication in the matter of verbal interactions. Buddhism stresses that intrapersonal communication is not an act if solitude. But a social act in that in takes place in the context of implicit social norms and imperatives. Third, the Buddhist approach to verbal communication operates in a moral space with self-clarification and edification being and important desiderata of language use. This is hardly surprising in view of the fact that Buddhism is above all, a religion, a way of life that teaches people the path of spiritual liberation.

Fourth, flowing from this is the idea that when one says that language constitutes meaning, according to Buddhist thinkers, it also means that language constitutes novel meanings that are relevant to leading a good life. This focus on the creation of new meanings for life is a vital aspect of the Buddhist approach to verbal communication. As Buddhism evolved over the centuries, and spread to various countries in the world, different sects and schools emerged. In this chapter, my focus has been on the early Buddhism or the Theravada School.

The Mahayana schools and various other forms of later developments of Buddhism are also important in terms of the philosophy of language and verbal communication. I have discussed elsewhere the relevance of Nagarjuna, who was instrumental in paving the way for the popularization of Mahayana Buddhism, to modern communication theory. The later Buddhist schools sought to place emphasis on different aspects of communication. For example, if we pause to examine the Zen Buddhist attitude to verbal communication as concretized, for example, in the writings of Dogen, we see how he focuses heavily on the phenomenology of pre- reflexivity.

It is his conviction that compassion, wisdom, equanimity, and egolessness can be productively comprehended by paying close attention to the pre- reflective dimensions of human experience. The implications of such a line of inquiry for understanding the dynamics of verbal communication are different from the ones foregrounded by early Buddhist perspectives that I have discussed in this chapter. Similarly, we can focus our attention on aspects of later esoteric Buddhism as represented, say, in the expository works of Kukai. He was deeply interested in the truth of words, and he sought to understand this by exploring the ritualistic structures of language.

For him, truth is manifested in ritual, and consequently sacred incantations and ritualistic usages of language became exceedingly important. Kukai evinced a great interest in the mysteries of language, and in his mind, biological gestures, reflective thinking, and verbal incantations were inseparably linked. This interest of his grows out of his privileged epistemology and ontology. Hence, it is hardly surprising that he chose to pay close and sustained attention to the ritualistic, incantational facets of verbal communication. Clearly, this marks a different approach to language and verbal communication from the one that is inscribed in the writings of early Buddhism.

This celebration of mysteries of language, the emphasis on ritual, is one that did not find favour in early Buddhism. When we discuss traditional Asian theories of communication, there is a tendency to think in large and capacious categories such as Hinduism, Buddhism, Taoism, and so on. This is, of course, understandable; however, in order to comprehend the true complexities of the situation, it is important, I think, to make finer discriminations and subtler assessments. In all religious traditions, there are different schools, sects, cults, with their own specific agendas and interests. Each claims to interpret the central doctrinal core of its professed religion, but in distinctive ways using different vocabularies of interpretation and different methodologies of investigation.

8

Hinayana and Mahayana with Chronology of the Mahayana

The unique beliefs and characteristics of Mahayana Buddhism (Dai Thua Phat Giao) is that it is essentially very different from the old teachings and literature of Theravada or Hinayana Buddhism. The differences between Hinayana Buddhism (Tieu Thua Phat Giao) and Mahayana Buddhism is such that:

- Hinayana holds psychological realism, Mahayana idealism. Hinayana sees suffering as real while Mahayana sees it as an illusion.
- Hinayana denies a "true being" behind a phenomena and avoid making metaphysical statements, the Mahayana teaches an Eternal Absolute under many names. Beings in all forms of rebirth are said to be identical in their cores with the absolute.
- The Historical Gautama is seeing as the projection of the absolute. In essence Gautama holds the core of being absolute but possesses a frail mortal frame of illusion. Hinayana regards the Gautama as a natural teacher, and at most a superman.
- Hinayana sees that liberation can only be achieved through one's own effort, while Mahayana considers assistance from outside as possible. Deliverance through other's power.

- The followers of Hinayana see the immediate goal as in achieving nirvana. Those who follow Mahayana see the immediate goal as in following the ways of the Bodhisattva in leading all beings to liberation.
- Nirvana, to Hinayana is the final exit from the world, while it to Mahayana considered becoming conscious of one's own absoluteness and gaining a state of mental aloofness from all. Hinayana has to create nirvana while Mahayana sees all beings as holding liberation from very begining but not aware of its existence.
- The attitudes of Mahayana are such that a person should lend a hand to help the world and educate its followers to be selfless. The Hinayana attitude is to defeat the world by analysing its elements and using that knowledge for individual conduct. It is pragmatic in its approach.

BUDDHOLOGY

The Buddha Gautama (Thi'ch Ca) is regarded by Mahayana Schools as the universal saviour and bestower of deliverance. He is master over space and time. Gautama's early life and his nirvana are illusions projected onto the world in order to lead mankind to knowledge and virtuous conduct. In fact he was already enlightened before he took the form of the historical Gautama. It is the Mahayana's conviction that there are also many other Buddhas aside from Gautama. There are as many Buddha as grains of sand on the bank of the Ganges (Song Hang). Buddhas appear in all region of the world taking many forms to shows beings the Buddha Vehicle.

THE THREE BODIES DOCTRINE

Buddha was regarded as human, super- human, and a heavenly being. From the earlier separation of view of the Buddha of the earlier Buddhists, the Mahayanans adopted the doctrines of three bodies of the Buddha.

1. The Dharmakaya (Dharma- body) is the inner nature of the Buddha. In all the immunerable earthly Buddhas and the countless transcesdental Buddhas, there is only one

Dharmakaya. It is the absolute reality, besides which there is no other reality. Dharma is the partial manifestation of natural laws, namely "facts". Dharma is the technical term for "factors of existence". The Dharmakaya thus is the base- consciousness of existence.

2. Sambhogakaya is the transcendental Buddhas, that cannot be interpreted or preceived by the senses, but only experience spiritually. Sambhogakaya- Buddhas are seen as mental creations, the idea of the Bodhisattva. It is the manifestation of the absolute. Transcendental Sambhogakaya Buddhas are regarded as objectively existing, supramundane and subtle beings. The most popular transcendental Buddha is the Amida Buddha (A Di Da Phat). The transcendental Buddhas are said to possess paradises, in which believers are reborn there. They are teachers of the Bodhisattvas and the spiritual fathers of the Earthly Buddhas. They project their compassions for all beings into the world by their meditation.
3. Nirmanakaya (Physical Body) belongs to those Buddhas like historical Gautama Buddha, appearing in the world in physical shape. They are called Nirmana or "manifest beings". They are subject to misery and aging, illness and death, because they are persons of flesh and blood. They are distinguished by thirty- two bodily characteristics and some supernatural abilities. The function of the Earthly Buddha or Nirmankaya Buddha is to teach and spread Dharma, the formulate truth into the world.

THE BODHISATTVA

The Bodhisattva is the name ascribed to those beings that strive to systematically for enlightenment, or who have already obtained it but postpone their own Static post- mortal nirvana until all beings are liberated. Bodhisattva lives exclusively for others. They have mercifulness and compassion, wishing, without self interest, only for the happiness of others. The Bodhisattva encompasses wisdom to give, compassion to help others in any way to bring others closer to enlightenment. The Bodhisattva is willing to take sufferings onto his shoulders to help others, sacrificing all to bring other beings closer to enlightenment.

The Bodhisattva has wisdom to see what is necessary for him to do to help others. There are 2 types of Bodhisattva, the Earthly ones and the transcendental ones. The Earthly Bodhisattva are said to be those who follow a way of life striving for enlightenment while helping others also to seek happiness in enlightenment like them. Everyone can be an Earthly Bodhisattva, from any walk of life in any situation if they follow the Bodhisattva way of life and vows.

The Transcendental Bodhisattva are those who through realizing perfection and wisdom and thus sainthood and liberation, have refuse to enter static nirvana to stay in active nirvana in a state of deliverance in which they can work for the benefit of the world. They can assume any form, playing the illusory reality to help those caught in it seek the truth and absolute. Of the famous and important of the Transcendental Bodhisattva is Avalokites'vara (The one who gracously looks down). In the Far East, the Bodhisattva Avalokites'vara is sculptured as a woman who resembles the Virgin Mary in the west and symbolic of a compassionate mother to all.

ALL IS SUFFERING

"All existance is suffering!" is the main doctrine of Buddhism. Mahayana too regards existance as sorrowful. In all forms of being there are grief and pain, longing and dissappointment. Life for a time may appear to be happy, and things one has grown fond of seem lasting, but what is loved has to perish as well as the person loving it. Parting and suffering are the inevitable course anyone must take.

There are 8 different types of suffering that Buddhism defined:

- *Suffering of birth*-No one comes into life smiling, we call come with tears. Through growing up, we experience the pain of growing new teeth, puberty, and the pain of finding our own identiy in life. Life is full of sorrows and happiness seemed not to last a long time.

- *Suffering of old age*-We all grow old, it is the inevitable course of life. With old age, we grow frail and weak. Unable to help ourselves and bear the pain of growing old.
- *Suffering of illness*-Even the strongest man becomes ill. With illness we experience pain, whether psychological or physical. No one can claim that they have never been sick. The suffering of illness is a part of life.
- *Suffering of death*-Everyone must die. With death, we experience the pain of the body. We twitch and turn, as our last breaths are released. Even the most powerful, successful, or riches person must die leaving their love ones behind to feel the pain of their departure. Death is the unavoidable consequence of life.
- *Suffering of unfullfilled desires*-We all want something in life, whether for ourselves or others. When our desires are unfullfilled, we suffer pain. The pain of not having what we want is great. To a child, the pain of not being able to have a toy is just as great as an adult not being able to have wealth, or a successful career, or love.
- *Suffering of being in the company of dislikes ones*-We all like to spend time with the ones we love. But that is not true many times. When we are in the company of those we fear, those we hate, it is like having a needle to our eyes. This is another part of living.
- *Suffering of separation from those we love*-We all like to be with those we love. But separation is a part of life. When we lose those we love to death, to war, to life's circumstances, we all suffer pains. It is an unavoidable part of life.
- *Suffering of health*-Many would ask: "Why would being healthy is also suffering?" It is that when we are healthy, we dwell in running our lives with envy, lust, greed, passion and waste our time not knowing that death is just a breath away. We are like those who play in a house of fire not knowing that it is burning around us. Many healthy people cause their own suffering with drugs, alcohol, and other addictions when they regard themselves as immortal, not knowing that death is near.

We all see and hear suffering around us, even to ourselves. But does not understand the reality of it. Ignorance in our views causes us to look for illusory happiness that does not last forever. Even the happinest person would suffer death. The healthiest person will also suffer illness, and the least wanting person the suffering of loss. The Buddha's teachings of suffering are to lead all to see that life is but a illusory existence.

We should not drown in depressing conceit in light of life's suffering, but take bold actions to end it and find the enternal happiness in our existence. We must seek the absolute truth to find our eternal self again. For our existence are that of illusions which is not as immutable as we think, but very mutable. Everything changes as the world turns. No matter how we try, no one can hinder death, or life. As the words of famous Romantic poets "Pershy Bysshe Shelley" puts it:

We are as clouds that veil the midnight moon;
How restlessly they speed; and gleam and quiver.
Streaking the darkness radiantly!- Yet soon!
Night closes round and they are lost forever:
Or like forgotten lyres whose dissonance strings,
Give various responses to each varying blast,
To whose frail frame no second motion brings,
One mood or modulation like the last.
We rest-a dream has power to poison sleep;
We rise-one wandering thought pollutes the day;
We feel, conceive or reason, laugh or weep
Embrace fond woe, or cast our cares away:
It is the same-for, be it joy or sorrow,
The path of its departure still is free;
Man's yesterday may ne'er be like his morrow
Nought may endure but mutability.

The way of Mahayana's deliverance through self-discipline corresponds with the "Eightfold Path" of the

Hinayana. The eighfold way is effective for liberation by its use of the law of *Karma*n (Wheel of Rebirth). But the Mahayana goes further as to see liberation as the removal of all ignorance and by the realization of the absolute in which the Eightfold Path helps to attain. To reach deliverance is not possible by mere ethical actions of which the karmic effects are confined. The Hinayana way sees that if one rise high and above in the Karmic circle to be reborn in a higher status and realm, it is easier to attain enlightenment there.

So what is the Eightfold Path? It is clearly as listed that if one possesses all of the characteristics below, he is on the eightfold path:

- Right View is gaining insight into the Dharmakaya of the Enlightened One.
- Right Resolve is the pacification of all imaginations.
- Right Speech is the realization that language confronted with the Dharmas falls silent; to speak the truth that does not consist lies, gossip, abuse and idle talk.
- Right Conduct is abstinence from any actions aiming at Karmic merit.
- Right Livelihood consists of the insight that all Dharmas are without origination and destruction, harmless breadwinning which would not cause suffering to anyone.
- Right Effort means relinquishing Energy and Method to obtain deliverance in the knowledge that Dharmas (the state of deliverance) rise out of action.
- Right Awareness means to stop brooding over being and non- being. Being mindfullness of the body, sensations, mind and mental objects. A person overwhelmed with rage would more easily rid of it once he is aware of his own rage and its destructiveness to himself and others.
- Right Meditation is freedom of opinion by non- grasping Dharmas. To be able to seek the ways and understand fully the methods of meditations as prescribed by the Buddha. One must choose one of many ways of meditation to go on the way of enlightenment. No one has ever attained Nirvana without meditation.

To the Mahayanan, the Eightfold Path serves as a vehicle to help one seek the Absolute. It is not the only way, but the fundamental way as the Buddha has taught. The Mahayana understands the teachings of the Hinayana, and it is use as basic a basic core. The core of these teachings is the denial of self in the Five Groups which constitutes the impirical person, and the theory of rebirth according to the quality of *Karman*. The consciousness of a dying being occasions in a mother's womb the origination of a new impirical person without entering into this person. The proprelling force causing the consciousness to do this is ignorance and craving. Their annihilation leads to Nirvana.

There are two types of Dharma (Pha'p), the Unconditioned Dharma (asamskrta) and the Conditioned Dharma (samskrta). The Uncondtioned Dharma are not dependent on anything, not influenced by devoid or impermanence. It constitutes Nirvana, the seed of Buddha nature. The Conditioned Dharmas are combinations of which that compose the impirical person, originating from previous Dharmas formed by an individual's *Karman*, moving from the previous body to the next in rebirth. Through out a life time, Conditioned Dharmas are in a continual process of disintergration, renewal, and rearrangement.

Of all the shortest being the thought. They barely exist for a split second before they yield to new Dharmas (or new thoughts). Man is comparable to a melody, made up of various chords and sounds. The continuous successions of chords produce the phenomenon of melody. The dissonance in the melody does not mean the end of music. Like death does not mean the end of the chain of Conditioned Dharmas. Death itself is a Dharma of the chain as dissonance is an element of the melody. We are enchanted by the melody as long as we perceive it as an ensouled pattern of sounds. The moment we are aware of the separate tones, the enchantment collapses.

In a way when we see the world as something essential, and when we see it as a phenomena produced by Conditioned Dharmas, as illusory as a melody with its chords and sounds components, we found wisdom. It is from this realization that

Nirvana is recognized. Knowledge is a matter of the mere intellect which can only grasp fragments of reality; wisdom on the other hand is intuitive identification of the reality of all existence and being an experience which is made with the whole of the personality after all rational limitations, views and doctrines have been discarded. It is defined as "omniscience" and in the Mahayana is synonymous with "enlightenment".

What is wisdom? Wisdom as taught in the *Prajnaparamitas* is the realization of non- selfness, or "emptiness". That the Conditioned Dharmas (Pha'p) are empty in nature, such that it is made of unison of others factors. Once all the factors made up the Condition are free, the Condition ceased to exist. Just as a chair robed of its shape, wooden nature, and nails would ceased to be a chair. But be aware that "emptiness" too is empty. For without a thing to be empty of, there wouldn't be emptiness. But wisdom is first born by the realization of emptiness.

By developing wisdom, it destroys craving and ignorance, the two causes of suffering. Craving feeds through contact of the senses and the illusory perception of a "self". This self is created through ignorance of the true nature of Contioned Dharmas; its destruction will lead to end of craving and ignorance. By seeing that the world is illusory, and the Dharma-Phenomenon is like a melody, ignorance vanishes leaving emptiness as the Asolute. Therefore suffering through attachment is uprooted. He who has rooted both causes of suffering is no longer threatened by rebirth.

THE BODHISATTVA WAY

The way of Self- discipline and of Wisdom presupposes in a follower self- restraint, intelligence and concentration power - abilities which, in the experience of Buddhism, are possessed by only a small portion of mankind. For the many who are untalented in these ways, the Mahayana therefore teaches three more methods of liberation: The Bodhisattva Way, the Way of Faith, and the Cultic Way. Let us first observe the Bodhisattva Way. On the Bodhisattva Way, the seeker relies of Great Compassion of the Bodhisattvas.

To obtain Nirvana, the followers of the Bodhisattva way themselves take the vows of the Bodhisattva to practise selflessness in helping others and seek for guidance from the Transcendental Bodhisattva to help remove unwholesome karmic seed and replace it with wholesome karmic merit assisting to speedier emancipation. There are ten stages of which the Earthly Bodhisattva follows to speed up his/her emancipation.

The Ten Stages

- The joyful (pramundita)-The believer takes the Bodhisattva vow to dedicate himself completely to the liberation of others and to postpone his own total extinction until all beings are free from suffering. Full of joy about his being on the way to help others, the young Bodhisattva cultivates in particular virtue- perfection of openhandedness. Without egoistic ulterior motives, he gives his possessions away to those in need.
- The Immanculate (vimala)-He perfects his self disciplines in the way the Buddha had taught.
- The Radiating (prabhakari)-The Bodhisattva gains insight into the transient nature of the world and develops the virtue of patience (ksanti). Patience here means willing endurance of adversities and perserverance in efforts for the deliverance of the world.
- The Blazing (arcismati)-As with flames, the Bodhisattva burns the remnant of false ideas. He cultivates will- power (virya) which he needs to be victorious in his struggle for the liberation of all beings.
- The Extremely Difficult to Conquer (sudurajya)-He perfects himself through meditation in order to grasp intuitively the true nature of existence.
- The Stage of Facing Wisdom (abhimukhi) - The Bodhisattva gains insights into Conditioned Origination which is the cause of sorrowful individual existance. His wisdom becomes perfect as he relies on the Emptiness of all beings and things and cognises it as the Absolute. On this stage he had realized Nirvana, but refuses to enter

Static Nirvana in order to help those who still see suffering as real.

- The Far- going (durangama) - The Bodhisattva changes over to a new mode of being, he becomes the Transcendent Bodhisattva, no longer tied to a physical body. He in his free will can assume any conceivable appearance for the deliverance of others.
- The Immovable (acala)-He gains the power to transfer his karmic merit to unliberated beings. Their well being in his vows.
- The Good Thought (sadhumati)-With strengh he devotes himself to the task of executing his vow to guide all beings to deliverance. The Bodhisattva on this ninth stage is the Avalokitesvara.
- The Clouds of Doctrine (Dharmamegha)-The Bodhisattva realizes his own knowledge. His body begins to radiate and to illuminate the universe. Amidst the Bodhisattvas of the ten directions, he sits on the lotus in the Tsusita heaven. One more chance of existence, and he will attain Buddhaship. Maitreya is the Bodhisattva on this tenth floor of perfection.

Accompanying are the six virtues of the Bodhisattva which play a role in his career.

- Open- handedness (dana)
- Discipline ('sila)
- Patience (ksanti)
- Will- power (virya)
- Meditation (dyana)
- Wisdom (prajna)

These six perfections are said to be true friends of the Bodhisattva and the cause of his omniscience. The other four which determins his path are:

- Right Method (upaya)
- Vow (pranidhana)
- Strengh (bala)
- Knowledge (jnana)

The Bodhissattva Way is the most prominent teachings of Mahayana Buddhism that differs from the older Hinayana Buddhism Schools. Mahayana Buddhism regard the Hinayana Buddhism as only taking the Monks and Nuns to The Wisdom Stage, where Nirvana is realized. There the person would stay in the Static Nirvana and be contented with his/her own deliverance and not help others to attain it also. The Bodhisattva Way also allows not only the Monks and nuns to follow but also the laymen and women to follow as well.

It is a way that increases the compassionate nature of the world and helps to better it as one awaits salvation from rebirth though True Wisdom. The voluminous Chinese literature concerning Buddhism offers valuable assistance, for the Chinese, unlike the Hindus, have a natural disposition to write simple narratives recording facts and dates. But they are diarists and chroniclers rather than historians. The Chinese pilgrims to India give a good account of their itinerary and experiences, but they have little idea of investigating and arranging past events and merely recount traditions connected with the places which they visited. In spite of this their statements have considerable historical value and on the whole harmonize with the literary and archæological data furnished by India.

The Tibetan Lama Târanâtha who completed his History of Indian Buddhism in 1608 is a less satisfactory authority. He merits attention but also scepticism and caution. His work is a compilation but is not to be despised on that ground, for the Tibetan translations of Sanskrit works offer a rich mine of information about the history of the Mahayana. Unfortunately few of these works take the historical point of view and Târanâtha's own method is as uncritical as his materials. Dire confusion prevails as to chronology and even as to names, so that the work is almost useless as a connected account, though it contains many interesting details.

Two epochs are of special importance for the development of later Indian Buddhism, that of Kanishka and that of Vasubandhu and his brother Asanga. The reader may expect me to discuss at length the date of Kanishka's accession, but I do not propose to do so for it may be hoped that in the next few years archaeological research in India or Central Asia will fix the chronology of the Kushans and meanwhile it is waste of time to argue about probabilities or at any rate it can be done profitably only in special articles. At present the majority of scholars place his accession at about 78 A.D., others put it back to 58 B.C. and arrange the Kushan kings in a different order, while still others think that he did not come to the throne until the second century was well advanced.

The evidence of art, particularly of numismatics, indicates that Kanishka reigned towards the end of his dynasty rather than at the beginning, but the use of Greek on his coins and his traditional connection with the beginnings of the Mahayana are arguments against a very late date. If the date 78 A.D. is accepted, the conversion of the Yüeh- chih to Buddhism and its diffusion in Central Asia cannot have been the work of Kanishka, for Buddhism began to reach China by land about the time of the Christian era. There is however no reason to assume that they were his work. Kanishka, like Constantine, probably favoured a winning cause, and Buddhism may have been gradually making its way among the Kushans and their neighbours for a couple of centuries before his time.

In any case, however important his reign may have been for the Buddhist Church, I do not think that the history of the Mahayana should be made to depend on his date. Chinese translations, supported by other evidence, indicate that the Mahayanist movement had begun about the time of our era. If it is proved that Kanishka lived considerably later, we should not argue that Mahayanism is later than was supposed but rather that his relation towards it has been misunderstood. The date of Vasubandhu has also been much discussed and scholars have generally placed him in the fourth or fifth century but Péri appears to have proved that he lived from about 280 to 360 A.D. and I shall adopt this view.

This chronology makes a reasonable setting for the development of Buddhism. If Kanishka reigned from about 78 to 123 A.D. or even later, there is no difficulty in supposing that Aœvaghosha flourished in his reign and was followed by

Nâgârjuna. The collapse of the Kushan Empire was probably accompanied by raids from Iranian tribes, for Persian influence appears to have been strong in India during the confused interval between the Kushans and Guptas (225- 320). The latter inaugurated the revival of Hinduism but still showed favour to individual Buddhists, and we know from Fa- Hsien that Buddhism was fairly flourishing during his visit to India (399- 415). There is nothing improbable in supposing that Vasubandhu, who is stated to have lived at Court, was patronized by the early Guptas.

The blank in Buddhist history which follows his career can be explained first by the progress of Hinduism at the expense of Buddhism and secondly by the invasions of the Huns. The Chinese pilgrim Sung- Yün has left us an account of India in this distressful period and for the seventh century the works of Hsüan Chuang and I- Ching give copious information. In investigating the beginnings of the Mahayana we may start from the epoch of Asoka, who is regarded by tradition as the patron and consolidator of the Hinayanist Church. And the tradition seems on the whole correct: the united evidence of texts and inscriptions goes to show that the Buddhists of Asoka's time held the chief doctrines subsequently professed by the Sinhalese Church and did not hold the other set of doctrines known as Mahayanist.

That these latter are posterior in time is practically admitted by the books that teach them, for they are constantly described as the crown and completion of a progressive revelation. Thus the Lotus illustrates the evolution of doctrine by a story which curiously resembles the parable of the prodigal son except that the returned penitent does not recognize his father, who proceeds to reveal gradually his name and position, keeping back the full truth to the last. Similarly it is held in the Far East that there were five periods in Sâkyamuni's teaching which after passing through the stage of the Hinayana culminated in the Prajñâ- pâramitâ and Amitâbha sutras shortly before his death. Such statements admit the historical priority of the Hinayana: it is rudimentary (that is early) truth which needs completion and expansion.

Many critics demur to the assumption that primitive Buddhism was a system of ethics purged of superstition and mythology. And in a way they are right. Could we get hold of a primitive Buddhist, we should probably find that miracles, magic, and superhuman beings played a large part in his mind and that the Buddha did not appear to him as what we call a human teacher. In that sense the germs of the Mahayana existed in the life- time of Gotama. But the difference between early and later Buddhism lies in this, that the deities who surround the Buddha in the Pali Pitakas are mere accessories: his teaching would not be affected if they were all removed. But the Bodhisattvas in the Lotus or the Sutra of the Happy Land have a doctrinal significance.

Though in India old ideas persist with unusual vitality, still even there they can live only if they either develop or gather round them new accretions. As one of the religions of India, Buddhism was sensitive to the general movement of Indian thought, or rather it was a part of that movement. We see as clearly in Buddhist as in non- Buddhist India that there was a tendency to construct philosophic systems and another tendency to create deities satisfying to the emotions as well as to the intellect and yet another tendency to compose new scriptures. But apart from this parallel development, it becomes clear after the Christian era that Buddhism is becoming surrounded by Hinduism.

The influence is not indeed one- sided: there is interdependence and interpenetration but the net result is that the general Indian features of each religious period overpower the especially Buddhist features and in the end we find that while Hinduism has only been profoundly modified Buddhism has vanished. If we examine the Pali Pitakas, including the heresies mentioned in the Kathâvatthu, we find that they contain the germs of many Mahayanist ideas. Thus side by side with the human portrait of the Buddha there is the doctrine that he is one in a series of supernatural teachers, each with the same life- history, and this life is connected with the whole course of nature, as is shown by the sympathetic earthquakes which mark its crises. His birth is supernatural and had he willed it he could have lived until the end of the present Kalpa. So, too, the nature of a Buddha when he is released form that is after death is deep and unfathomable as the ocean.

The Kathâvatthu condemns the ideas (thus showing that they existed) that Buddhas are born in all quarters of the universe, that the Buddha was superhuman in the ordinary affairs of life, that he was not really born in the world of men and that he did not preach the Law himself. These last two heresies are attributed by the commentary to the Vetulyakas who are said to have believed that he remained in the Tushita heaven and sent a phantom to preach on earth. Here we have the rudiments of the doctrine afterwards systematized under the name of the three bodies of Buddha. Similarly though Nirvana is regarded as primarily an ethical state, the Pali Canon contains the expression Nirvânòadhâtu and the idea that Nirvana is a sphere or realm (*âyatanam*) which transcends the transitory world and in which such antitheses are coming and going, birth and death, cease to exist.

This foreshadows the doctrine of Bhûta- tathatâ and we seem to hear a prelude to the dialectic of Nâgârjuna when the Kathâvatthu discusses whether Suññatâ or the void is predicable of the Skandhas and when it condemns the views that anything now existing existed in the past: and that knowledge of the present is possible (whereas the moment anything is known it is really past). The Kathâvatthu also condemns the proposition that a Bodhisattva can be reborn in realms of woe or fall into error, and this proposition hints that the career of a Bodhisattva was considered of general interest.

The Mahayana grows out of the Hinayana and in many respects the Hinayana passes into it and is preserved unchanged. It is true that in reading the Lotus we wonder how this marvellous cosmic vision can represent itself as the teaching of Gotama, but the Buddhacarita of Aœvaghosha, though embellished with literary mythology, hardly advances in doctrine beyond the Pali sutras describing the marvels of the Buddha's nativity and the greater part of Nâgârjuna's Friendly Epistle, which purports to contain an epitome of the faith, is in phraseology as well as thought perfectly in harmony with the Pali Canon.

Whence comes this difference of tone in works accepted by the same school? One difficulty of the historian who essays to account for the later phases of Buddhism is to apportion duly the influence of Indian and foreign elements. On the one hand, the Mahayana, whether we call it a development or perversion, is a product of Indian thought. To explain its trinities, its saviours, its doctrine of self sacrifice it is not necessary to seek abroad. New schools, anxious to claim continuity and antiquity, gladly retained as much of the old doctrine as they could. But on the other hand, Indian Buddhism came into contact with foreign, especially Iranian, ideas and undoubtedly assimilated some of them.

From time to time I have drawn attention to such cases in this work, but as a rule the foreign ideas are so thoroughly mastered and indianized that they cease to be obvious. They merely open up to Indian thought a new path wherein it can move in its own way. In the period following Asoka's death Buddhism suffered a temporary eclipse. Pushyamitra who in 184 B.C. overthrew the Mauryas and established the Sunga dynasty was a patron of the Brahmans. Târanâtha describes him as a ferocious persecutor, and the Divyâvadâna supports the story. But the persecution, if it really occurred, was probably local and did not seriously check the spread of Buddhism, which before the time of Kanishka had extended northwards to Bactria and Kashmir. The latter territory became the special home of the Sarvâstivâdins.

It was in the reign of Pushyamitra that the Græco- Bactrian king Menander or Milinda invaded India (155- 3 B.C.) and there were many other invasions and settlements of tribes coming from the north- west and variously described as Sakas, Pahlavas, Parthians and Yavanas, culminating in the conquests of the Kushans. The whole period was disturbed and confused but some general statements can be made with considerable confidence. From about 300 B.C. to 100 A.D. we find inscriptions, buildings and statues testifying to the piety of Buddhist and Jain donors but hardly any indications of a similar liberality to Brahmans.

In the second and third centuries A.D. grants of land to Brahmans and their temples begin to be recorded and in the fourth century (that is with the rise of the Gupta Dynasty) such grants become frequent. These facts can hardly be interpreted otherwise than as meaning that from 300 B.C. to 100 A.D. the upper classes of India favoured Buddhism and Jainism and did not favour the Brahmans in the same way or to the same extent. But it must be remembered that the religion of the Brahmans continued throughout this period and produced a copious literature, and also that the absence of works of art may be due to the fact that their worship was performed in sacrificial enclosures and that they had not yet begun to use temples and statues. After the first century A.D. we have first a gradual and then a rapid rise in Brahmanic influence.

Inscriptions as well as books indicate that a linguistic change occurred in the same period. At first popular dialects were regarded as sufficiently dignified and current to be the medium for both scripture and official records. Sanskrit remained a thing apart- the peculiar possession of the Brahman literati. Then the popular language was sanskritized, the rules of Sanskrit grammar being accepted as the standard to which it ought to conform, though perfect conformity was impracticable. In much the same way the modern Greeks try to bring Romaic into line with classical Greek. Finally Sanskrit was recognized as the proper language for literature, government and religion.

The earliest inscriptions in correct Sanskrit seem to date from the second century A.D. Further, the invaders who entered India from the north- west favoured Buddhism on the whole. Coins indicate that some of them worshipped Siva but the number and beauty of Buddhist monuments erected under their rule can hardly be interpreted except as a sign of their patronage. And their conversion was natural for they had no strong religious convictions of their own and the Brahmans with their pride of caste shrank from foreigners. But Buddhism had no prejudice of race or class: it was animated by a missionary spirit and it was probably the stronger creed at this period.

It not only met the invaders on their entry into India but it sent missionaries to them in Bactria and Afghanistan, so that to some extent they brought Buddhism with them. But it was a Buddhism combined with the most varied elements. Hellenic art and religion had made the figures of Apollo, Herakles and Helios familiar in Bactria, and both Bactria and northern India were in touch with Zoroastrians. The mixed cults of these borderlands readily professed allegiance to the Buddha but, not understanding Indian ideas, simply made him into a deity and having done this were not likely to repudiate other Indian deities. Thus in its outward form the Buddhism of the invaders tended to be a compound of Indian, Greek and Persian ideas in which Sun worship played a large part, for not only Indian myths, but Apollo and Helios and the Persian Mithra all entered into it.

Persian influence in art is discernible as early as the architecture of Asoka: in doctrine it has something to do with such figures as Vairocana and Amitâbha. Græco- Roman influence also was powerful in art and through art affected religion. In Asoka's time likenesses of the Buddha were unknown and the adoration of images, if not entirely due to the art of Gandhara, was at least encouraged by it. But though coins and sculpture bring clearly before us a medley of deities corresponding to a medley of human races, they do not help us much in tracing the growth of thought, phases of which are preserved in a literature sufficiently copious though the record sometimes fails at the points of transition where it would be of most interest.

It is natural that sacred books should record accepted results rather than tentative innovations and even disguise the latter. But we can fix a few dates which enable us to judge what shape Buddhism was taking about the time of the Christian era. The Tibetan historian Târanâtha is not of much help, for his chronology is most confused, but still he definitely connects the appearance of Mahayanist texts with the reign of Kanishka and the period immediately following it and regards them as a new phenomenon. Greater assistance is furnished by the Chinese translators, whose dates are known with some exactitude.

Thus the earliest Buddhist work rendered into Chinese is said to be the sutra of forty- two sections, translated by Kâœyapa Mâtanga in 67 A.D. It consists of extracts or resumés of the Buddha's teaching mostly prefaced by the words "The Buddha said," doubtless in imitation of the Confucian Analects where the introductory formula "The master said" plays a similar part. Its ideas and precepts are Hinayanist: the Arhat is held up as the ideal and in a remarkable passage where the degrees of sanctity are graded and compared no mention is made of Bodhisattvas. This first translation was followed by a long series of others, principally from the Sûtra- Pitòaka, for very little of the Vinaya was translated before the fifth century.

A great number of Hinayanist sutras were translated before 300 A.D. but very few after 450. On the other hand portions of the sutra about Amîda's Paradise, of the Prajñâ-pâramitâ, and of the Avatamòsaka were translated about 150 A.D. and translations of the Lotus and Lalita- vistara appeared about 300. Great caution is necessary in using these data and the circumstances of China as well as of India must be taken into account. If translations of the Vinaya and complete collections of sutras are late in appearing, it does not follow that the corresponding Indian texts are late, for the need of the Vinaya was not felt until monasteries began to spring up.

Most of the translations made before the fifth century are extracts and of indifferent workmanship. Some are retained in the Chinese Tripitaka but are superseded by later versions. But however inaccurate and incomplete these older translations may be, if any of them can be identified with a part of an extant Sanskrit work it follows that at least that part of the work and the doctrines contained in it were current in India or Central Asia some time before the translation was made. Applying this principle we may conclude that the Hinayana and Mahayana were flourishing side by side in India and Central Asia in the first century A.D. and that the Happy Land sutras and portions of the Prajñâ- pâramitâ already existed.

From that time onwards Mahayanist literature as represented by Chinese translations steadily increases, and after 400 A.D. Hinayanist literature declines, with two exceptions, the Vinaya and the Abhidharma books of the Sarvâstivâdins. The Vinaya was evidently regarded as a rule of life independent of theology, but it is remarkable that Hsüan Chuang after his return from India in 645 should have thought it worth while to translate the philosophy of the Sarvâstivâdins. Other considerations render this chronology probable. Two conspicuous features of the Mahayana are the worship of Bodhisattvas and idealist philosophy.

These are obviously parallel to the worship of Siva and Vishnu, and to the rise of the Vedanta. Now the worship of these deities was probably not prevalent before 300 B.C., for they are almost unknown to the Pali Pitakas, and it was fully developed about the time of the Bhagavadagîtâ which perhaps assumed its present form a little before the Christian era. Not only is the combination of devotion and metaphysics found in this work similar to the tone of many Mahayanist sutras but the manifestation of Krishna in his divine form is like the transformation scenes of the Lotus.

The chief moral principle of the Bhagavad- gîtâ is substantially the same as that prescribed for Bodhisattvas. It teaches that action is superior to inaction, but that action should be wholly disinterested and not directed to any selfish object. This is precisely the attitude of the Bodhisattva who avoids the inaction of those who are engrossed in self- culture as much as the pursuit of wealth or pleasure. Both the Gîtâ and Mahayanist treatises lay stress on faith. He who thinks on Krishna when dying goes to Krishna just as he who thinks on Amitâbha goes to the Happy Land and the idea is not unknown to the Pali texts, for it finds complete expression in the story of Matòtòhakunòdòali.

The idea of a benevolent deity to be worshipped with devotion and faith and not with ceremonies is strange to old Buddhism and old Brahmanism alike. It was a popular idea which became so strong that neither priests nor Bhikshus could ignore it and in its ultimate result it is hard to say whether Buddhist or Brahmanic elements are more prominent. Both Avalokita and Krishna are Devas. The former has the beauty of holiness and the strength which it gives, but also the weakness of a somewhat abstract figure: the latter is very personal and springs from the heart of India but to those who are not Hindus seems wanting in purity and simplicity.

The divine character of both figures is due to Brahmanism rather than Buddhism, but the new form of worship which laid stress on a frame of mind rather than on ceremonial and the idea of Avatâras or the periodic appearance of superhuman saviours and teachers indicate the influence of Buddhism on Brahmanism. There is a similar parallel between the newer Buddhist philosophy and the Vedantist school represented by Sankara, and Indian critics detected it. Sankara was called a Pracchanna- bauddha or crypto- Buddhist by his theological opponents and the resemblance between the two systems in thought, if not in word, is striking.

Both distinguish relative and absolute truth: for both the relative truth is practically theism, for both absolute truth is beyond description and whether it is called Brahman, Dharma-kâya or Sûnyatâ is not equivalent to God in the Christian or Mohammedan sense. Just as for the Vedantist there exists in the light of the highest knowledge neither a personal God nor an individual soul, so the Mâdhyamika Sûtra can declare that the Buddha does not really exist. The Mahayanist philosophers do not use the word Mâyâ but they state the same theory in a more subjective form by ascribing the appearance of the phenomenal world to ignorance, a nomenclature which is derived from the Buddha's phrase, "From ignorance come the Sankhâras."

Here, as elsewhere, Buddhist and Brahmanic ideas acted and reacted in such complex interrelations that it is hard to say which has borrowed from the other. As to dates, the older Upanishads which contain the foundations but not the complete edifice of Vedantism seem a little earlier than the Buddha. Now we know that within the Vedantist school there were divergences of opinion which later received classic expression in the hands of Sankara and Râmânuja. The latter rejected the doctrines of Mâyâ and of the difference between relative and absolute truth.

The germs of both schools are to be found in the Upanishads but it seems probable that the ideas of Sankara were originally worked out among Buddhists rather than among Brahmans and were rightly described by their opponents as disguised Buddhism. As early as 520 A.D. Bodhidharma preached in China a doctrine which is practically the same as the Advaita. The earliest known work in which the theory of Mâyâ and the Advaita philosophy are clearly formulated is the metrical treatise known as the Kârikâ of Gaudòapâda. This name was borne by the teacher of Sankara's teacher, who must have lived about 700 A.D., but the high position accorded to the work, which is usually printed with the Mânòdòûkya Upanishad and is practically regarded as a part of it, make an earlier date probable.

Both in language and thought it bears a striking resemblance to Buddhist writings of the Mâdhyamika School and also contains many ideas and similes which reappear in the works of Sankara. On the other hand the *Lankâvatâra Sûtra* which was translated into Chinese in 513 and therefore can hardly have been composed later than 450 is conscious that its doctrines resemble Brahmanic philosophy, for an interlocutor objects that the language used in it by the Buddha about the Tathâgatagarbha is very like the Brahmanic doctrine of the Âtman. To which the Buddha replies that his language is a concession to those who cannot stomach the doctrine of the negation of reality in all its austerity.

Some of the best known verses of *Gaudòapâda* compare the world of appearance to the apparent circle of fire produced by whirling a lighted torch. This striking image occurs first in the *Maitrâyana Upanishad* (VI. 24), which shows other indications of an acquaintance with Buddhism, and also in the *Lankâvatâra Sûtra*. A real affinity unites the doctrine of Sankara to the teaching of Gotama himself. That teaching as presented in the Pali Pitakas is marked by its negative and deliberately circumscribed character. Its rule is silence when strict accuracy of expression is impossible, whereas later philosophy does not shrink from phrases which are suggestive, if not exact.

Gotama refuses to admit that the human soul is a fixed entity or Âtman, but he does not condemn (though he also does not discuss) the idea that the whole world of change and becoming, including human souls, is the expression or disguise of some one ineffable principle. He teaches too that the human mind can grow until it develops new faculties and powers and becomes the Buddha mind, which sees the whole chain of births, the order of the world, and the reality of emancipation.

As the object of the whole system is practical, Nirvana is always regarded as a *terminus ad quem* or an escape (*nissaranam*) from this transitory world, and this view is more accurate as well as more edifying than the view which treats Brahman or Sûnyatâ as the origin of the universe. When the Vedanta teaches that this changing troubled world is merely the disguise of that unchanging and untroubled state into which saints can pass, it is, I believe, following Gotama's thought, but giving it an expression which he would have considered imperfect.

Bibliography

Anacker, Stefan, *Seven Works of Vasubandhu*. Delhi: Motilal Banarsidass, 1984.

Basham, A.L., ed. *Papers of the Date of Kaniska*. Leiden: E.J. Brill, 1968.

Dutt, Nalinaksha, *Aspects of Mahayana Buddhism*. London: Luzac, 1930.

Kalupahana, David, *The Principles of Buddhist Psychology*. Albany: SUNY Press, 1987.

Cleary, Thomas, trans., *The Flower Ornament Scripture*. Boston: Shambala, 1983.

Conze, Edward, *Buddhist Wisdom Books*. London: George Allen & Unwin, 1958 (also New York: Harper & Row, 1972). Contains Diamond-Cutter Sutra and Heart Sutra; translation with commentary.

Eckel, Malcolm David, *To See the Buddha: A Philosopher's Quest for the Meaning of Emptiness*. Princeton: Princeton University Press, 1992.

Garfield, Jay L., *The Fundamental Wisdom of the Middle Way: Nagarjuna's Mulamadhyamakakarika*. New York: Oxford University Press, 1995. Both the translation and the author's notes follow the Gelug interpretation of the text.

Harris, I.C. *The Continuity of Madhyamaka and Yogacara in Indian Mahayana Buddhism*. Leiden: E.J. Brill, 1991.

Huntington, C. W., Jr., *The Emptiness of Emptiness: An Introduction to Early Indian Madhyamika*. Honolulu: University of Hawaii Press, 1989.

Inada, Kenneth K., *Nagarjuna. A Translation of His Mularmadhyamaka- karika with an Introductory Essay.* Tokyo: Hokuseido Press, 1970.

Kalupahana, David J., *Nagarjuna: The Philosophy of the Middle Way.* Albany: SUNY Press, 1986.

Lindtner, Christian, *Master of Wisdom.* Berkeley: Dharma Publishing, 1986.

Kiyota, Minoru, ed., *Mahayana Buddhist Meditation: Theory and Practice.* Honolulu: University Press of Hawaii, 1978 [M].

Pye, Michael. *Skilful Means: A concept in Mahayana Buddhism.* London: Duckworth, 1978.

Nagao, Gadjin, *Madhyamika and Yogacara: A Study of Mahayana Philosophies.* Albany: SUNY Press, 1991.

Napper, Elizabeth, *Dependent-Arising and Emptiness.* Boston: Wisdom Publications, 1989.

Powers, John, trans., *Wisdom of Buddha: The Samdhinirmocana Sutra.* Berkeley: Dharma Publishing, 1994.

Ramanan, K. V., *Nagarjuna's Philosophy as Presented in Maha-Prajnaparamita-Sastra.* Tokyo, 1966; Delhi: Motilal Banarsidass, 1978.

Robinson, Richard H., *Early Madhyamika in India and China.* Madison: University of Wisconsin Press, 1967. Read pp. 21-70.

Ruegg, D.S., and L. Schmithausen, eds. *Earliest Buddhism. Madhyamaka.* Leiden: E.J. Brill, 1990.

Sprung, Mervyn, trans., *Lucid Exposition of the Middle Way.* Boulder, Colo.: Great Eastern, 1980.

Sprung, Mervyn, ed., *The Problem of Two Truths in Buddhism and Vedanta.* Boston: Reidel, 1973.

Stcherbatsky, Theodore, *The Conception of Buddhist Nirvana.* Leningrad: Office of the Academy of Sciences of the U.S.S.R.,1927.

Streng, Frederick J., *Emptiness: A Study in Religious Meaning.* Nashville, Tenn.: Abingdon Press, 1967.

Suzuki, D. T., trans., *Lankavatara Sutra.* London: Kegan Paul, 1932 and 1956.

Williams, Paul, *Mahayana Buddhism: The Doctrinal Foundations.* Routledge & Kegan Paul, 1989.

Williams, Paul. *Altruism and Reality: Studies in the Philosophy of the Bodhicaryavatara.* London: Curzon, 1998.

Index

V

W

Y